CRIME CONTROL STRATEGIES

CRIME CONTROL STRATEGIES

**An Introduction
to the Study of Crime**

Harold E. Pepinsky

OXFORD UNIVERSITY PRESS
New York   1980   Oxford

Copyright © 1980 by Oxford University Press, Inc.

Library of Congress Cataloging in Publication Data
Pepinsky, Harold E
  Crime control strategies.
  Bibliography: p.
  Includes index.
  1. Crime prevention. 2. Crime and criminals.
I. Title.
HV7431.P45 1980   364.4   79-15374
ISBN 0-19-502607-1

Printed in the United States of America

To Les Wilkins

pioneer
teacher
inspiration
and friend

Preface

The purpose of this book is straightforward, if ambitious. It attempts to help novices and experts use information about crime and criminal justice for social purposes. To this end, the book has several unusual features.

It is customary to separate information about criminology and criminal justice. Criminologists have traditionally limited themselves to the study of why people commit crime, students of criminal justice to the study of the behavior of officials of crime control. It seems to make little sense to divide the two fields. Whether people are more or less likely to commit crime depends largely on how officials do their jobs, and how and why officials act as they do depends largely on the nature of the crime problem they face. Considering it a waste of effort to study the two fields separately, I have grouped them together under the heading of criminology, which literally means "the study of crime." The purpose of criminology is to learn how to control crime. To stress the need for integration in this field, I have drawn from the work of those trained in the humanities, natural sciences, social sciences, and professions such as engineering, law, medicine, and social work.

I reject the "value neutral" position held by many criminologists who hold that knowledge of the causes of crime has intrinsic value, that it should be mastered regardless of its practical utility. In the book I have evaluated information about crime and criminality in terms of its usefulness in aiding the control of crime.

The book is both comprehensible to the beginning student of

criminology (or criminal justice) and novel to the expert in the field. Much research in the field (including, unfortunately, some of my own) is written in such esoteric jargon as to be incomprehensible to the beginner. I know of no research that cannot readily be explained to the beginning student in simple language. I have tried to write simply without writing simplemindedly. And, just as in any scholarly article or monograph, I have tried to carry the analysis in this book beyond the existing limits of knowledge and understanding. If I have succeeded, both the beginner and the expert will finish this book with a more profound understanding of criminological issues.

It is a disservice to students for criminologists to disseminate their beliefs as certainties. I therefore invite readers to share my own skepticism about the validity of even my own beliefs. Readers are invited to transcend rather than to accept or memorize the author's conclusions. I invite readers to take issue with my propositions, try to give them enough information to do so, and conclude each chapter with questions (entitled "Food for Thought") rather than with answers on criminological issues.

Criminological knowledge is integrated with political consideration and ethical issues. The questions and answers of criminologists are tied to political and ethical presuppositions. It is only fair to make the connections explicit.

For teachers who share the above premises with me, this book is suitable as a primary text in either an introductory criminology or an introductory criminal justice class. The coverage of material in these areas is broad enough to prepare students for more specialized courses. For teachers who wish their students to review the literature in the manner of standard introductory texts, this book is concise and readable enough to be used as a supplement, exposing beginning students to a particular (social systems) point of view.

The book is also written to be read by a lay person without benefit of a lecturer or tutor, and yet (particularly from Chapter 4 on) has enough original material to challenge the advanced student. In sum, the book is designed to transcend the need to classify and compartmentalize workers in criminology.

AN OVERVIEW

Chapter 1 of the book resembles an abridged edition of a traditional criminology text. Here, a sketch is drawn of various schools of criminological thought, from Beccaria and the utilitarians (or classical school) to Wilkins and the systems theorists. Obviously, the survey is incomplete, but it does indicate how diverse approaches to studying crime can be.

Chapter 2 outlines the topics of each of the remaining chapters, and Chapter 3 introduces themes and issues that recur throughout the book. Then follow four chapters on controlling crime, four on controlling criminals, a chapter on cost-benefit analysis, and a conclusion. Chapter 7 reviews the material in Chapters 4 to 6, Chapter 11 the material in Chapters 8 to 10, and 13 the entire book.

Note that for reasons given at the beginning of Chapter 9, that chapter is twice the length of any other. On the other hand, as integrative chapters tying together loose ends, Chapters 11 to 13 are shorter than the others. A teacher allocating course time for various parts of the book can plan accordingly.

Most students who have used this book in manuscript form have become depressed by the end of Chapter 3. Chapters 2 and 3 emphasize the problems and ambiguities in criminological knowledge; students may begin to wonder, at this point, what criminological knowledge can be good for. The tone of Chapter 4 is cautious, too. Chapter 5 is somewhat bolder, however, and by Chapter 11, I affirmatively emphasize personal views and ideas for crime control. By this time, readers should be more optimistic about the utility of criminological knowledge, but should be well armed and prepared to read my arguments with an independent, critical eye.

For easy reference two appendices are provided, one describing stages of the criminal justice process and the other defining crimes and elements of crimes.

While readers can glance at different parts of the book in any order they please, the chapters are written progressively, each chapter presuming familiarity with prior material. The reader would probably do best to read them in order.

Many serious issues are considered in this book, but the reader still ought to be able to—have fun! (I did)

H. P.

Bloomington, Indiana
November 1978

Acknowledgments

Of the many fine teachers I have had in recent years, Leslie T. Wilkins is outstanding. Formally a colleague of Les's at the State University of New York at Albany, I team-taught a seminar with him for four years. With his rich experience and keen insight, he gave me far more than I could possibly have given him.

Les has always treated me as a peer, like all his students. He thrives on a good intellectual fight, and we have often argued fundamental research and policy issues. In the course of these debates and exchanges, even if I did not let on at the time, Les has consistently taught me a great deal.

In the field of criminology (and criminal justice), Les is a true pioneer. He has developed a social systems perspective on the study of crime and deviance. His book *Social Deviance* is a classic. I owe whatever integration has been achieved of my own research on crime control to a vision that Les has shared with me. That debt is reflected in the many citations to Les's ideas and work that appear in this book.

Above all, Les represents uncompromising commitment to free scientific inquiry as a keystone of his larger commitment to humanity. Les's friendship, example, and guidance remain precious to me. Now that we work in different places, I continue to seek his counsel on issues that perplex me, and he never fails to help me clarify my thinking. It is as a small token of my appreciation that I dedicate this book to him.

I also owe a great deal to the support, encouragement, and intellectual exchange that I enjoy with my colleagues in Forensic Studies at Indiana University. I have continually been refreshed and enlightened by Bob Borkenstein, Jim Miller, Barton Parks, John Ramirez, Myke Spicker, Vic Streib, Hill Trubitt, and Cathy Widom. Particularly as we have begun to teach and write together, Phil Parnell has done me a major service by opening the richness of anthropological literature to my view and sharing his thorough understanding of it with me.

Thanks in large measure to Ellen Dwyer, a demanding though sympathetic critic, I have been introduced to the work of historians on crime—notably that of Tom Duesterberg, Barbara Hanawalt, and Eric Monkkonen—which has forced me to extend my own theoretical horizons.

Special thanks go to Doug Smith for enlightening me about self-report research.

The heart of my support and learning comes from my wife, Jill, my daughter, Kate (who at three months was already busy helping me to type a draft of this book), and my parents, Harold B. and Pauline Pepinsky.

I am very grateful to Donna Littrell and Martha Geter for the help they have given me in preparing the manuscript, and to the many students who have read and commented on the manuscript for their invaluable feedback.

Special thanks go to Jim Anderson, Ellie Fuchs, Helen Greenberg, and the editorial staff at Oxford, without whose encouragement and expert assistance this book would not have been possible.

There are countless other friends and colleagues without whole help I could not have written this book. I hope they forgive my failure to mention them all by name, and accept my thanks as well.

Contents

PART III.   CONTROLLING RATES OF CRIMINALITY

PART ONE

INTRODUCTION

CHAPTER ONE

A History
of the Study of Crime

As you begin reading this book, you are entering the field of criminology. Reflect for a moment on what that means. In the scholarly world, a field is not an area where everyone does the same thing, like going door-to-door and asking people questions. Instead, the people working in a scholarly field try to make discoveries in any way they can about a common phenomenon—in this case, about crime. You are embarking on the study of crime, which should bring you surprise and delight (together with some perplexity).

This is probably not your first entry into the field of criminology. These days, it is almost impossible to glance at a newspaper, watch television, listen to radio, or carry on a conversation without learning something new about crime. And it is fair to say that whenever you try to make sense of this new information, you are in the field of criminology.

People have probably been moving in and out of the field of criminology from time immemorial. A decade ago, a task force of an American national crime commission noted: "Virtually every generation since the founding of the Nation and before has felt itself threatened by the spectre of rising crime and violence" (President's Commission on Law Enforcement and Administration of Justice, 1967a: 19). Not surprisingly, practically every available criminological study has, implicitly at least, been founded on a concern about controlling crime. Most writers on the subject have assumed or concluded that one or more varieties of crime required more effective control than was then available. A few writers have opposed the very idea of crime control (e.g., Berkman, 1971), generally reflecting minority (but perhaps correct?) views. Among those who make careers out of the study of crime in the Western world today, there is general consensus on grouping common perspectives on crime into "schools of criminology." Beccaria (1968), whose book on crime control was originally published in Italy in 1764, first drew together the ideas of a Western school of criminology—the "classical school." From this origin, we can trace the historical development of the field of criminology.

CLASSICAL CONCEPTS OF CRIME

Beccaria wrote at a time when people believed it was possible to create new forms of government to respond to "typical" behavior. It was assumed that most people responded in the same way to the same stimuli; that most people were rational; and that all people had the same kind of rationality. Given this assumption, it followed that each crime would bring the same advantage to every potential criminal. If laws were written and made known to all, if the punishments slightly outweighed the advantage to be gained from the crime, and if a law enforcement system were established which almost guaranteed punishment for any crime, then one could hope that crime would be almost wiped out. This thesis was by no means unique to Beccaria. It was espoused at about the same time by Bentham (1970, substantially completed in 1782 and first published in 1839) in England. Perhaps Beccaria is more commonly cited by criminologists today because of the concise detail with which he described how criminal law should be written and applied. It was Beccaria who rationalized the separation of legislative and judicial powers, precision in legal provisions, and abolition of capital punishment.

Beccaria's work implied an explanation of crime: people who commit a crime do so because they gain more than they lose. The assumption that practically everyone is capable of committing a certain kind of crime sets Beccaria's explanation of crime apart from those of many other criminologists. Beccaria believed that a threat of legal punishment sufficient to deter one person would discourage most people as well. As we shall see, despite later developments in criminological thought, Beccaria's position has a number of adherents today; these include Van den Haag (1976) and Wilson (1975).

THE LATE DYNASTIC TRADITION IN CHINA

We Westerners are apt to forget that other cultures have developed alternative theoretical approaches to crime. This short-sightedness can lead us to believe that ways of thinking about crime are limited and fixed. To avoid parochialism, let us note at least one other position that had already been carefully articulated in the East by Becarria's time.

China had a series of detailed penal codes from the seventh century T'ang dynasty until the fall of the Ch'ing dynasty in 1911. During this period, legal response to crime stressed preservation of the dynasty rather than making citizens behave according to certain rules. Although, by the seventh century, the Chinese generally accepted the notion that China would be ruled by some dynastic order, the rise and fall of particular dynasties was held to be inevitable.

Each dynasty, it was believed, survived only so long as the emperor retained "the mandate of heaven." The emperor was believed to serve as the link between heaven and earth. He was responsible for keeping the social order below him in harmony with the principles of the heavenly order above him. This meant that his success depended, in part, on guiding his people by the example of his own principled behavior. It also depended on his demonstrating to the heavenly order his capacity to respond appropriately to social disorder. Heaven and earth were ruled by the interaction of two competing principles, *yin* (the submissive principle) and *yang* (the dominant principle). It was a law of heaven that each instance of improper behavior be controlled by a dominance (so long as the response of the emperor was *yang* and sponse to disorderly behavior retained heavenly principled dominant response of the heavenly order. So long as the emperor's reimproper behavior among the people remained *yin*), the emperor would retain his mandate of heaven. If improper behavior among the people became dominant (*yang*) in relation to the conduct of the emperor (*yin*), the heavenly order would reassert its dominance, displacing the weak emperor and establishing the rule of a new, strong emperor in a successor dynasty.

Each case of improper behavior which came to the attention of the emperor or of one of his representatives (down to the level of the district magistrate) called for a measured, dominant imperial response. A distinct body of law governed official misconduct (*ling*), but one branch (*lü*), analogous to our penal law, designated the response fitting each officially known case of misconduct. Appropriate punishments, ranging from degrees of corporal punishment, through degrees of banishment, to various kinds of capital punishment (strangulation, beheading, and slicing) were set by law. According to Ch'ing law, the magistrate who imposed the wrong punishment was liable to that punishment himself (or one degree less if the punishment had not yet been executed).

The security of the emperor's mandate depended not only on proper application of the law but also on swift disposition of cases. In Ch'ing law, a magistrate who let a case go for more than a year without passing sentence was liable to punishment. To protect each dynasty and the positions of its representatives, people were deterred from bringing cases to any higher functionary than the magistrate. In fact, it was even better to avoid the law completely. People were encouraged to settle disputes within the organization of families, guilds and informal village management, and by using experienced mediators who communicated between the quarreling factions. People were inhibited from complaining to officials by the prospect of being tortured into admitting that they had made false accusations. By obtaining such confessions, magistrates could bring cases to a speedy resolution. The issue was not so much justice for the parties involved as demonstrating that the dynasty was secure in its mandate to rule. (See Van der Sprenkel, 1962, and Bodde and Morris, 1967, for detailed accounts of Ch'ing law.)

To Beccaria, the primary issue posed by crime was, how should the lives of average citizens be regulated? In China, in contrast, the question was, who should govern? By extension, while Western criminologists in the Beccarian tradition see crime prevention primarily as a matter of maintaining orderly relationships among citizens, the Chinese tradition sees crime control as the preservation of the authority of hereditary rulers. Westerners since the eighteenth century have looked on a sophisticated body of written criminal law as a means to equalize the social position of all citizens. The Chinese have assumed that a well-developed criminal code is a way of maintaining a stable social hierarchy of rulers and ruled. Given the Communist Chinese commitment to the development of social equality, the Chinese legal tradition accounts for their continued failure to adopt a criminal code (see Pepinsky, 1973).

WESTERN THINKING ON CRIME INTO THE NINETEENTH CENTURY AND BEYOND: THE MARXIST PERSPECTIVE

Beccaria's position gained ascendancy in the West as absolute monarchies were replaced by democratic governments. In the eighteenth century, democracy was already displacing monarchy in England by evolution; it would later do so in the United States and France by revolution. Criminal law institutions were made to conform to Beccaria's assumption that individual differences between persons were legally irrelevant. Because Beccaria had argued that this assumption required that legislation be kept independent of individual cases, legislative and judicial functions were separated in Western countries. England anticipated Beccaria by half a century in ruling that judges could not control jury verdicts through punishment (England, Court of Common Pleas, 1670). In the United States, the right to have lay juries decide guilt or innocence was incorporated into the Sixth Amendment of the Bill of Rights. In France, the doctrine was that judges who heard cases were to be guided only by the criminal code to determine what law applied to each case (David and Devries, 1958). Some provisions of the United States Constitution reflect other Beccarian principles. For instance, *ex post facto* legislation is prohibited, as are laws which apply to specific individuals (bills of attainder, in Article I, section 9, paragraph 3).

However, by the mid-nineteenth century, one well-known

social critic, Karl Marx, came to conclude, like the Chinese, that the criminal law inevitably served to maintain the social hierarchy rather than to establish and maintain social equality. Marx saw the state—the institution which enacts and applies the criminal law (referred to by Beccaria as the "sovereign")—as an instrument used by an elite economic class to retain its rule over an "oppressed" class. In the Western economic system of his day, which he and others called "capitalism," Marx believed that the law was used by "the owners of the means of production" ("the bourgeoisie") to dominate "the workers" ("the proletariat"). Marx was a prolific writer. His monumental attempt to synthesize his ideas was *Capital* (Marx, 1967, originally published in German in 1867, and as edited and translated into English by Friedrich Engels, first published in 1887).

Small wonder, then, that in toppling an established social hierarchy, the Chinese Communists have demonstrated sympathy toward Marx's view of the role of law in society. In the West, too, some writers have accepted the assumption that the use of written law to prevent crime is an inherently inequitable or oppressive approach to social control. For instance, in the United States today, Quinney (1974, known as a "radical criminologist") argues that law serves to keep the ruling class in power.

Others, who reject Marx's idea that a dictatorship of workers must lead society beyond class exploitation, still agree that law is oppressive. These include persons who call themselves anarchists (see Berkman, 1971) and existentialists (see Sartre, 1965).

Although seriously questioned by many thinkers, the assumption that law is necessary to protect individual liberty and to secure social equality predominates in Western criminological thought. Written law is important even for the Soviet Communists in carrying through the "socialist revolution" on an explicitly Marxist foundation (Berman and Spindler, 1972). It is now quite respectable in American criminology to say that the criminal law is written and applied unevenly, to benefit the rich and to disadvantage the poor. However most American criminologists who accept this premise (like Sutherland, 1940, who coined the term "white-collar crime") also argue that we should attempt to realize the ideal of equal treatment under law *through* the use of the law rather than *in spite of it*. In the United States, the dramatic increase in prosecutions for white-collar crimes in recent years (Mc-Carthy, 1975) reflects widespread acceptance of Beccarian assumptions about crime control. The Chinese concept of the purpose of written criminal law stand in stark contrast to generally accepted Western ideas.

WESTERN THINKING INTO THE NINETEENTH CENTURY AND BEYOND: THE POSITIVIST PERSPECTIVE

Though Western criminologists generally agree with Becarria that written law is desirable for the development of personal liberty and social equality in any society, many have come to disagree with another of Beccaria's assumptions. Beccaria believed that the criminal law should ignore personal characteristics. The only important question was, did this person commit a proscribed act? In contrast, criminological thinkers of the nineteenth century began to argue that other individual differences had to be taken into account in determining what should legally be done to various kinds of people who committed crimes.

Just as they had developed the right to trial by jury, the English anticipated Beccaria in yet another respect. It stood to reason that if the criminal law was based on personal accountability, people must be intellectually capable of understanding the consequences of their actions. Based on this reasoning, English law from the beginning of the fourteenth century stated that a child under the age of seven could not be held responsible for a crime. Over the next three centuries, this principle was extended. Children aged fourteen and up were held responsible, while those aged seven to thirteen were presumed to lack the intellectual capacity for criminal liability (LaFave and Scott, 1972: 357).

Forty years before Beccaria's treatise was published, a lower court judge in England extended this logic to apply to adults. He ruled that persons who had no greater capacity to understand what they were doing "than an infant, than a brute, or a wild beast" could not be punished for a crime (England, Kingston Assizes, 1724: 724). In 1843, a variant of this rule was accepted by the House of Lords (in judicial matters, the English equivalent of the United States Supreme Court). They held that a person who did not have "a sufficient degree of reason to know that what he was doing was wrong" could not be held legally responsible for a crime—even homicide (England, House of Lords, 1843). Since the defendant in this case was named M'Naghten, the holding of the case has come to be known as the "M'Naghten Rule." The rule is still law in England, and the rule or one of its variants is also law in every jurisdiction in the United States. (This includes rules based on whether the crime is a product of "an irresistible impulse"—e.g., Alabama Supreme Court, 1886; or, for a while, of "mental disease or defect," United States Court of Appeals, D.C. Circuit, 1954; or defendant "by reason of mental disease or defect lacks substantial capacity either to appreciate the criminality of his conduct or to conform his conduct to the requirements of law," United States Court of Appeals, D.C. Cir., 1972.) In recent years, a law has also been developed in England (1957) and in some American jurisdictions (as in California; California Supreme Court, 1966) of "diminished" or "partial responsibility," in which premeditation in the crime of murder can be rebutted by a finding of mental incapacity.

English recognition of the idea that forces beyond "rational" control might lead a person to commit a crime created issues which the classical criminologists could not resolve. Problems proliferated in the nineteenth century. English jurists had once seen factors beyond personal control leading to crime in only rare, extreme, and inexplicable cases. Now, however, others began to believe that *most* crime might be explained by factors beyond rational control. Darwin (1970, first published in 1842–1844) had awakened the Western world to the wonders of inductive explanation of how humanity had come to be as it is. Perhaps, by looking at characteristics other than behavior, one could discover *why* people evolved into criminals. Perhaps some people could be diagnosed as predestined to commit crimes if left at liberty. If so, for these people retribution or deterrence was not a viable strategy to prevent or control crime. Such people would have to be isolated from society, as in asylums, or otherwise *incapacitated*. Or if the causes of crime were conditions which could be changed, then the strategy would be *treatment* or *rehabilitation*. Theorists who promote such solutions are known as members of the "positive school" of criminology.

BIOLOGICAL EXPLANATIONS OF CRIME

Two Italians named for the Roman emperors (Caesars) have been called the founding fathers of two schools of criminological thought. Cesare Beccaria is one father of the classical school; a doctor, Cesare Lombroso (1968, first published in Italian in 1899), is a founder of the positive school. Based on research he conducted while working for the Italian Army, Lombroso concluded that true criminals, who he believed to be evolutionary throwbacks or *atavisms*, could be identified by physical features: the shapes of their bodies, faces, and hands. Lombroso held that these atavistic persons were genetically incapable of behaving according to a Beccarian legal order.

Still, Lombroso conceded that atavistic persons constituted a minority (he estimated 40 percent) of those who committed crimes. In a few other cases, crimes were committed by criminaloids—those with a touch of (biological) degeneracy who were unusually susceptible to illicit behavior because of social circumstances. Lombroso detected physiological abnormalities as well in criminals of passion. Only "habitual criminals" and "pseudo-criminals" were full products of social circumstance.

Politically, the most effective rebuttal to Lombroso's biological theory was the research first published by an Englishman, Goring (1972), in 1913. Goring compared the physical features of convicts to those of soldiers and university students. He found none of the distinctive features of convicts reported by Lombroso, but did find that the convicts were on the whole lower in stature, weight, and intelligence than the average soldier and student. He concluded that some persons inherited a stature, weight, and intelligence that predisposed them to commit crimes, although persons inheriting these characteristics were not inevitably criminals and were thought amenable to preventive treatment. Today, most criminologists (though by no means all; see Hirschi and Hindelang, 1977) are skeptical that inherited low intelligence causes crime. This is primarily because they believe that intelligence tests measure people's social circumstances rather than their gene structures.

Other notions of physiological causes of criminal behavior are also supported in the literature. For example, the XYY chromosome (an extra male sex chromosome in men) has been cited as a cause of antisocial behavior (see Burke, 1969), as have abnormal hormone levels (Valenstein, 1973: 128) and unusual brain function (Hare, 1970).

WARNINGS TO THE CRIMINOLOGIST

The research literature on the role of these factors is, unfortunately, of little use to the person who wants to determine whether any of these factors is "really" a cause of crime. Problems of proof include the following.

Defining the subject populations   This problem is considered in detail in the following two chapters. To determine a "real" cause of crime, one must be able to compare populations of "true" criminals with normal populations. How does one know that a person has committed a crime? Is a jury verdict of guilt infallible? If so, how does one account for (admittedly infrequent) decisions to release people from prison because it appears that they are innocent after all?

Even if one assumes that certain people are really criminals, how does one locate a comparison (or "control") group of noncriminals? In the United States, when children or adults are polled on whether they have committed crimes, the vast majority report that they are guilty (see Chapter 9). To be sure, some of these people report having committed fewer and less serious offenses than others, but do their responses indicate "reality"? Criminologists like Sutherland have argued that while all persons might commit an equal amount of crime, the higher one's socioeconomic status, the less likely one is to be officially labeled a criminal. If we cannot absolutely determine who has and has not committed *any* crime, let alone particular kinds of crime, how can one isolate characteristics which separate criminals from noncriminals? Bear in mind that even a small amount of error in selecting subject populations could falsify the correlations researchers typically find between any set of characteristics and criminality.

Committing the fallacy of affirming the consequent Even if one researcher fails to find a correlation between a particular characteristic and criminality, the correlation may still be found in subsequent research. For instance, though Goring did not find a clear physical difference between criminals and noncriminals, these differences might later be found using more refined measures. Many research physicists have long assumed, for example, that an elemental particle of matter called a "quark" exists, though until very recently no one claimed to see a picture or trace of a quark. The problem is like looking for a missing needle in a haystack; until the object is found, how long must one look before concluding that it is not there? Criminologists have spent far less research effort in trying to find physical correlates of criminality than social correlates. Would they have found physical factors if they had looked longer and harder? No one can tell.

Interaction of explanatory factors Consider the possible relationship between the XYY chromosome and antisocial behavior. A disproportionate number of males institutionalized for antisocial behavior have been found to have the XYY chromosome. They also tend to be taller than males with the normal XY chromosome (Burke, 1969: 265). If, as a social or cultural matter, males are seen as a threat and treated accordingly, this could account for the disproportionate number of antisocial XYY males. The aggressiveness attributed to XYY males could also be a stereotyped inference from their height. Alternatively, judges may have the cultural stereotype that taller males are more dangerous than others found guilty of aggressive, antisocial behavior. Therefore, they may sentence to institutions a disproportionate number of taller males (among them, males who happen to have the XYY chromosome). If so, why does a disproportionate number of males end up in institutions for aggressive or even violent behavior: genetic or cultural reasons? Perhaps the answer is: neither by itself and both together. Genetic and cultural factors may *interact* to produce a certain effect. (A more mundane example: what causes a sunburn? God, the sun, ultraviolet radiation, a person's genetic makeup, the chemical structure of the skin, a chemical reaction, social pressure to get a tan, a psychological predisposition to stay outside on a clear day as part of the resolution of one's Oedipal complex? All of the above, some of the above, none of the above, something else?)

A personal characteristic may be related to criminality, but this does not imply that the characteristic is the *cause* of criminal behavior. Indeed, it is unlikely that a particular gene structure will produce the same type of behavior under all circumstances. We would do better to trace behavior to *combinations* of a range of genetic structures, physical stimuli, cognitive processes, and social and cultural settings, acting not independently of one another but in concert. And just as we should not expect to isolate a single cause for behavior, we should not hope to find ultimate causes of behavior, unless we can carry our investigations back to the beginning of time.

For this reason, it is not appropriate to call a Lombrosian notion of criminal cause a "theory." In classical scientific terms, a theory must be refutable to determine its validity. There is no way to test the proposition that a particular gene structure is or is not *the* cause of criminality (or *ultimately* is even an independent cause). Empirical evidence cannot prove or invalidate the Lombrosian or any other explanation of crime. Only propositions developed within each approach, not the approach itself, can be made testable (Kuhn, 1974). We may even find a situation in which researchers pursuing differing approaches find a one-to-one correspondence between criminal behavior (measured in a certain way) and simultaneously, a particular genetic structure, a particular psychological history, a particular set of social and cultural factors, and so forth.

Explaining the rare event   A few kinds of crime, such as possession of heroin, may imply distinctive behavior patterns which dominate the person's life. For many if not most crimes, this is probably not the case. For example, burglars with minimal experience can enter a house and carry the goods back to their car in less than five minutes. Ordinarily, they will try to get rid of these stolen goods as soon as possible. The entire operation, from the search for a place to burglarize until the moment the goods are fenced, may take only an hour. Even during the burglary, the burglars will behave like noncriminals in many respects. They will drive and walk like noncriminals, speak to fences in basically everyday language, and so forth. The most of the burglars' day will probably be spent in noncriminal activity. In most respects, then, the criminals behave like noncriminals. To be discriminating, a cause of their criminal behavior must not be a cause of their general behavior. For instance, if a brain dysfunction distinctively causes the criminal behavior, the dysfunction must be of a kind that does not interfere with noncriminal behavior most of the time. Or a gene that causes criminal behavior must, in most instances, be compatible with noncriminal behavior. Or if low intelligence causes many kinds of criminal behavior, it must also generally lead to noncriminal behavior.

The fact that criminal behavior is uncommon even for repeat offenders implies that other characteristics unique to criminals are very difficult to locate. If persons are picked out for having characteristics which make them especially likely to commit a certain kind of crime, the prediction is apt to be wrong. In a recent California study described in detail in Chapter 10, the most sophisticated techniques currently available were used to select the 10 percent of the sample most likely to commit violent crimes. (The most important predictor was whether the subject had previously been convicted of a violent offense.) Upon release, only 10 percent of the group was subsequently found to commit a violent crime, and half of all the violent crimes later committed by the *total* sample of just over 2,000 people were not the work of the chosen 10 percent (Wenk and Emrich, 1972). Given the difficulties of isolating the causes of rare criminal behavior, this result is not surprising.

Implying a cure worse than the disease　Did you ever try to adjust the speed of the mechanism on a cheap wind-up alarm clock? There is usually a screw that can be turned to make the clock slower or faster. The trouble is that the whole clock mechanism is imprecise. If you try very carefully to slow down a clock that is, let us say, a minute fast per day, you are liable to end up with a clock that is two minutes slow.

The same problem arises in trying to eliminate criminal behavior, especially with persons from whom crime is rare. Any behavior change is likely to alter more than the criminality. If the change is unpleasant or punitive, as treatment of criminals usually is, there is a good chance that equally undesirable traits may be produced. The problem, like that of adjusting the alarm clock, is not the inability to change behavior but the likelihood of changing it too much. If the change is coercive, if the offender is treated as an adversary, the treatment is apt to make the offender act more than ever like a deviant. Over time, this change is the process Lemert (1972) describes as "secondary deviation." As Gove (1975) points out, and Lemert acknowledges, the problem is not that the treatment makes a person a criminal. It is that after the treatment, the person's behavior will probably be more criminal or otherwise undesirable than before.

In part, this problem can be alleviated by treating a variety of conditions instead of isolated behavior. For instance, in an area where a lot of muggings are taking place, it may be more effective to light and patrol the streets than to treat every individual robber for whom robbing is relatively rare behavior.

Another way to make the cure more effective is to design it not merely to stop bad behavior, with the new behavior left to chance, but to encourage some specific kind of good behavior. As Skinner (1971) suggests, social control based on reward is likely to work better than social control based on punishment. Mind you, punishment is just as powerful a way to change behavior as reward. But if the behavior change is triggered by a reward, one gets the behavior one wants; while if the behavior change results from (threat of) punishment, the new behavior may be worse than the old. The use of reward permits the control of the new behavior. Punishment, in contrast, can do no more than specify a few things a person is not to do, while what the person does do is open to chance.

Remembering that the cure may be worse than the disease, whenever strategies of crime control are considered, I will project what behavior the strategy would *produce* as well as what it would discourage.

If finding the causes of criminal behavior is so difficult, why should we try to explain how certain crimes occur in any society? Every criminological study is implicitly directed to one (or both) of two practical ends: finding a new strategy to stabilize or reduce crime, or finding other consequences of a particular approach to crime control. To illustrate, Lombroso's research was implicitly designed to identify people who should be incapacitated by the state to prevent crime. Goring's criticism of Lombroso was that identifying such people by their physical features would lead to a lot of error and could not be expected to reduce crime. Goring's own assertion that low intelligence led to crime implied at least two strategies of crime prevention: either incapacitating or giving special education to those of low intelligence. By contrast, Chinese criminological thought focused on crime control strategies designed to perpetuate a dynasty, while Sartre (1965) concentrated on a personal sense of responsibility in shaping one's own life.

We can discuss the consequences of different strategies of crime control without trying to determine what "really" causes crime. This book analyzes which consequences are to be expected from following strategies of crime control implied by various criminological ideas. This analysis is difficult and has problems of its own, but it is an attempt to develop practical knowledge from criminological thinking and research.

Before turning to this analysis, however, let us complete the history of criminological thought, bearing in mind the problems about explanations of crime.

PSYCHOLOGICAL EXPLANATIONS OF CRIME

At the turn of the century, an Austrian physician, Freud (1969, first published in authorized translation in 1920), spurred attempts to explain behavior in terms of personal experiences in growing up. Through the technique of psychoanalysis, subjects were able to reconstruct their early childhood experiences. Freud considered the relationship between children and their parents to be crucial in determining behavior patterns throughout life. Freud's contemporary, Aichhorn (1955, first published in 1935), another Austrian psychiatrist and director of a correctional institution, traced criminal behavior to a failure to develop normal ego control of one's impulses.

Many other explanations have traced delinquency and crime to problems of early psychological development. Miller (1958), an American anthropologist, studied boys in street gangs and concluded that their behavior was an exaggerated attempt to assert their masculinity to compensate for lack of identification with adult male figures in fatherless homes. In associating fatherless homes with poverty and explaining gang delinquency as an indirect outcome of poverty, Miller made a connection that is common to most Western explanations of crime: class distinctions are either a cause of crime or effects of the same cause as that of crime. Earlier, Healy and Bronner (1936) had traced delinquency directly to emotional problems of adjustment to poverty.

The word "delinquency" has been used here for the first time. Freud's work helped to show that the treatment of criminals should start as soon as problems were diagnosed in childhood, to make treatment of criminality most effective. A juvenile court movement began to develop at the turn of the century. Children might once have been ignored by the state as being too immature to commit crimes. However, throughout the United States today, special court procedures and treatment programs are reserved for delinquent youths. Delinquency has now taken its place beside crime as a major social problem in the Western world. But does the juvenile court movement provide tighter and more onerous state control over children than they would suffer if treated under the criminal law as adult offenders? In a series of rulings in the last decade, a number of American courts, led by the U.S. Supreme Court, have attempted to extend some of the protections of adult criminal defendants and convicts to children in the juvenile system. However, the idea of the juvenile court is still subject to criticism. (See Faust and Brantingham, 1974, for an overview of American juvenile justice history.)

The raft of psychological explanations of delinquency, including poverty, disrupted family life, and other types of poor learning environments are not alone. Another series of explanations has traced delinquency to problems in school. The work of Cohen (1955), an American sociologist, exemplifies this approach. Cohen suggests that delinquency may be a "reaction formation" to failure in school. This consists of hostility to middle-class norms among boys who had found middle-class society unattainable but still attractive.

Except for self-report research in Chapter 9, problems of delinquency will not be covered in later chapters. Whole books (e.g., Cavan and Ferdinand, 1975) and courses are devoted to this problem, and detailed integration of issues of crime control with those of delinquency would be unmanageable in this introduction to the study of crime.

Psychological and sociocultural approaches to categorizing criminals have led to the development of alternatives to imprisonment (like probation) and of other ways to serve sentences beginning with imprisonment (such as parole). While Beccaria advocated one kind of punishment for each type of crime, positivism has influenced Western criminal justice systems to consider differences among individual offenders.

CULTURAL EXPLANATIONS OF CRIME

Cultural explanations trace crime to values and norms of behavior. These are learned by people in a group (such as a society) and passed on from one generation to the next.

If suicide is considered a form of criminal behavior, the earliest major work developing a cultural explanation of crime is that of the French sociologist Durkheim (1951, first published in French in 1897). In this study, Durkheim introduced the concept of the "social fact," which stated that suicide rates in various societies might be explained without determining which individuals were suicide prone.

Durkheim arrived at four explanations of suicide. In an organization like the army, where a positive value was placed on sacrificing one's life for one's country, he found a high rate of "altruistic" suicides. In areas where the higher church authority of Roman Catholicism had been replaced by Protestant faiths, which stressed individual responsibility for salvation, Durkheim concluded that this responsibility resulted in part in a high rate of "egoistic" suicide. In areas where technology had made life so easy that people no longer felt bound to cooperate in using scarce resources, Durkheim concluded that a feeling of meaninglessness about life would result in a high rate of "anomic" suicide. Members of particularly oppressed groups, like slaves, might be particularly subject to "fatalistic" suicide.

Other theorists have described whole social groups whose values dictate a commitment to crime, such as the Thugs who dedicated themselves religiously to murder and robbery in India (Venugopal Rao, 1967: 19–28). The research begun by an American sociologist, Wolfgang, and an Italian psychiatrist, Ferracuti (1967), suggests that "subcultures of violence" may exist in many places. In the United States, it is widely believed that a group of Sicilians have imported the cultural heritage of an organization known as the Mafia to control vices like gambling, prostitution, and narcotics traffic throughout the country (President's Commission on Law Enforcement and Administration of Justice, 1967b). This idea is controversial. Some studies, like a recent historical one by Smith (1975), have concluded that the notion of Mafia-controlled organized crime is a myth. But regardless of what people may think, these ideas about the Mafia exemplify the widespread belief that cultural values are a cause of some kinds of crime.

Another explanation of some kinds of crime is that migrants to a new culture may continue to follow norms of the old culture which are illegal in the new environment, such as avenging the honor of one's family. This idea was initially developed by a Swedish-American sociologist, Sellin (1938). It has been supported by subsequent studies (Wolfgang, 1968).

In his study, Sellin also proposed a variant of the idea of culture conflict. Sellin referred to Sutherland's (1924) thesis that criminal behavior is learned from associating mostly with people who favor solving problems by committing crimes. This is known as "the theory of differential association." Sellin suggested that the special life experiences of individuals would lead them to develop unique ideas of what behavior was right and wrong. Hence these persons, in doing what they thought was right, might be surprised to discover that others considered their behavior criminal.

In the 1930s, too, still another American sociologist, Merton (1957: 131–194), developed a conception of how cultural values could be a source of crime. Known as "the theory of anomie," it was based on the assumption that practically everyone in a society knew and shared a belief that each person should work toward the same ends (like getting rich) using agreed-upon means. However, not enough legitimate means and ends would be available to everyone. In this situation of scarcity, some people would be pressed to abandon their commitment to the ends or the means or both. Those who held fast to both ends and means Merton called "conformists." Those who accepted the ends but rejected legitimate means to reach them (like some robbers) Merton called "innovators." Those who continued to follow the means but abandoned hope of reaching the ends Merton called "ritualists." Those who rejected both ends and means, with no commitment to try to establish new cultural standards (like some habitual heroin users), Merton called "retreatists." Those who rejected both ends and means and committed themselves to the establishment of new cultural standards (like some political terrorists) Merton called "rebels."

Another pair of American sociologists, Cloward and Ohlin (1960), studied street gangs and carried Merton's conception a step further. True, they claimed, illicit behavior might begin in a geographical area in ways suggested by Merton. But before long, groups of people would emerge who shared a pattern of nonconformist behavior (like theft as a form of "innovation"). These groups would become "subcultures" unto themselves. When this happened, people would adopt the nonconformist behavior in order to conform to the subcultural group.

Almost by definition, subcultural explanations of crime imply treatment or rehabilitation strategies of crime control, to retrain people to conform to the law. Greater tolerance of deviant subcultures might be implied by subcultural research but usually is not, since most deviant subcultures are cast as poor or otherwise inferior to middle-class culture. Despite the many rationales and supporting evidence for such strategies, there has been a recent wave of disenchantment with rehabilitation or treatment in the United States. Critics, like Von Hirsch (1976) argue that the many programs that have been tried don't work. We will consider the merits of such strategies in later chapters.

SOCIAL EXPLANATIONS OF CRIME

Some thinkers—like Yablonsky (1959), who observed American street gangs—have concluded that illicit behavior can be a reaction to the situation of the moment. For instance, if a rumor spreads among an unorganized group of boys that a small fight has started somewhere, this can become the occasion for a large gang fight, according to Yablonsky. In his study of criminal homicide, Wolfgang (1975, originally published in 1958), concluded that many people were aroused to kill their victims because of chance provocative acts by the victims themselves.

As indicated above, it has also been argued that repeated illicit behavior can result from a social interaction process known as "labeling" (from the recent work of the American sociologist Lemert, 1972, borrowing from an earlier book by Tannenbaum, 1938). Lemert describes the process as follows. First, a person inexplicably and uncharacteristically commits a deviant act ("primary deviation"). This act is detected by others, who label the person "deviant" (or "delinquent" or "criminal"). The person then begins to see himself or herself as a deviant, and thereafter behaves accordingly ("secondary deviation"). This leads to reaffirmation of the label by others in a self-fulfilling prophecy.

It is a short step from the process of labeling to the question of why or how people decide that others are criminals or have committed crimes. A long line of criminologists (Marx; the Dutchman Bonger, 1969, first published in the United States in 1916; the Americans Robison, 1973 [originally published in 1936], on delinquency, and Sutherland, 1940; and many thereafter) have concluded that because of the power of the rich or the vulnerability of the poor, or both, the search for criminals is concentrated in the lower socioeconomic classes. This approach to crime and criminals is the focus of the controversy over the "real" causes of crime. If Piliavin and Briar (1964) conclude that the behavior, not the socioeconomic class, of juveniles gets them into trouble with the police, the rebuttal is that lower-class children tend to be antagonistic to the police because of a history of discrimination. If Terry (1967) finds that a prior offense record is the primary determinant in treating children as delinquent, the argument may be that the prior record is a result of discrimination. If Green (1970) finds that adults are arrested in Philadelphia not because of their race (as an indicator of class) but because of where they were born (in the U.S. South) or their occupational status, he is open to the response that these other factors are, after all, only signs of class discrimination. And so it goes.

Leslie Wilkins (e.g., 1964), an English statistician who works in the United States suggests that the way information is presented, rather than its content, may affect official decisions about crime. For example, if, at the beginning of a case, the suspect's race is mentioned first, the investigator may discriminate on the basis of race. If other information were presented instead, this might not occur.

Still other sociologists (e.g., Coser, 1956; Erikson, 1966; and Garfinkel, 1956) state that all societies (especially large, heterogeneous ones) will define a quota of persons as deviant or criminal. The size of the quota depends on factors like the capacity of available jails and prisons. This is done to establish what societal membership means.

Beginning fifty years ago, a group of Chicago sociologists, including Thrasher (1963), and Shaw and McKay (1972), and known collectively as "the Chicago School" or "the ecological school," began a new line of research. They explained delinquency and crime as the interaction between "social disorganization" and physical environment (such as overcrowded areas or those that fall between different kinds of neighborhoods). Their work has generated a good deal of research on the link between individual decisions to commit crime and crime rates in certain geographic areas. These problems are referred to collectively as "the ecological fallacy" (Hammond, 1973).

How can so many explanations of crime be integrated? Indeed, is such integration possible? This is the concern of a group of thinkers known as "systems theorists." One model that has emerged from such research is Wilkins's (1964) model of "deviance amplification." This model relates such factors as norms of behavior, opportunities for crime, and defiance of norms to concepts like information processing and feedback. The purpose is to account for the increase of deviance in society. Systems theorists do not look for particular causes of crime. Instead, they first try to show how the interaction of many factors produces crime. Then, they explore how changes in the social system might affect crime. To systems theorists, the issue is not why crime occurs, but how the probability of crime can be changed.

CONCLUSION

If this historical review has stirred your imagination about ways of looking at crime, it has served a good purpose. Stereotypes about crime abound, and it is worth getting a sense of the many approaches that have been used in the study of crime.

With notable (or notorious?) exceptions, the bulk of criminological literature in this century has taken a positivist perspective. There have been two major focuses: (1) the factors which distinguish criminals from noncriminals and (2) how society should respond to such distinctions. The practical application of these findings are discussed beginning in Chapter 8.

Persons with a continuing interest in criminology should read the sources cited in this chapter. This author's interpretation of others' work should be approached with healthy skepticism. There is some bias in anyone's summary of another's work, and readers must finally reach their own conclusions. It is also fascinating to spend some time with a thinker like Beccaria, to share a vision of the world of someone who lived centuries ago.

The survey of literature in this chapter is by no means exhaustive. If you are reading this book for a course, you may hear your teacher mutter (or even exclaim): "How could the author have not mentioned so-and-so's work!" Students of criminology are fortunate enough to have such a rich body of literature that new ideas and knowledge always remain to be discovered. If you have the chance, try visiting the libraries of several career criminologists. You will begin to get an idea of how wide a range of literature is available. Those of us who work regularly in the field tend to have pet notions of whose work is "important" or "seminal" or is a "major contribution to the literature" or "something every student in the field has to know." Not surprisingly, disagreement abounds. This is an open invitation to beginning students to explore the literature and to choose freely which work best suits their own purposes.

This author favors the systems approach. That is, each of the perspectives mentioned in this chapter is integrated with the others in planning crime control strategies. This will become apparent as you read on. But the purpose of this book is not so much to persuade as to stimulate you to ask new questions and develop your own ideas and commitments. By now, you can choose one of many views of crime and explore where and how far it takes you. As you read, feel free to be opinionated about crime, but also to change your opinions and perspectives if one seems untenable. In the process, you, like all of us, will be exploring the potentially limitless field of criminology.

REFERENCES

Aichhorn, August. 1955. *Wayward Youth*. New York: Meridian.

Alabama Supreme Court. 1886. *Parsons v. State*. 81 Ala. 577.

Beccaria, Cesare (Henry Paolucci, trans.). 1968. *On Crimes and Punishments*. Indianapolis: Bobbs-Merrill.

Bentham, Jeremy (H. L. A. Hart, ed.). 1970. *Of Laws in General*. Atlantic Highlands, N.J.: Humanities.

Berkman, Alexander. 1971. *ABC of Anarchism*. London: Freedom.

Berman, Harold J., and James W. Spindler. 1972. *Soviet Criminal Law and Procedure*. Cambridge, Mass:. Harvard (2nd ed.).

Bodde, Derk, and Clarence Morris. 1967. *Law in Imperial China*. Cambridge, Mass.: Harvard.

Bonger, Willem (Austin W. Turk, ed. and trans.). 1969. *Criminality and Economic Conditions*. Bloomington, Ind.: Indiana University Press.

Burke, Kenneth J. 1969. "The 'XYY syndrome': genetics, behavior and the law." *Denver Law Journal* 46 (Spring): 261–284.

California Supreme Court. 1966. *People v. Conley*. 64 Cal. 2d 321.

Cavan, Ruth Shonle, and Theodore N. Ferdinand. 1975. *Juvenile Delinquency*. Philadelphia: Lippincott (3rd ed.).

Cloward, Richard A., and Lloyd A. Ohlin. 1960. *Delinquency and Opportunity: A Theory of Delinquent Gangs*. New York: Free Press.

Cohen, Albert K. 1955. *Delinquent Boys: The Culture of the Gang*. New York: Free Press.

Coser, Lewis. 1956. *Functions of Social Conflict*. New York: Free Press.

Darwin, Charles. 1970. *The Origin of Species*. New York: Macmillan.

David, Rene, and Henry P. Devries. 1958. *The French Legal System*. Dobbs Ferry, N.Y.: Oceana.

Durkheim, Emile (John A. Spaulding and George Simpson, trans.). 1951. *Suicide*. New York: Free Press.

England. 1957. *Homicide Act*. 5 & 6 Eliz. 2, chap. 11.

———, Court of Common Pleas. 1670. *Bushell's Case*. 1 Vaughn's Rep. 135.

———, House of Lords. 1843. *M'Naghten's Case*. 8 Eng. Rep. 718.

————, Kingston Assizes. 1724. *Trial of Edward Arnold.* 16 How. St. Tr. 695.

Erikson, Kai T. 1966. *Wayward Puritans: A Study in the Sociology of Deviance.* New York: Wiley.

Faust, Frederic L., and Paul J. Brantingham. 1974. *Juvenile Justice Philosophy: Readings, Cases and Comments.* St. Paul, Minn.: West.

Freud, Sigmund. 1969. *General Introduction to Psychoanalysis: The Authorized English Translation.* New York: Simon & Schuster.

Garfinkel, Harold. 1956. "Conditions of successful degradation ceremonies." *American Journal of Sociology* 61 (March): 420–424.

Goring, Charles. 1972. *The English Convict: A Statistical Study to Which is Added the Schedule of Measurements and General Anthropological Data.* Montclair, N.J.: Patterson, Smith (1913 ed.).

Gove, Walter R. (ed.). 1975. *The Labeling of Deviance: Evaluating a Perspective.* New York: Wiley.

Green, Edward. 1970. "Race, social status, and criminal arrest." *American Sociological Review* 35 (June): 476–490.

Hammond, John L. 1973. "Two sources of error in ecological correlations." *American Sociological Review* 38 (December): 764–777.

Hare, Robert. 1970. *Psychopathy: Theory and Research.* New York: Wiley.

Healy, William, and Augusta F. Bronner. 1936. *New Light on Delinquency and Its Treatment.* New Haven, Conn.: Yale.

Hirschi, Travis, and Michael J. Hindelang. 1977. "Intelligence and delinquency." *American Sociological Review* 42 (August): 571–586.

Kuhn, Thomas S. 1974. *The Structure of Scientific Revolution.* Chicago: University of Chicago Press (2nd enlarged edition).

LaFave, Wayne R., and Austin W. Scott, Jr. 1972. *Criminal Law.* St. Paul, Minn.: West.

Lemert, Edwin M. 1972. *Human Deviance, Social Problems, and Social Control.* Englewood Cliffs, N.J.: Prentice-Hall (2nd ed.).

Lombroso, Cesare (Henry P. Horton, trans.), 1968. *Crime, Its Causes and Remedies.* Montclair, N.J.: Smith, Patterson.

McCarthy, Colman. 1975. "White collar crime." *Washington Post* (April 11).

Marx, Karl (Frederick Engels, ed. and trans.). 1967. *Capital: A Critique of Political Economy.* New York: International (3 vols.).

Merton, Robert King. 1957. *Social Theory and Social Structure.* New York: Free Press (rev. ed.).

Miller, Walter B. 1958. "Lower class culture as a generating milieu of gang delinquency." *Journal of Social Issues* 14 (November): 5–19.

Pepinsky, Harold E. 1973. "The people v. the principle of legality in the People's Republic of China." *Journal of Criminal Justice* 1 (March): 51–60.

Piliavin, Irving, and Scott Briar. 1964. "Police encounters with juveniles." *American Journal of Sociology* 70 (September): 206–214.

President's Commission on Law Enforcement and Administration of Justice. 1967a. *Crime and Its Impact: An Assessment.* Washington, D.C.: United States Government Printing Office.

———. 1967b. *Organized Crime.* Washington, D.C.: United States Government Printing Office.

Quinney, Richard. 1974. *Critique of Legal Order: Crime Control in Capitalist Society.* Boston: Little, Brown.

Robison, Sophia M. 1973. *Can Delinquency Be Measured?* Millwood, N.Y.: Kraus Reprint (1936 ed.).

Sartre, Jean-Paul (Robert Denoon Cumming, ed., and trans.). 1965. *The Philosophy of Jean-Paul Sartre.* New York: Random House.

Sellin, Thorsten. 1938. *Culture Conflict and Crime.* Millwood, N.Y.: Kraus Reprints.

Shaw, Clifford R., and Henry D. McKay. 1972. *Juvenile Delinquency and Urban Areas.* Chicago: University of Chicago (rev. ed.).

Skinner, B. F. 1971. *Beyond Freedom and Dignity.* New York: Knopf.

Smith, Dwight. 1975. *The Mafia Mystique.* New York: Basic.

Sutherland, Edwin H. 1924. *Criminology.* Philadelphia: Lippincott.

———. 1940. "Is 'white-collar crime' crime?" *American Sociological Review* 5 (February): 1–12.

Tannenbaum, Frank. 1938. *Crime and the Community.* Boston: Ginn.

Terry, Robert M. 1967. "The screening of juvenile offenders." *Journal of Criminal Law, Criminology, and Police Science* 58 (June): 58–71.

Thrasher, Frederic M. (James F. Short, Jr., ed.). 1963. *The Gang: A Study of One Thousand Three Hundred Thirteen Gangs in Chicago.* Chicago: University of Chicago (abridged ed.).

United States Court of Appeal (D.C. Circuit). 1954. *Durham v. United States.* 214 F. 2d 862.

———. 1972. *United States v. Browner.* 471 F. 2d 969.

Valenstein, Elliot S. 1973. *Brain Control.* New York: Wiley.

Van den Haag, Ernest. 1975. *Punishing Criminals: Concerning a Very Old and Painful Question.* New York: Basic.

Van der Sprenkel, Sybille. 1962. *Legal Institutions in Manchu China.* London: Athlone.

Venugopal Rao, S. 1967. *Facets of Crime in India.* New York: Allied.

Von Hirsch, Andrew. 1976. *Doing Justice: The Choice of Punishment.* New York: Hill and Wang.

Wenk, Ernst A., and Robert L. Emrich. 1972. "Assaultive youth." *Journal of Research on Crime and Delinquency* 9 (July): 179–196.

Wilkins, Leslie T. 1964. *Social Deviance: Social Action, Policy, and Research.* Englewood Cliffs, N.J.: Prentice-Hall.

Wilson, James Q. 1975. *Thinking About Crime.* New York: Basic.

Wolfgang, Marvin E. 1975. *Patterns of Criminal Homicide.* Montclair, N.J.: Smith, Patterson.

——— (ed.). 1968. Crime and Culture: Essays in Honor of Thorsten Sellin. New York: Wiley.

————, and Franco Ferracuti. *The Subculture of Violence: Towards an Integrated Theory in Criminology*. London: Tavistock.

Yablonsky, Lewis. 1959. "The delinquent gang as a near-group." *Social Problems* 7 (Fall): 108–117.

FOOD FOR THOUGHT

(This book is intended to be heuristic. That is, the information, instead of being presented to you as an end in itself, is intended to stimulate you to think about important social issues. Thus, each chapter ends with a few questions for you to consider, under the heading "Food for Thought." If you are reading this book for a class, your teacher may raise the questions for class discussion, or ask you to write essays in answer to some of the questions. But don't wait for a teacher to take the initiative. If you know other people who are reading the book, try getting together with them to debate and discuss the issues raised. Try writing some brief answers to the questions just as a challenge to yourself. If nothing else, take some time to sit and reflect on how you would answer the questions for someone asking your opinion. Remember: this or any book is only as good as the thinking it makes you do for yourself.)

1. One way to weigh approaches in explaining any phenomenon, including crime, is to ask what kind of power you would want to give people—to choose an approach on political grounds. Thus, you might favor a biological approach to crime because it is easier to imagine success in changing people by manipulating their body chemistry—as by surgery—than by using other forms of influence, like psychotherapy or social reorganization. On the other hand, a biological technique like psychosurgery may seem too powerful and dangerous a weapon to risk putting in the wrong hands. Instead, you might decide that psychotherapy is as far as we dare go. Hence, you might favor using psychological approaches to learn about crime and criminality. Going a step further, it might seem that unjust social discrimination would probably result from applying knowledge of crime or criminality—including biological and psychological knowledge. That is, particular individuals, rather than the social structure, would be identified and

isolated as the source of the crime problem. Hence, you might favor a sociocultural approach as the least dangerous, even if potentially weakest, alternative.

On political grounds, which approach do you think should be supported most, and which least, in funding criminological research? As a criminologist yourself, which approach would you prefer taking?

2. In his book *Thinking About Crime*, James Q. Wilson, a political scientist, states that trying to figure out why people commit crimes is futile. After all, he argues, one can design a system to deter people from crime even without knowing what factors would promote crimes in the absence of deterrence.

Travis Hirschi, a sociologist and author of the book *Causes of Delinquency*, has declared (in the School of Criminal Justice's 1976 Pinkerton Lecture at the State University of New York at Albany) that for criminologists to neglect research on why people commit crimes is morally indefensible. He argues that this is what criminologists are paid to do and what they ought to deliver.

How much emphasis do you think criminologists ought to give to research on why people commit crimes?

3. How strongly should criminologists consider the possibility of abandoning law as a means of controlling crime?

4. A number of criminologists, such as Alexander Berkman, in his book *ABC of Anarchism*, have stated that success in capitalist society amounts to stealing. According to this argument, the only difference between legal profit making and illegal theft is that the law happens to support one person and oppose the other. Generally speaking, laws are structured to favor accumulation of wealth by the rich but not by the poor. The thief may work as hard and enterprisingly as the businessperson, and consumers and workers may be as powerless in unequal exchange with the businessperson as victims are in regard to the thief.

If protection of good business in capitalist society amounts to license to steal, what rehabilitation objectives for thieves or property offenders are justified?

5. Should all criminologists use the same approach in answering the same questions about crime, or should diverse approaches be encouraged?

CHAPTER TWO

What Should We Control?

What kind of evidence is adequate to show success or failure in crime control? If you think the answer is simple, think again. Apart from general problems of error in any measure of success or failure (see Chapter 3), which measure should be used in the first place? The range of choice is broad. There are three general ways of portraying the crime problem. Some measures are of amounts of *crime*. Others are measures of *criminality*. Still others concern the *costs* of crime and of criminality, which may be weighed against the costs of crime control.

It is easy to imagine reducing crime in one way while increasing it in another. We might succeed in reducing crime by focusing on stopping confirmed criminals, only to reduce the system's capacity to control first offenders. The Prosecutor's Management Information System (Institute for Law and Social Research, 1974) rests on the assumption that it is more important to identify career criminals and give priority to their control. This could lead to more criminals but fewer crimes, as people without criminal records learn that they can commit one crime with relative impunity.

Which is more important to reduce, crime or criminality? Reducing crime implies that people run a lower risk of being victimized. But if this means that more people commit their first crimes, then we might be protecting people from crime at the expense of their own degeneracy. This argument is implicit in the debate between the proponents of legalizing crimes without victims, like Morris and Hawkins (1970), who argue for legalization as a move to efficient crime control, and those who favor enforcing laws against immorality, as by combating the distribution of obscenity (the argument of minority opinions in the report of the President's Commission on Pornography, 1970). One side argues for protecting the public from crime; the other side for protecting the public from immorality. Scientific logic cannot help us decide which danger is greater, but this issue may be crucial in deciding how to control crime.

The cost of crime and crime control is yet another matter. We could attempt to reduce theft by protecting rich would-be victims, thus (a) reducing the total amount stolen in our society and (b) driving thieves to steal from the poor instead, thereby (c) increasing the number of thefts and of people victimized. To cite another example, it has been suggested (as by Quinney, 1974) that a few wealthy businesspersons steal more than all the street burglars put together. If we stop this white-collar crime, we may reduce the cost of crime more than by stopping the burglars, and yet stop fewer crimes and criminals. No matter which benefits of crime control we choose, we may end up increasing its cost more than we gain from reducing crime or criminality. For instance, we might find ourselves spending 10 percent more money on burglary enforcement in order to reduce the burglary rate by 5 percent or catch 3 percent more burglars. But perhaps intangible gains of crime control—like reducing the public's fear of crime—more than outweigh any disparity between the cost of crime control and reduction of crime, criminality, or even the direct cost of crime. This issue, too, is crucial in deciding how crime should be controlled. And again, it is an issue that scientific logic cannot resolve.

If we have trouble in controlling crime, it is in part because we cannot agree on what we most want to control or reduce.

MEASURES OF CRIME—CONVICTIONS

Each of the three categories of crime measurement consists of various competing measures. The oldest way of measuring crime is by counting the number of court convictions. Court records are the oldest source of information about the amount of crime and whether crime is increasing or decreasing. Recently, historians have begun using court records to trace crime trends in England as far back as the fourteenth century (Hanawalt, 1976; Samaha, 1973). Nationwide conviction statistics were first published in France in 1827 (Sellin and Wolfgang, 1964: 7). The earliest U.S. statewide crime statistics were prosecution and conviction data for New York in 1829 (Robinson, 1911).

Should conviction statistics be the basis for deciding whether crime is being prevented? There are two points in favor of their use. One line of argument (Tappan, 1947) is as follows: Respect for our legal system implies that the courts alone must decide whether a crime has been committed. Thus, it is presumptuous for people to determine this themselves. No crime has "really" occurred unless and until evidence has been weighed in a court and found sufficient for conviction. Without due process of law, it is only a short step to accusing people of crimes without giving them a fair chance to defend themselves. Requiring court conviction prevents fear and loss of reputation with wild, unproven, and probably unprovable charges.

Another purpose of limiting crime statistics to court convictions is to restrain government officials from intruding into people's lives. If crimes can become crime statistics without court conviction, then crime statistics will increase greatly. If this happens, then—by definition—the crime problem is larger. If the crime problem is defined as larger, officials can (and do) press the claim that more officials are needed to control crime more forcefully than ever. A vicious circle can be created in which officials take on more power and private citizens learn to depend on them more for protection and management of their problems. Citizens become less reliant on themselves and each other, and try to take advantage of each other in self-defense. The crime problem grows accordingly, and officials must take on still more power to protect the citizens from themselves. To control the criminal justice bureaucracy and official power, we would do well to be conservative about reporting crime—for example, by requiring that crime reports be preceded by a court hearing (Pepinsky, 1977).

In general, people favor using conviction data to determine whether crime is increasing or decreasing if they are especially worried about the dangers of *over*reporting crime.

In the history of U.S. crime measurement, there has been overriding concern about the dangers of *under*reporting crime (Pepinsky, 1976b). It is commonly believed that using conviction statistics as crime indicators amounts to ignoring crime. The argument is this: Many crimes are never reported, police fail to arrest suspects for many reported crimes, and many suspects who are arrested are not convicted. In addition, many children are "taken into custody" rather than arrested, and "adjudicated delinquent" rather than convicted of crimes, simply because of their youth. Findings that children as old as eighteen have committed offenses may therefore be excluded from conviction figures, or more rarely, from arrest figures.

Since the likelihood of underreporting crime probably fluctuates as conviction figures go up and down, a decrease or increase in conviction figures does not tell us whether crime is really decreasing or increasing. We may therefore be deluding ourselves if we rely on lower conviction figures to indicate that crime is being prevented, or on higher conviction figures to indicate failure of crime prevention. Worse yet, if we understate the crime problem by defining it in terms of conviction figures, we cannot protect ourselves from danger. In our complacency, we will fail to strengthen our criminal justice system enough to control crime. One early U.S. argument to this effect is that by Robinson (1911).

Because conviction figures have traditionally been used to indicate the magnitude of crime, and because there are plausible arguments in favor of this choice, Chapter 4 is devoted to considering the control of crime conviction rates. Perhaps we should be satisfied that we are preventing crime if we decrease the conviction rates. As you continue to read this book, do not hasten to rule this possibility out. Conviction rates are still used as the authoritative indicator of crime in many parts of the world, including European countries with a long history of crime measurement. It remains to be seen whether the United States has made the right choice in developing ways to measure crime more completely.

Police data   The first police department to begin regular compilation of arrest figures was that of New York City, in 1840. As early as 1858, these figures were used to show that crime was rising and hence that the police department budget needed to be increased (Inciardi, 1976: 179–180). To this day, the only nationwide record of police figures is the Federal Bureau of Investigation's annual arrest data (except for seven "Index Offenses," described below).

After arrest but before conviction, cases can be resolved in many ways. Prosecutors may drop or reduce charges in order to induce defendants to plead guilty and save the time and expense of a trial. Defendants may be diverted into community programs, like Alcoholics Anonymous, or agree to informal arrangements, like making restitution, so that conviction is avoided. Defendants may abscond. Witnesses may decline to take the trouble or risk of giving evidence to convict, or may even die before testifying. A defendant wanted in another jurisdiction may be turned over to prosecutors without first being prosecuted. Under these circumstances, arrest data will include reports of crimes that fail to appear in conviction data.

Furthermore, a person who has been arrested may not be convicted because someone decides that no crime has occurred. For various reasons, more than 18 percent of arrests in the United States ended in dismissal or acquittal in 1974, according to the Federal Bureau of Investigation (F.B.I., 1975: 174). However, arrest records almost always remain untouched. In many jurisdictions today, defendants who have had cases dismissed or been acquitted can have their arrest records expunged. However, perhaps out of ignorance, they seldom bother to do so.

All these adjustments to cases after arrest provide a basis for the argument that arrests both underreport *and* overreport crime.

Again, in the United States, most people believe that arrest figures vastly underreport crime. They point out that the police fail to identify suspects in most reported cases of major crimes. For instance, nationwide, the police fail to get enough evidence to arrest a suspect in more than 80 percent of reported burglaries (F.B.I., 1975: 166). Furthermore, even when those arrested confess to or are charged with several crimes, only one offense is recorded for that case in arrest statistics. One reflection of this discrepancy: F.B.I. (1975: 166, 174) figures suggest that police "clear" five burglary cases "by arrest" for every three arrests they make. (On the other hand, police occasionally report several arrests of suspects for single offenses.) And increasingly, defendants may be summoned to court and ultimately convicted of minor offenses without being arrested.

Those who criticize the use of arrest and conviction data as a measure of crime often state that arrest and conviction data refer to criminals, not crimes. This is debatable. Many defendants are arrested and convicted repeatedly, so that annual arrest and conviction figures are overstatements of the number of persons involved. And of course, many criminals may never be apprehended or prosecuted at all. Arrest and conviction statistics are hybrids: they overstate numbers of official criminals by reporting cases as those of crimes, and they understate numbers of official crimes by reporting cases as those of criminals. Arrest (and conviction) data warrant serious criticism as crime indicators, but not because they indicate the number of criminals.

U.S. police themselves have long been dissatisfied with arrests as a measure of crime. In 1927, the International Association of Chiefs of Police recommended that national crime data be based instead on offense reports made by the police, whether or not arrests followed (National Commission on Law Observance and Enforcement, 1931: 10). The F.B.I. has been trying to implement this recommendation since 1930. At present, the F.B.I. annually reports the numbers (and rates per 100,000 total population) of "offenses known to the police" in seven categories: murder and nonnegligent manslaughter, forcible rape, robbery, aggravated assault, burglary or breaking or entering, larceny or theft, and motor vehicle theft. Many U.S. police departments report "offenses known" figures for all offenses in their jurisdictions.

The procedure for setting up "offenses known" data is a little involved. Whenever a police officer sees or hears of reasonable grounds for believing that an offense has occurred, a written report of it must be filed. The report is then supposed to be reviewed by a detective, who may "unfound" it. (Every year, the F.B.I. reports that detectives across the country unfound 4 percent of all offense reports.) From this point on, the offense report is supposed to remain in "offenses known" data, even though a police officer, prosecutor, judge or jury may later decide that the crime never occurred. (By contrast, the British Home Office subtracts such cases from police murder figures [Gibson and Klein, 1961, 1969]).

After clearing the investigative officer, the reports by U.S. police are then to be compiled by a departmental statistician. If two or more offenses are reported for a single incident (e.g., rape and murder), the statistician is supposed to record only the most serious offense. The department then sends its figures to the F.B.I., which reviews them and changes the figures it believes to be incorrect or implausible (President's Commission on Law Enforcement and Administration of Justice, 1967: 211).

Many liberties are thought to be taken in compiling "offenses known" data. To begin with, police officers inevitably exercise discretion as to which offenses should be reported. Black (1970) and Pepinsky (1976a) have found that this occurs in various ways—for example, based on wishes of complainants and decisions of the police dispatcher. Second, detectives in many departments, flooded with cases, are reputed to be somewhat cavalier about their review and investigation of many reports. Third, some departments apparently feel free to increase or decrease their figures for political purposes. This author has been told of various cases—typically in large cities—in which supervisors tell their patrol officers to report major offenses as minor ones, or to stop reporting some kinds of complaints altogether, in order to prove that police are succeeding in preventing crime. Statisticians have been rumored to add or subtract freely from the figures in order to meet departmental objectives—for demanding larger budgets or for showing that crime is being prevented. Seidman and Couzens (1974) conclude that from 1969 to 1971, there is good reason to believe that the Washington, D.C., police revised offense reports downward to indicate success in crime prevention, and that changes in F.B.I. reporting procedures facilitated this subterfuge. Some absurdities even get published. By changing its reporting procedures, the New York City Police Department managed to report 72 percent more offenses in 1966 than in 1965 (Weinraub, 1967). Finally, as mentioned, if the F.B.I. does not believe the reported figures for a jurisdiction, the figures are adjusted.

The strength of "offenses known" data is also their weakness. The data include reports of offenses regardless of whether suspects can be identified and apprehended. This makes "offenses known" figures more inclusive than arrest figures, but officials can also play around with and perhaps even abuse these data precisely because no defendant's fate hangs on their accuracy.

Whatever their weaknesses, police data remain the most widely used referent for the size of crime in the United States. The reduction of police-produced crime rates is discussed in Chapter 6.

Even "offenses known" data have been criticized for being substantially underreported. In response, in the mid 1960s a new crime measurement technique was developed: the victim survey.

Victimization The first three major U.S. victim surveys were commissioned by the President's Commission on Law Enforcement and Administration of Justice in 1965 (Biderman et al., 1967; Ennis, 1967; Reiss, 1967). Numerous victim surveys have followed and their popularity continues to mount, especially in the United States, as successive surveys begin to make year-to-year comparisons possible (National Criminal Justice Statistics and Information Service, 1976b, 1977).

In the typical victim survey, a random sample of households or businesses is asked whether they as individuals, or in some cases any of their members, has been a victim of certain offenses during the preceding year. Affirmative answers are followed by requests to describe the incidents.

It is difficult to make direct comparisons between victim survey figures and other indicators of the size of crime, but it is nonetheless common to compare victim surveys to police "offenses known" data. One victim survey, of what was then the Model City area of Minneapolis, found ten times as much crime as in police "offenses known" figures (Reynolds, 1972). Differences are normally not this large. For instance, the largest difference shown from a comparison of 1974 figures for the entire United States is that more than six times as many thefts of less than $50 were reported in the victim survey as were reported to police. At the opposite extreme, it was found that 90 percent of business robberies were reported to police (Hindelang et al., 1977: 358). But the 1974 figures also show the problems of comparing victim survey and police figures. According to the victim survey, 869,700 robberies were reported to the police (Hindelang et al., 1977: 358). According to the F.B.I. (1975: 56), there were only 441,290 such reports. Does this mean that the police unfound almost half the robbery reports they receive? The F.B.I. has never reported as high as a 20 percent unfounding rate for any offense, and robberies would probably be among the less likely offenses to be unfounded. (The same victim survey/police data discrepancy appears for all other index offenses.) It is possible that the police receive many more complaints than they admit (although this was not the case, at least in this observer's presence [Pepinsky, 1976a]). It could be that victim survey respondents have bad memories or lie freely. If this is the case, it is not simply that victim survey respondents exaggerate in saying that they have made reports to police. Reiss (1967: 150) interviewed a sample of people in Detroit whom he knew had reported offenses to the police in the preceding month. Twenty percent of these people denied making any reports. Discrepancies between victim survey and "offenses known" data range so widely that it is hard to know who or what to blame for the inconsistencies.

Moreover, victim surveys make it hard to know whether crime is increasing or decreasing. Because of their expense, only limited random samples of people in private households and businesses are interviewed. When the amount of a particular crime increases or decreases in the samples, there is a wide margin for error in generalizing from these samples to the larger population. If numbers of crimes for the overall populations change by just one or a few percentage points a year, the sample figures are bound to change so little that analysts will hesitate to draw any conclusions regarding the whole population. As is to be expected, the first comparisons of victim figures from one period to the next are inconclusive. Researchers generally find insufficient reason to believe that amounts of victimization are changing (National Criminal Justice Information and Statistics Service, 1976b, 1977).

Suffice it to say that victim survey figures are consistently higher than police "offenses known" figures, and that who is over- or underreporting is far from clear. However, because victim survey data as indicators of the crime problem have been widely publicized, Chapter 7 discusses whether and how victimization rates might be reduced.

What does a measure of crime measure? What is this thing called "crime"? By now, you can see just how slippery a term "crime" is. Crime comes in many amounts and sizes, depending on who—judges and juries, police or private citizens—defines it. Amid all this confusion, people repeatedly ask: How much crime is there *really*, and is crime *really* increasing or decreasing? When all the hidden crime has been detected, and all the lies and errors of memory and perception accounted for, what is the *true* crime rate, and how much does it change from one time to the next?

For better or for worse, these questions are unanswerable.

A crime is not a simple event like a flood or transportation of goods or a death. Consider the crime of murder. People die all the time without being considered murder victims. And people kill each other all the time without being considered murderers. Further, unintentional killing of another person is not necessarily considered a crime at all, let alone murder. Even when all concerned agree that an intentional killing has taken place, the killing is often partly excused or justified. Though the common law and the statutory law of murder may have taken centuries to develop and clarify, there is still uncertainty and controversy over whether the police officer who shoots the fleeing youth, or those who shoot their spouse or lover, or the apparent rape victim who stabs her attacker, is guilty of murder; or whether the eyewitness correctly identified the slayer; or whether the confession of murder was truthful.

In many cases, the law leaves ample room for honest disagreement over whether a particular crime has occurred. There is bound to be a lot of disagreement; such decisions involve not only whether there has been a crime, but what the official response should be. Crime is a serious offense to society, requiring that the person's life ought to be specially managed by the state. This moral and political judgment is at the heart of the meaning of the word "crime," and there is no way to be value neutral in deciding whether a crime has really occurred.

By extension, to conclude that crime is being prevented is to decide that the state has fewer occasions to take custody of people and of their affairs. This is what a decreasing crime rate really means. Another way of looking at it is this: If we decide that the courts, or the police, or victim survey respondents are the authorities who truly decide how big the crime problem is, we must rely on *their* moral and political judgment regarding state intervention in private affairs. Who should we trust to tell us that we can get along better together without official intercession: judges and juries by convicting fewer defendants, police by arresting fewer suspects or by filing fewer offense reports, or victim survey respondents by describing fewer incidents? To put it another way, do we need criminal justice officials more if: judges and juries convict more, police arrest more or file more offense reports, or victim survey respondents report more incidents? Inferring whether crime is "really" decreasing or increasing involves these issues.

When we, as citizens, call something a measure of crime, we use it to determine how much we want officials to take the problem out of our hands. If we are skeptical of such state intervention, we may want to measure the crime problem in terms of convictions—to err, if at all, on the side of conservatism. If we are inclined to have officials take care of our lives and our fortunes, if we are worried about being left officially unprotected, we may want to measure crime in terms of victim survey reports—to exaggerate the problem and to err on the side of protecting ourselves from each other more than we need.

Keep this issue in mind as you read and consider Chapters 4 through 7.

MEASURES OF CRIMINALITY—INCARCERATION

While the traditional way to measure crime was to count convictions, the traditional way to count criminals was to count prisoners. In the United States, Massachusetts began publishing an annual state census of prisoners in 1834 (Robinson, 1911). The U.S. government now publishes censuses of state and federal prisoners convicted and sentenced to serve more than a year (National Criminal Justice Information and Statistics Service, 1976c). Today, figures on incarceration (placement in jail or prison) can be compared worldwide (Waller and Chan, 1974).

Perhaps people once believed that the number of people in jail and in prison represented the number of criminals in a society. Few would hold this view today. For one thing, many people who are incarcerated are awaiting trial. In some countries, they are simply held; there is no hearing process. Holding people who have not (yet) been convicted is known as "detention." In the United States, only jails—county or city lock-ups designed to hold people for short periods (seldom more than a year)—are used for this purpose. Jails are also used for people sentenced to short terms after conviction. Hence, if jail inmates are included in U.S. incarceration figures, the figures will cover not only convicts but detainees as well. If, instead, only people in state and federal prisons (more centrally managed places than jails, designed to hold serious offenders for longer periods) are included, the incarceration data will exclude the many jail inmates convicted of crimes. Jail figures can make quite a difference in incarceration statistics. This is discussed in detail in Chapter 8. For now, note that the U.S. jail population (more than 140,000 on July 1, 1972; Hindelang et al., 1977: 237) now approaches the size of the prison population (just over 196,000 as of Dec. 31, 1972; Hindelang et al., 1977: 686).

Distinctions between those incarcerated and other categories of people seem arbitrary. Many convicts are under government supervision but remain in the community. They may be in halfway houses. They may never have been sentenced to jail or prison, but instead placed under a form of supervision called "probation." They may have been released from prison before expiration of their terms, under a form of supervision called "parole." U.S. state and local figures are hard to obtain, but it is known that almost three times as many persons are under other forms of supervision as are held in federal penitentiaries (Hindelang et al., 1977: 665, 686). Defendants may also be convicted but simply fined or released without supervision, sometimes unconditionally.

As the juvenile justice system developed (Platt, 1969), its supervision of juveniles became separated from that of adults. Juveniles have their own probation and parole officers. In many places, there are separate facilities to detain juveniles awaiting a hearing, and separate state facilities for delinquents. There were reportly 30,000 persons in U.S. juvenile facilities in 1973 (National Criminal Justice Information and Statistics Service, 1976a: table B-7).

There is also the elusive distinction between legal offenders and mental patients or incompetents. Many ostensibly ill or defective persons commit crimes that precipitate their commitment, but no figures are available. However, the population in other than criminal justice custody is substantial. For instance, there were 315,000 patients in U.S. psychiatric hospitals in 1972 (Bureau of the Census, 1974: 77).

How long should someone who has committed a crime be considered a criminal? Is the burglar today a burglar tomorrow? Next year? While under criminal justice supervision? For life?

Does the length of time a person remains a criminal depend on the seriousness of the offense? Does a murderer thus remain a criminal longer than a car thief?

Does the length of time a person remains a criminal depend on how many offenses have been committed? Does a person with four prior convictions for robbery remain a criminal longer than someone convicted for the first time?

Consider that a person may commit a crime without being caught. If *any* offender thus becomes a criminal for life, then perhaps most Americans are crooks. As reported in greater detail in Chapter 9, 64 percent of the men and 29 percent of the women in one survey (of a total of 1,698 persons, including workers, professionals and businesspersons, housewives, students, and farmers, mostly from the New York City area) confessed to having committed acts as adults which carried a prison sentence of more than a year (Wallerstein and Wyle, 1947: 112). Does that mean that more than a third of adult Americans are crooks?

As you can see, the problems of deciding how many people are criminals are formidable. No wonder few people believe that the number of criminals equals the number of people incarcerated. On the other hand, the amount of incarceration can be seen as an index of the ability of a society's members to live together. The fact that the Dutch incarcerate only one-tenth the fraction of their population that Americans do on any given day (Waller and Chan, 1974) suggests that the Dutch live together in greater harmony and tolerance for one another. Thus there is ample justification for considering ways that incarceration rates might be lowered. This is done in Chapter 8.

Self-reporting As the victim survey was developed to discover unofficial *crime*, so the self-report survey was developed to discover unofficial *criminality*. The first self-report studies—one of children just north of Boston, one of college students in Texas, and one of adults mainly in New York City—were done as World War II ended (Wallerstein and Wyle, 1947). In these studies, respondents are given descriptions of offenses either on questionnaires or in interviews, and asked to indicate which offenses they themselves have committed, how often, and approximately when.

Invariably, in the U.S. studies at least, practically all respondents claim to have committed at least one crime, and most respondents claim more. In Wallerstein and Wyle's (1947: 110) survey of adults, men claimed to have committed an average of 18 offenses after age sixteen (the age in New York State at which persons are first treated as adults in criminal courts), while women averaged 11. In addition, men reported committing an average of 3.2 offenses before age sixteen, while the figure for women was 1.6.

Self-report studies are done not primarily to measure crime but to determine what kinds of persons are more criminal than others. Since self-reporting is used to help find out what makes people more or less likely to become criminals, surveys of children rather than adults are the norm. To compare children's self-report figures with police "offenses known" figures is highly problematic. To make the comparison, the number of offenses known or attributable to children of the ages surveyed must be estimated, and the number of offenses per child must be known for a particular year (as in certain self-report surveys, like that of Gold and Reimer, 1975). Self-report figures are less applicable in counting crime as in counting the criminal tendencies of various kinds of people. For this reason, self-reporting is considered an index of criminality, rather than crime. This is discussed in detail in Chapter 9.

Recidivism Suppose you started a program to treat a group of convicted offenders. How would you know how well the treatment was going? It would be a little grandiose to look at crime rates in the overall community, and, if the rates dropped, to attribute the drop to your own program. You might not trust the offenders to confess their crimes on a self-report questionnaire. As a measure of your success, you would probably use some indicator of whether officials thought your clients had done something wrong since coming into your program.

Many different indicators could show that you had failed to turn your clients away from crime. Your clients might be considered failures if they were rearrested. Or you might want to give them a chance to be vindicated in the courts, and count them as failures only if they were convicted of a new offense. If the clients were released to you conditionally, either by a court on probation or by a parole board (from prison) on parole, you might consider them failures if their probation or parole were revoked. Revocation might occur if they committed a new offense or a technical violation—of one of the rules of probation or parole—such as leaving town without permission, associating with felons, or drinking. (Glaser, 1964, has even used combined reconviction and revocation measures of recidivism.) If you run a unique program for offenders in a jurisdiction—such as the only women's prison in the state—you might count as failures only those clients who returned to your own care or custody. Or you might include all those who wind up in any jail or prison.

Failures of this kind are called "recidivism." Recidivism indicates that a person has relapsed into criminal behavior. In practice, it means that official action has been taken against a convict.

Deciding which measure of recidivism to use—arrest, conviction, revocation, or reentry into a program or institution—is as problematic as deciding whether to measure crime by convictions, police reports, or victim survey data. Generally speaking, revocation and arrest are far more liberal measures than conviction and reentry into specific programs. Recidivism will usually be much higher using the former measures than the latter. Thus, those predisposed to find that programs are failures favor the liberal measures, while those who see them as successes favor the conservative ones.

The reduction of recidivism rates will be considered and compared in Chapter 10. Here, let us note that recidivism is an index of criminality that is very useful in evaluating treatment programs.

What does a measure of criminality measure? The distinction between punishment, and treatment and incapacitation is the same as that between the classical and the positivist schools of criminology (see Chapter 1). Punishment and classical criminology assume that practically all members of any society have the same sense of rationality. Thus, they will attempt to avoid a criminal act so as not to incur a certain expected cost of the punishment (perceived likelihood of punishment times severity of punishment) that follows. Treatment and incapacitation, like positive criminology, on the other hand, assume that some persons are more prone to criminal behavior than others. Thus, special measures are needed to keep them from wrongdoing.

In choosing among crime control strategies, we must try to determine whether the crime problem stems mainly from forces at work on all equally rational persons, or whether it is the work of a few evil, sick, or otherwise defective persons. If the latter, a few criminals can be brought under control and the rest of society will live together in harmony. If the former, the number of criminals who are controlled is irrelevant. The forces in society at large will continue to make crime occur at the same rate among the remaining population. The problem is like that of deciding what to do with a car that keeps breaking down. Do you assume that there are just a few bad parts, and hence repair the car and keep driving it? Or do you assume that the whole car is a lemon—that if some parts are fixed, others are bound to go bad—and trade it in? Changing parts is like isolating chronic or potential offenders as a means of preventing crime. Changing cars is like changing the general forces that operate in society as a means of controlling crime.

Reducing *crime* basically involves a classical approach. Offenders cannot even be identified from the two leading sources of crime measurement data: police offense reports and victim surveys. Concern for reducing crime does not necessarily entail knowing who the criminals are. Some common ways of trying to reduce crime are increasing police patrols, putting deadbolt locks on doors, and trying to establish uniform punishments for each crime, regardless of individual differences among offenders.

Reducing *criminality* basically involves a positivist approach. Measures of criminality identify those who contribute most to crime. To deal with *criminality* is to invoke special treatment for special people. Special penalties for repeat offenders, classification of offenders, and diagnosis and treatment of individual problems are common ways of trying to reduce criminality.

Some criminologists, like Berkman (1971) and Quinney (1974), believe that crime control is inherently unjust. They feel it is no accident that under the criminal justice system, rich people stay comfortable and safe while poor people must choose between being victims of crime or of crime control. To these students of crime, *crime* data show who the criminal justice system protects (the rich), while *criminality* data show who the system punishes (the poor). The distinction between measures of crime and measures of criminality remains significant even for those who criticize crime control.

For those who wish to reduce criminality, the issue is: How liberal can a society be about a criminal's chance of redemption? How much can we hope that criminals can yet be like other people? Incarceration as a measure of criminality suggests that once people are out of jail or prison, their criminality is automatically over. But who, including the criminal, can be expected to believe this? To hold that incarceration is the *sole* criterion of criminality probably means that anyone who has been incarcerated is regarded as a criminal forever.

If we really want to give the ex-convict a chance to get over the stigma of being a criminal, we may look for a way to show that the criminal is not so different from the rest of us. Self-reporting fills this need, for it shows that practically all of us have committed criminal offenses. We are all criminals. Or are we? As it turns out, we still compare those who get in trouble with the law with those who have not, and find that those with official police records admit to more serious and more numerous offenses. And so, more than ever, we end up stigmatizing those who have been incarcerated. Self-report data show that those incarcerated have made themselves criminal by committing not merely one crime, but probably many of them.

Sympathy for the criminal can then move us to measure criminality in ways that allow the incarcerated person to stay out of our criminality statistics. This can be done by using recidivism rates to show how well we are preventing criminality. If an ex-convict is not rearrested, reconvicted, revoked, or sent back to prison, that person is not a criminal in terms of recidivism data. This eases the stigma on the criminal—or does it? What of the many who recidivate? If recidivism is our measure of criminality, those who become our criminality statistics bear the heaviest stigma of all.

This is one of the reasons Szasz (1965) states that those whom we now treat as mentally ill should be punished instead as criminals. The more compassion we show toward those whose behavior we do not like, the less dignity and worth we give them; the more sympathy and understanding we give to wrongdoers, the less chance we give them to redeem themselves. If we choose the measure of criminality that is most lenient toward the criminal, those we now count as criminal will seem intolerable.

In deciding which form of criminality you most want to reduce, consider, too, that your choice implies both greater tolerance and greater intolerance of the criminal than any other measure you might use. This problem of choosing how to reduce criminality is unavoidable.

COST-BENEFIT ANALYSIS OF CRIME CONTROL

Some persons agree that crime and criminality are harmful, and favor decreasing crime and criminality. But these persons also recognize the costs of preventing crime. They assume it would be absurd, irrational, to invest more in crime control unless the investment were at least equalled by the amount of harm prevented. If a million dollars invested to prevent theft reduced the amount stolen by half a million dollars, the investment would be foolish. As long as the reduction of crime exceeds the added investment in crime control, they argue, investment in crime control should continue (potentially until all stealing has been eliminated). The cutoff point is that at which the added cost (or, in economic terms, the *marginal* cost) of investment begins to exceed the added (marginal) benefit of crime or criminality reduction. This point is known to cost-benefit analysts as the *optimum* (plural is *optima*), and arriving at that point, *optimization*. The object of cost-benefit analysis is to optimize crime control.

Most work on cost-benefit analysis is theoretical and recent. McPheters and Stronge's (1976) collection of essays gives an idea of the range of this literature. Most models of cost-benefit analysis are based on economics. Here, the basic issue is: What things are considered costs and benefits? For instance, Harris (1976) cites Becker (1976) for failure to include in his equations the cost of mistakenly punishing innocent people as criminals. The logic of cost-benefit analysis provides no rules for choosing what to count as costs and benefits. The range of choice is practically limitless. Any of the measures of crime and criminality thus far discussed could be used in figuring benefits—which, in turn, could be computed in a number of ways.

One of the few applications of cost-benefit analysis involves California's probation subsidy program (Reid, 1976: 698–699). Under this program, the State of California paid subsidies to local communities to invest in probation services. The subsidies increased as the number of persons sent from the communities to state correctional facilities decreased. The cost was the state subsidy, and the benefit was the amount of money the state saved by maintaining fewer persons in correctional facilities. The benefit was found to outweigh the cost.

No attempt was made to optimize the subsidies by raising them to spur local communities to withhold still more offenders from state facilities until marginal costs equaled marginal benefits. And some people criticized the cost-benefit analysts for failing to take other measures of recidivism—of potential benefits of crime reduction in the local communities—into account (Serrill, 1975: 512–515).

Whatever its shortcomings, it is likely that cost-benefit analysis will be used more and more to evaluate attempts at crime control. Because of its growing importance, cost-benefit analysis is considered in detail in Chapter 12.

CONCLUSION

Many factors are involved in crime control, are there not? There are so many manifestations of crime that those who say they intend to attack the problem have not said much. Many people believe that knowledge of crime and criminal justice is practically useless. This is partly because it is so hard to decide how the knowledge should be used. The knowledge itself does not—and cannot—answer this question for us. It cannot even give us an indication of whether we should use it to attack social conditions (crime) or people (criminals).

There is a bright side. It is a lot easier to control crime if one knows whose figures are to be controlled. For instance, if one is interested in lowering the rate of prison returnees—instead of adding to police forces or arranging more expensive treatment programs for offenders—one might work with parole officers to make them try more alternatives before revoking parole for offenders who run into trouble. If one aims to reduce police "offenses known" figures, hiring more police and asking them to work harder to detect crime would probably not help. Instead, this could well increase police figures. Being specific about the measures of crime or criminality to be reduced helps in planning workable strategies by indicating who must be involved in the change.

In addition, if we can accept the idea of limited, specific forms of crime control—rather than imagining that we can control all forms of crime at once—we will not be so disappointed by our failures. If we become a little humbler about our inability to reduce all reasonable measures of crime at once, we can be more satisfied by our success in reducing it measure by measure.

No doubt, you believe that some measures of crime or criminality are more worth reducing than others. If so, the chapter(s) dealing with those measures will be especially interesting to you. But try to be flexible. By the time you have evaluated the pros and cons of decreasing crime and criminality in different ways, you may want to change your mind.

REFERENCES

Becker, Gary S. 1968. "Crime and punishment: an economic approach." Pp. 5–65, in Lee R. McPheters and William B. Stronge (eds.), *The Economics of Crime and Law Enforcement*. Springfield, Ill.: Charles C. Thomas.

Berkman, Alexander. 1971. *ABC of Anarchism*. London: Freedom Press.

Biderman, Albert D., Louise A. Johnson, Jennie McIntyre, and Adrienne W. Weir. 1967. "Incidence of crime victimization," Chap. 2, pp. 26–118, in President's Commission on Law Enforcement and Administration of Justice, *Field Surveys I: Report on a Pilot Study in the District of Columbia on Victimization and Attitudes Toward Law Enforcement*. Washington, D.C.: United States Government Printing Office.

Black, Donald J. 1970. "Production of crime rates." *American Sociological Review* 35 (August): 733–747.

Bureau of the Census. 1974. *Statistical Abstract of the United States: 1974*. Washington, D.C.: United States Government Printing Office.

Ennis, Philip H. 1967. "Crime victimization in the United States: report on a national survey." In President's Commission on Law Enforcement and Administration of Justice, *Field Surveys II*. Washington, D.C.: United States Government Printing Office.

Federal Bureau of Investigation. Annual. *Uniform Crime Reports.* Washington, D.C.: United States Government Printing Office.

Gibson, Evelyn, and S. Klein. 1961. *Home Office Studies in the Causes of Delinquency and the Treatment of Offenders, No. 4: Murder—A Home Office Research Unit Report.* London: Her Majesty's Stationery Office.

————. 1969. *Home Office Research Studies, No. 3: Murder, 1957–1968.* London: Her Majesty's Stationery Office.

Glaser, Daniel. 1964. *The Effectiveness of a Prison and Parole System.* Indianapolis: Bobbs-Merrill.

Gold, Martin, and David J. Reimer. 1975. "Changing patterns of delinquent behavior among Americans 13 through 16 years old: 1967–72." *Crime and Delinquency Literature* (December): 483–517.

Hanawalt, Barbara A. 1976. "Violent death in fourteenth- and early fifteenth-century England." *Comparative Studies in Society and History* 18 (July): 297–320.

Harris, John R. 1976. "On the economics of law and order." Pp. 66–77, in Lee R. McPheters and William B. Stronge (eds.), *The Economics of Crime and Law Enforcement.* Springfield, Ill.: Charles C. Thomas.

Hindelang, Michael J., Michael R. Gottfredson, Christopher S. Dunn, and Nicolette Parisi. 1977. *Sourcebook of Criminal Justice Statistics— 1976.* Washington, D.C.: United States Government Printing Office.

Inciardi, James A. 1976. "Criminal statistics and victim survey research for effective law enforcement planning." Pp. 177–189, in Emilio Viano (ed.), *Victims and Society.* Washington, D.C.: Visage.

Institute for Law and Social Research. 1974. *Prosecutor's Management Information System: Briefing Series.* Washington, D.C.: Institute for Law and Social Research.

McPheters, Lee R., and William B. Stronge (eds.). 1976. *The Economics of Crime and Law Enforcement.* Springfield, Ill.: Charles C. Thomas.

Morris, Norval, and Gordon Hawkins. 1970. *The Honest Politician's Guide to Crime Control.* Chicago: University of Chicago Press.

National Commission on Law Observance and Enforcement. 1931. *Number 3: Report on Statistics.* Washington, D.C.: United States Government Printing Office.

National Criminal Justice Statistics and Information Service. 1976a. *Children in Custody: Final Report on the Juvenile Detention and Corrections Facility Census of 1972–73.* Washington, D.C.: United States Government Printing Office.

————. 1976b. *Criminal Victimization in Eight American Cities: A Comparison of 1971/72 and 1974/75 Findings.* Washington, D.C.: United States Government Printing Office.

————. 1976c. *Prisoners in State and Federal Institutions on December 31, 1974.* Washington, D.C.: United States Government Printing Office.

————. 1977. *Criminal Victimization in the United States: A Compari-*

son of 1974 and 1975 Findings. Washington, D.C.: United States Government Printing Office.

Pepinsky, Harold E. 1976a. "Police offense-reporting Behavior." *Journal of Research in Crime and Delinquency* 13 (January): 33–47.

———. 1976b. "The growth of crime in the United States." *Annals of the American Academy of Political and Social Science* 423 (January): 23–30.

———. 1977. "Despotism in the quest for valid U.S. crime statistics: historical and comparative perspectives." Pp. 69–82, in Robert F. Meier (ed.), *Theory in Criminology: Contemporary Views.* Beverly Hills, Calif.: Sage.

Platt, Anthony. 1969. *The Child Savers: The Invention of Delinquency.* Chicago: University of Chicago Press.

President's Commission on Law Enforcement and Administration of Justice. 1967. *Crime and Its Impact: An Assessment.* Washington, D.C.: United States Government Printing Office.

President's Commission on Pornography. 1970. *Obscenity Report.* New York: Stein and Day.

Quinney, Richard. 1974. *Critique of Legal Order: Crime Control in Capitalist Society.* Boston: Little, Brown.

Reid, Sue Titus. 1976. *Crime and Criminology.* Hinsdale, Ill.: Dryden.

Reiss, Albert J. Jr. 1967. "Measurement of the nature and amount of crime." Vol. 1, pp. 1–183, in President's Commission on Law Enforcement and Administration of Justice, *Field Surveys III: Studies in Crime and Law Enforcement in Major Metropolitan Areas.* Washington, D.C.: United States Government Printing Office.

Reynolds, Paul D. 1972. *Victimization of the Residents and Their Perceptions of Community Services—1971.* Minneapolis: Metropolitan Council of the Twin Cities.

Robinson, Louis Newton. 1911. *History and Organization of Criminal Statistics in the United States.* Boston: Houghton Mifflin.

Samaha, Joel B. 1973. *Law and Order in Historical Perspective: The Case of Elizabethan Essex.* New York: Academic.

Seidman, David, and Michael Couzens. 1974. "Getting the crime rate down; political pressure and crime reporting." *Law and Society Review* 8 (Spring): 457–493.

Sellin, Thorsten, and Marvin E. Wolfgang. 1964. *The Measurement of Delinquency.* New York: Wiley.

Serrill, Michael S. 1975. "Profile/California." Pp. 510–531, in Seymour Halleck, Paul Lerman, Sheldon L. Messinger, Norval Morris, Patrick V. Murphy, and Marvin E. Wolfgang (eds.), *The Aldine Crime and Justice Annual: 1974.* Chicago: Aldine.

Szasz, Thomas S. 1965. *Psychiatric Justice.* New York: Macmillan.

Tappan, Paul W. 1947. "Who is the criminal?" *American Sociological Review* 12 (February): 96–102.

Waller, Irvin, and Janet Chan. 1974. "Prison use: a Canadian and international comparison." *Criminal Law Quarterly* 17 (December): 47–71.

Wallerstein, James S., and Clement J. Wyle. 1947. "Our law-abiding law-breakers." *Probation* (March–April): 107–112, 118.

Weinraub, Bernard. 1967. "Crime reports up 72% here in 1966: actual rise is 6.5%." *New York Times* (February 21).

FOOD FOR THOUGHT

1. At the annual meeting of the International Association of Chiefs of Police, three police chiefs, who are old friends, get together to compare how things are going. Chief Worse says, "My city council had better authorize our hiring more officers. We've been doing well, but we need to do a lot better. I've got to give my officers credit. We have young officers all over the city, and they really hustle. They're getting citizens to report offenses, and our figures are way up for all index offenses except homicide. Our arrests are up, too, but we can't keep up with the increases in offenses known. Our crime is going to get out of hand unless we get help."

Chief Better chuckles. "I have our city council eating out of my hand. My officers know they're only supposed to file reports on offenses we have a decent chance of clearing. Our offenses known have gone way down. Our arrests have gone down a little, too, but not nearly as much as the offenses known. So, we make arrests for a larger percentage of the offenses we report. We can claim that we're preventing crime because we're getting the criminals off the street in a larger percentage of the cases we report, and we're showing that crime is decreasing. Nothing succeeds like success. The city council keeps giving us more money to keep doing better. I don't know where this is going to end (what if we run out of offenses to 'slough'?), but so far we're doing fine."

Chief Sowhat shrugs. "Why try to change things? My officers know to keep cool. Instead of sticking their necks out, they manage to make reports and arrests for about the same number of offenses month after month. Life goes on. We get authorized just enough new officers to keep up with the growing population of our town. Since nobody expects much to change, nobody's unhappy."

Whose approach is best?

2. Chief Worse has another problem. The criminal court judges in his city do not like the kind of arrests his hard-working officers are making. The judges complain that now that they are making so many more arrests and trying to clear still more reported offenses, they are overburdening the criminal justice system, which could not even handle its former smaller caseloads well. Hence, the judges have repeatedly thrown cases out of court. Conviction figures are even dropping below previous levels. If you were called in as a consultant by the regional criminal justice planning agency, how would you advise them to find out whether the crime problem in the city is getting bigger or smaller? As a guess, what might you expect the planning agency would find?

3. Most probation and parole officers with clients in Metro County have decided that the prisons and jails in their state and county are so bad that they will go to great lengths to keep their offender-clients out of trouble. The probation and parole agents work tirelessly with arresting police officers, prosecutors, and judges to work out informal arrangements short of revocation and conviction. How would you measure the recidivism rate for this clientele?

4. The United States incarcerates about as large a percentage of its population, before and after trial for crimes, as any country. Does this mean that the U.S. crime problem is among the most serious in the world?

5. If we found (as we well might) that the cost of incarcerating property offenders exceeds the cost to their victims, should property offenders be left alone to commit their crimes? Should they be given corporal or capital punishment instead, if these were much cheaper than incarceration?

CHAPTER THREE

How Can Strategies of Crime Control Be Evaluated?

As we have seen, it makes little sense to speak of crime control in general. We must first decide which crime rate we wish to change. But once we have chosen, a number of other issues remain. These must be tentatively resolved before we can even guess how crime control of any kind can be accomplished.

SOURCES OF ERROR IN PREDICTING ANYTHING

The best laid plans to change crime rates can consist of no more than some educated guesses. The planner looks into the future, trying to predict the outcome of a new course of action. Predictions are fallible. One thing the well-trained scientist soon learns is that no one can foresee the future with certainty. Planners can hope to minimize but not to preclude the chances of failure. We can forget about trying to discover foolproof strategies of crime control, but we can aspire to find some strategies with a reasonable chance of success.

Hence, an issue of central concern is: What needs to be done, and what can be done, to minimize the margin for error in planning crime control? The first thing to remember is how many different kinds of errors are possible. To illustrate, suppose we must decide what to do with a child who has just given a neighbor a black eye. We want to reduce the child's chances of hurting other people, and increase the child's ability to get along with other people. To prevent further assaults, we might decide to lock the child in his or her room. This minimizes the immediate risk of the child's repeating wrong behavior.

By locking the child away, we run the risk of making an error known to statisticians as a "type I error" or a "false positive." This means that the child might have learned to get along with others, without any problems, had we done nothing. It is the chance that we are wrong in guessing that the child, left untreated, would have assaulted anyone in the future.

On the other hand, we could make a mistake in leaving the child alone. If we guessed that the child would not hit anyone if left alone, we might be wrong. Such a mistake would be a case of "type II error," or a "false negative."

A planner commits type I error by doing something unnecessary and type II error by failing to do something that will make a situation better, or keep it from getting worse.

Since predictions with groups of people are fallible, it may be possible to avoid either type I or type II error, but never both. If everyone who might conceivably commit an offense is treated effectively, there will be no false negatives, but false positives will be maximized. If no one is treated, there will be no false positives, but false negatives will be maximized. As Wilkins (1969: 125–129) notes, this important issue of choice between types of error has largely been overlooked in criminological research.

The problem of risking error is not one of conflicts of errors alone. In addition, the planner runs the risk of errors compounding one another. Suppose we ourselves did not see the child's assault but had it reported to us by someone else. We now run the risk not only of being wrong in guessing that the child will assault other people even with a prior record of assault, but also of the report's being false. If the chances of further assaults are one in ten, and the chances of the report's being false are fifty-fifty, then the chances of further assaults after the reports are only one in twenty.

As Schumacher (1973) shows, simple predictions—which require only paper and pencil—are at least as accurate as and often better than predictions combining so many data at once that only computers can process them. As possible sources of error increase so much that we cannot keep track of them, we lose our ability to make errors cancel one another out. Left to accumulate, errors tend to be compounded. The problem is like that of error in shooting pool. A simple plan to make a straight shot, so that the ball goes into the pocket, has a better chance than a sophisticated plan to carom the cue ball off some cushions before it hits its target. One might expect any error in one angle to be canceled by the error off another, but there are so many directions the errors can take—so many ways they can combine—that the chances are greater that one error will be compounded by the next.

In planning crime prevention strategies, we must consider the various stages at which the risk of error is introduced, knowing that these risks multiply as the plan becomes more complex.

Wenk and Emrich's (1972) study, as described and discussed in Chapter 10, is an excellent illustration of the problems (a) of choosing between and (b) of compounding type I and II error.

Another source of error, illustrated by and alluded to in Chapter 1, comes from predicting the rare event. Wenk and Emrich (p. 192) despair of the possibility of improving their predictions when the target is so small. After all, less than 3 percent of their offender sample ultimately recidivated violently. As the prevalence of any phenomenon increases, the likelihood of prediction error decreases. For instance, one can predict much more accurately the age at which all Americans born in 1977 will die than the age at which they will die of brain tumors. Similarly one can predict more accurately which of a group of repeaters will be re-arrested in a given period than which of a group of citizens will be arrested for the first time. As we shall see, changes in crime rates can generally be predicted more accurately than changes in recidivism rates for particular individuals.

To summarize, error in prediction can be minimized by (a) maximizing the amount of the phenomenon to be predicted while (b) minimizing the amount of information used to make the prediction; however (c) there will still be substantial room for error in any prediction, and (d) implicit in the prediction will be a tradeoff between type I and type II error.

ERROR IN CRIME RATE MEASUREMENT

The first stage at which the possibility of error arises is in measuring the rate(s) of crime one hopes to change. This is the most troublesome kind of error for the planner because it is so likely to go undetected before, during, and after implementation of a crime control strategy. If the measure of success contains too many false positives (i.e., if failure is exaggerated), or if enough offenders fail to be counted before implementation, planners may abandon a strategy that is actually working in the erroneous belief that the crime rate(s) are not changing as rapidly as desired.

Wilkins (1975) shows how evaluations of treatment strategies can be confounded by false negatives in follow-up measures of success. Patuxent Institution, a penal institution in Maryland, claims to have an especially effective psychiatric treatment program. Its director implies that its recidivism rate of 7 percent shows that its treatment is superior to that in most prisons, where the recidivism rate is closer to 65 percent. Patuxent counts the first three years its inmates are released as a treatment period, and does not begin reckoning recidivism until that period is over. Wilkins notes that most recidivism takes place in the first months following release. After three years, one would normally expect only 7 percent of former inmates of any prison still at large to recidivate. Wilkins charges that the false negatives in Patuxent's measurement of its recidivism rate, compared to other prisons, leads Patuxent to a type I error of treatment. Inmates at Patuxent do no better than those at other prisons, and there is no call to abandon simple imprisonment in favor of the extra treatment Patuxent provides. Patuxent's special treatment of inmates is superfluous in preventing recidivism. Candidates for Patuxent's special treatment are misdiagnosed, are false positives, although the Patuxent staff's diagnosed measurement error has misled them into thinking otherwise.

On the other hand, after "offenses known" figures were criticized for being incomplete, U.S. police departments revised their reporting procedures in the 1960s. This revision could have been responsible for the discovery that crime rates were rapidly increasing in that period. If crime rates were not really increasing, if the reported increases were just a result of police artifice, then a false alarm over a crime wave resulted from type I measurement error. If the statistical revisions were warranted, if police had been failing to find as much crime in the past, then they were eliminating type II measurement error by reporting more offenses, but the alarm that crime rates were increasing was still false.

The issue of error in crime measurement is central in the field of criminal justice. In particular, have the recent change in U.S. police reporting practices—which led to greater resources for police and other criminal justice agencies—overcome type II measurement error? The motives of each side have been called into question. One side claimed that officials were trying to deceive the public into giving more money for law enforcement. The other side claimed that its critics were showing a callous disregard for crime victims. To one side, the increase in crime was a political gimmick; to the other side, crime that had previously been hidden was being publicized for the first time.

As we saw in the discussion of police "offenses known" data (Chapter 2), the debate was turned on its head five years later, when police began to report reduced rates of some offenses in Washington, D.C. Officials cited these reductions as evidence that a federal war on crime was succeeding, while critics argued that manipulations of the crime rate data implied a cynical disregard for the victims of crime. The issue of whether a crime control strategy was working was lost in the debate over the validity of the criteria used to evaluate it. (See Pepinsky, 1976, for a review of this history.)

There is no satisfactory way of resolving this kind of debate. Does one try to determine the validity of an offense report by reading the report and personally evaluating its plausibility? This approach is known as "content validation." For instance, Ennis (1967) had "experts" read over victim survey reports to rule out those which did not seem to report true offenses. The critics of this approach argue that it is too intuitive to be reliable. Can the validity of official crime rates be evaluated by comparing them to rates measured by other means, such as victim surveys? Reiss (1967: 150) used this approach in his victim survey. He interviewed a subsample of persons who had reported offenses to the police a month before, to see how complete the victim survey reporting was. This approach is known as "criterion validation." Its critics argue that it relies too heavily on the assumption that the criterion is valid in the first place. Can one evaluate the validity of crime rates measured at one time and place by *comparing* them to the rates for the same crimes at *another time or place?* This procedure is known as "construct validation." It was used by Beattie (1960), who criticized police crime rates for not being in the same proportion to one another everywhere in the country. Critics of this approach argue the tenuousness of the theoretical assumption that relative rates will remain stable from one time and place to another.

THE CONCEPT OF RATES

Crime and criminality figures are commonly expressed as *rates*. Instead of being a count of the number of reports of crime or criminality (known as measuring *incidence*), the figures are expressed as fractions—the raw numbers divided by a base number of events or persons. Thus, the Federal Bureau of Investigation reports (annually) not merely the number of offenses known to U.S. police from year to year, but the number of offenses known divided by the number of hundreds of thousands of U.S. inhabitants. These "offenses known" *rates* indicate how likely crime is to occur among the population regardless of its size. For instance, with a population of 100,000,000, there might be 12,000 murders; and, by the time the population climbs to 200,000,000, 20,000 murders. The *incidence* of murder would have risen 67 percent. And yet, the 12,000 murders occurred at the *rate* of 12 per 100,000 inhabitants, while the 20,000 murders occurred at the rate of 10 per 100,000—a decline of 17 percent. Even though there were a lot more murders by the time the population had reached 200,000,000, the probability of any inhabitant's being murdered would have declined, as the rate comparison shows.

As another example, when measuring recividism in order to evaluate a treatment program, the usual practice is to measure a recidivism rate—the percentage of all those in treatment who later recidivate—rather than simply the incidence of recidivism. If five offenders in a program of ten recidivate, it is a worse reflection on the program than if the rate is five out of twenty.

In a rate figure, the top part of the fraction—for instance, the number of crimes reported—is called the *numerator*. The bottom part of the fraction—for instance, the number of inhabitants—is called the *denominator*. The problems of measurement error we have thus far considered involve numerators. Even if one is satisfied that the numerator of a crime rate has been validly measured, one can still question the choice of denominator. To illustrate, the standard denominator used for offenses known to the police is the number of hundreds of thousands of people in the area that is being measured (i.e., offenses per 100,000 population). But should all people in the area be included in this denominator? Generally speaking, in England and the United States, children under the age of seven are held legally incapable of committing crimes (LaFave and Scott, 1972: 351). If this is true, then perhaps this age group should be excluded from the denominator. If the proportion of the population below the age of seven is declining, a crime rate that includes this group in the denominator will increase faster than one that does not. This problem is known to demographers as that of defining "the population at risk."

In sum, planners must address two issues in selecting a measure of a crime rate to change. There are issues of definition, both in the choice of a numerator (e.g., convictions or arrests) and in the definition of a population at risk for use in the denominator. There are also issues of measurement error; the measure used in practice may not correspond to the rate one is trying to change in theory. Planners must choose ways to resolve these issues, knowing that there can be no guarantee that the choices are right.

EVALUATING CHANCES OF CONTROLLING PARTICULAR CRIME RATES

Once the planners have selected a crime rate measure to change, they need to choose a strategy. This includes assessing the chances that a given strategy will change the rate as desired. The possibilities of committing type I and type II error create different kinds of political and ethical issues. In England, moral and political objections to risking type I error—to having the government intervene in citizens' lives unnecessarily—are called "liberal." In the United States, they are called "conservative." The position of the English liberal and the American conservative is that the necessity and effectiveness of a program of state control must be proved by its advocates. Otherwise, citizens should be left to their own devices.

Mill (1975, first published in 1854) is perhaps the best

known proponent of the view that unnecessary or ineffective crime control strategies are immoral. This assumption is an article of faith; readers can decide for themselves whether they accept it.

Politically, an unnecessary or superfluous strategy can be attacked as a waste of society's resources. But the planner's problem is more complex than deciding whether a certain strategy *is* unnecessary. Given the uncertainty of any prediction about the future, the issue is: *How much chance* is there that the strategy is unnecessary (Wilkins, 1969: 127–128)?

This raises further issues. The planner may not have enough information to calculate precisely the element of chance. In fact, as later chapters will show, in general the planner can only calculate whether a strategy is more likely than not to succeed.

Is a chance of success greater than fifty-fifty enough to warrant implementation of a strategy? Any answer to this question is arbitrary, but this issue, too, must be resolved when planning crime control.

The risk of making type II error—of failing to control crime by failing to treat it specially—raises similar issues. How great a risk of crime and criminality can be tolerated *without* intervening? Conventionally, the American liberal and the British conservative presume type II treatment error to be the greater risk to be avoided.

Once a strategy of crime control has been implemented, the planner can reassess the possibility of error. A recent reassessment concerns whether prison is necessary or sufficient to curtail crime (see Von Hirsch, 1976, for a review of the literature). Some people argue that imprisonment is unnecessary for many inmates. This is an accusation of type I error in imprisoning people for the sake of rehabilitation or specific deterrence. Others argue that imprisonment is insufficient to rehabilitate offenders, and that something new must be done. For example, Von Hirsch argues that imprisonment should rest on the principle of just deserts—that is, deserved retribution for wrongful acts. This amounts to an accusation that our present prison system is creating type II error. Of course, one might conclude that prisons do not work and that we are just as well off without them or anything in their place. This again amounts to a charge of type I error. To summarize, type I treatment error in a crime control strategy means that the strategy is unnecessary; type II treatment error means that the strategy is insufficient to bring about change. Given the uncertainty involved in evaluating strategies (e.g., the century-long, and inconclusive, debate over whether imprisonment rehabilitates—Rothman, 1971), plus the uncertainty of whether unprecedented change is practical (e.g., whether imprisonment can yet be made to rehabilitate offenders if it has not already done so), beliefs that type I and type II error have already occurred, like beliefs that they will occur in some future strategy, defy proof. Crime control planners may be called upon to decide whether type I or type II error has occurred or will occur in some strategy without knowing whether they are correct. The implications of the decision—whether to do less or more—are nonetheless so important that the planner cannot afford to overlook the distinction and simply decide that a crime control strategy "doesn't work."

THE POSSIBILITY OF SIDE EFFECTS

A crime control strategy may succeed in changing a crime rate, but at the same time it may achieve other—often undesirable—results. Consider again the case of the assaultive child. Locking the child away may be necessary and sufficient to prevent future harm to others and to teach the child to get along well with peers. However, it is possible that the child might stop speaking to his or her parents or begin eating poorly because of the treatment. So, the crime control planner must consider the possibility of other consequences as well.

A crime rate can scarcely be expected to change in isolation. Other factors are related. This is the case of a phenomenon biologists call "symbiosis." In the plant structure known as lichen, algae lives off food produced by a fungus, and the fungus lives by eating the algae. What crime control planners must ask themselves is, if the crime rate is changed, what else might change with it? This requires the planner to look at the crime rate as only one element in a larger social system.

If one of the possible side effects in crime control is deemed undesirable, the planner is again confronted with type I and type II error. Would the undesirable effect occur anyway, so that abandoning the strategy on the grounds that it would produce the side effect would entail type I error? Might the change in the crime rate produce desirable side effects, so that failure to implement the strategy would entail type II error? Recall, from Chapter 1, that the chances of planning successfully for what *will* occur are far better than those of planning successfully to suppress an effect. The planner does better to try to foresee which side effects *might* occur rather than might *not* occur, and then to look for room for error in the prediction. To sum up, the problem of possible side effects requires a search for things that might change with the change in a crime rate, assumptions about how serious or desirable such changes would be, and a calculation of the errors in the prediction.

A planner might want to *maximize* error in predicting side effects. One longstanding example of building in error is the wide latitude given to criminal trial judges in sentencing. The more potential damage planners foresee in sentencing some offenders (like young, remorseful, first-time offenders) to prison, the more discretion will be recommended. This is a way of building type II error into the application of the law in particular cases. The more discretion the judge has, the more latitude the judge has to risk leniency with a defendant. (Again, see Von Hirsch, 1976, for a review of issues of sentencing discretion.)

On the other hand, some criminologists, like Van den Haag (1975), argue that it is unnecessary to abolish capital punishment for murder, since at least as much killing would take place if it were abolished. People who are deterred by capital punishment would then kill. This suggests that there is a substantial risk of type I error built in the concept that discretion not to punish does good.

POLITICAL CONSIDERATIONS

My father, a psychologist, has a saying: "People are trouble." A planner may devise an almost foolproof crime control strategy, but getting people to follow it is another matter. Implementation of a strategy may require legislation. In that case, cooperation of legislators will be needed. It may require a change in police policy. In that case, cooperation of police administrators will be needed. It may require public vigilance. In that case, citizen cooperation will be needed. And so on. No viable strategy can be implemented by the planner alone.

There are, of course, many alternatives for getting people to do what you want them to do. One alternative is coercion (Etzioni, 1961: 5). The planner would do well to ignore this. Coercion leaves people with no other choice than to comply. For instance, if public vigilance is coerced, the strategy would need to deprive citizens of all means of avoiding that vigilance. In other words, the strategy must not only account for how vigilance is to be obtained but also for the suppression of other alternatives. Visions of a brave new world aside, no such broad management of human behavior has yet succeeded. Fortunately, there are simpler approaches to social control.

One such approach is to reward desired behavior (Etzioni, 1961: 5). For instance, cooperative legislators can be rewarded with campaign contributions. This approach may sometimes seem unethical, but its efficacy is undeniable. A major limitation of this alternative that considerable resources are usually needed to provide enough rewards—more than an individual planner can provide. The strategy must include persuading a number of people to donate rewards to others. Such planning can prove difficult.

A third alternative is to rely on what is known as "identification" and "personal authority" (Kelman, 1958: 53). People sometimes do things because of *who* is telling them to do it. One example is implementing recommendations of a consultant, who is thought to be an expert. If respected persons or authorities can be made to advocate a crime control strategy, that may be sufficient to persuade others to carry out the plan. Here, there are two problems. First, the planner may be in error in predicting that someone will be able to exercise the force of personal authority. Second, the planner must persuade the authority to advocate the strategy. Nonetheless, this alternative is potentially quite useful.

The final alternative is to lead people to do what they were already inclined to do, or thought they ought to do, by showing them new ways to pursue their interests (Kelman, 1958: 53). My experience in defending clients in criminal court illustrates the use of this alternative. After a probation program had been developed for a client, including work and private counseling, a judge could sometimes be persuaded that granting probation with this program would be more likely than a jail sentence to meet the judge's *own* concerns. This was not a matter of coercing the judge, rewarding him, or ordering him to do something, but simply indicating that there was a way for him to carry out his wishes by a means he had not previously considered. This tactic is more likely than the others to get people to cooperate in implementing a crime control strategy. However, there is generally a wide margin for error in projecting what others see as their own interest. In theory, this tactic, which sociologists call "cooptation," is powerful; in practice, it is hard to plan.

ETHICAL ISSUES

Thus far, we have been discussing what the planner *can* do. Another issue is, what *should* the planner do? At various points, the planner's strategies will be guided by assumptions of good or bad, right or wrong, better or worse.

An assumption is a matter of belief. Its truth is taken for granted but not proven. While arguments as to *how* things can be done rest on logic, suppositions about *why* things should be done are essentially articles of faith. They rest on a belief in divine prophecy, on a so-called "natural" order, on acceptance of other people's statements, or on purely personal feelings. In a scientific sense, no person's beliefs or assumptions are better or worse than anyone else's. In a moral sense, planners must still do or advocate what they believe to be right.

In this book, whenever I take a stand on an ethical issue, I try to leave the reader with a higher set of unresolved issues. For instance, I may say that if you hold a certain ethical position, it would be inconsistent with your own ethics to pursue a strategy without telling you which ethical position to take in the first place. Many ethical choices are left up to readers, for whom authors should not dictate right and wrong but rather push them to develop their own opinions.

Another ethical dilemma is that of ends and means. A certain strategy may be effective, but the means necessary to implement it may be so undesirable as to make the strategy unpalatable. For instance, many would resist the use of corporal punishment even if it were found to deter crime (see the debate by Korn, 1971, and Wilkins, 1971). Ethical issues arise about both ends and means in planning crime control strategies.

To make matters worse, we may be forced to choose not between right and wrong but between greater and lesser evils. Again, corporal punishment provides an example. It may be the only effective means we can see of reducing certain kinds of crimes. We may believe this crime to be wrong and want to prevent it. But if we also believe corporal punishment to be wrong in itself, we are faced with choosing between corporal punishment and unnecessary crime.

Another ethical issue involved whether police should carry guns. Their own lives may be put in greater jeopardy if the guns are taken away, but on the other hand, armed police are more often shot at than unarmed police. Either choice may well increase the risk of police. We must then try to decide which undesirable risk we prefer, rather than with minimizing all undesirable risks (see Takagi, 1974).

Confronting these issues may sometimes prove beneficial. We are led to develop new strategies in which many undesirable risks are minimized simultaneously. For instance, without disarming either police or citizens, planners have used various approaches to train police in new ways of responding to calls of family quarrels so as to reduce the probability of violence (Schonborn, 1975: 27–38). Here, as in many cases, an attempt to resolve an ethical dilemma has led to new approaches to social control.

SYNTHESIS OF CRIME CONTROL STRATEGIES

The synthesis of new approaches to crime control can be pushed to higher and higher levels. To what extent can strategies be developed to change more than one kind of crime rate at a time? For example, a strategy for reducing conviction rates might involve increasing arrest rates in the hope that more cases would be dismissed before trial. This could prove effective in reducing conviction rates, but we may wish to do more. We may want to reduce conviction rates and arrests together. More ambitiously, we may even want to reduce simultaneously all six of the crime and criminality rates considered here. Could a strategy be developed which would offer a good chance of accomplishing so much? This question is addressed in Chapters 7 and 11 through 13.

Here, let us anticipate some of the major difficulties involved in such syntheses. To begin with, the odds are high that a strategy that reduces one kind of crime or criminality rate will rely in part on an undesired change in another kind of rate, as illustrated above. In statistical terms, having six kinds of rates to change at once considerably reduces the "degrees of freedom" in planning a strategy. This is no small problem.

Second, the more a strategy has to accomplish, the greater the chances of partial failure. Thus, even if we could design a strategy with a 90 percent chance of reducing each kind of crime rate, the chances are more than 70 percent that at least one kind of rate would not be reduced. A grand strategy involves a considerable margin for error.

CONCLUSION

Readers may be overwhelmed by the problems that arise in planning a crime control strategy. They are not alone. The more we learn about the world, the more reason we have to feel uncertain about how it works. Many seniors scientists admit that they have learned far more of what they do not know than of what they do.

The demands on researchers and planners in solving social problems have grown dramatically in recent years. In one sense, this trend has merit. It indicates that people are increasingly committed to facing social problems squarely, and to think through carefully how to respond to them. In another sense, the trend has had unfortunate consequences. Many researchers and planners have been moved to spend a lot of time and effort in trying to prove that their predictions are correct. Errors in prediction have increasingly been taken as evidence of their incompetence.

The growing tendency is to confuse competence with infallibility. As researchers and planners are pressured to prove that they are correct, their predictions tend to grow so general that they are practically meaningless. Furthermore, the pressure mounts to demonstrate the ignorance or naiveté of their critics. Thus, the focus shifts from the predictions to the people who make or assess them. Narrow sets of qualifications are used to certify some people as experts, in order to disqualify their critics from judging their ideas.

This book is based, in part, on the assumption that the reader is qualified to create and evaluate strategies of crime control. A sense of uncertainty in the reader is a healthy sign, as is a sense of the difficulty involved. If we make errors in planning, it is because no human being can do otherwise. If we cannot foresee all contingencies, at least making errors indicates that we have made an honest attempt to foresee as many problems as possible.

Thus, the reader need not feel threatened or overwhelmed by the issues and possibilities for error. Presenting these problems is a way of saying, "It is all right to make mistakes; go ahead and try to plan your strategies as best you can."

While care in the planning of crime control strategies cannot eliminate all errors, it can make it easier to correct the errors when they do occur. Like a car mechanic, the social planner stands a better chance of fixing problems that are precisely located. Careful planning not only optimizes the chances for success but also specifies where mistakes can occur. Conscientious planners do make mistakes, they try their best to help others find them. I believe that failure is a sign of good rather than poor planning. The many issues in this chapter are presented as a challenge to the reader rather than as a source of fear.

REFERENCES

Beattie, Ronald H. 1960. "Criminal statistics in the United States." *Journal of Criminal Law, Criminology, and Police Science* 51 (May–June): 49–65.

Ennis, Philip H. 1967. "Crime victimization in the United States: report on a national survey." In President's Commission on Law Enforcement and Administration of Justice, *Field Surveys II*. Washington, D.C.: United States Government Printing Office.

Etzioni, Amitai. 1961. *A Comparative Analysis of Complex Organiza-*

tions: On Power, Involvement, and Their Correlates. New York: Free Press of Glencoe.

Federal Bureau of Investigation. Annual. *Crime in the United States: Uniform Crime Reports.* Washington, D.C.: United States Government Printing Office.

Kelman, Herbert C. 1958. "Compliance, identification, and internalization: three processes of opinion change." *Journal of Conflict Resolution* 2 (March): 51–60.

Korn, Richard. 1971. "Reflections on flogging: an essay review of the work of Leslie Wilkins and Tom Murton." *Issues in Criminology* 6 (Summer): 95–112.

LaFave, Wayne R., and Austin W. Scott, Jr. 1972. *Criminal Law.* St. Paul, Minn.: West.

Mill, John Stuart (David Spitz, ed.) 1975. *On Liberty.* New York: Norton.

Pepinsky, Harold E. 1976. "The growth of crime in the United States." *Annals of the American Academy of Political and Science* 423 (January): 23–30.

Reiss, Albert J. Jr. 1967. "Measurement of the nature and amount of crime." Vol. 1, pp. 1–183, in President's Commission on Law Enforcement and Administration of Justice, *Field Surveys III: Studies in Crime and Law Enforcement in Major Metropolitan Areas.* Washington, D.C.: United States Government Printing Office.

Rothman, David J. 1971. *The Discovery of the Asylum: Social Order and Disorder in the New Republic.* Boston: Little, Brown.

Schonborn, Karl. 1975. *Dealing With Violence: The Challenge Faced by Police and Other Peacekeepers.* Springfield, Ill.: Charles C. Thomas.

Schumacher, E. F. 1973. *Small Is Beautiful: Economics as if People Mattered.* New York: Harper & Row.

Takagi, Paul. 1974. "A garrison state in a 'democratic' society." *Crime and Social Justice* 1 (Spring–Summer): 27–33.

Van den Haag, Ernest. 1975. *Punishing Criminals: Concerning a Very Old and Painful Question.* New York: Basic Books.

Von Hirsch, Andrew. 1976. *Doing Justice: The Choice of Punishment.* New York: Hill and Wang.

Wenk, Ernst A., and Robert L. Emrich. 1972. "Assaultive youth: an exploratory study of the assaultive experience and assaultive potential of California Youth Authority wards." *Journal of Research in Crime and Delinquency* 9 (July): 171–196.

Wilkins, Leslie T. 1969. *Evaluation of Penal Measures.* New York: Random House.

––––––. 1971. "Reply to 'reflections on flogging.' " *Issues in Criminology* 6 (Summer): 113–114.

––––––. 1975. "Putting 'treatment' on trial: effiiciency, equity, and the clinical approach to offenders." *Hastings Center Report* 5 (February): 35–48.

FOOD FOR THOUGHT

1. What guidelines would you suggest to a planner or criminal justice administrator in deciding whether the chances of type II treatment error are great enough that a crime control strategy should be implemented?

2. If beating costs less and reduced recidivism much more than imprisonment, should beating be used as a punishment for crime?

3. Should a stronger case be made to justify abandoning an established crime control strategy than to justify not implementing a strategy?

4. Since there is much uncertainty whether legal crime controls reduce crime or criminality, should these controls be abolished?

5. What procedure should be used, and by whom, to decide which strategies of crime control should be implemented?

6. Should criminal justice planners, who design crime control strategies for state agencies, favor certain strategies over others from a practical standpoint? From a moral standpoint?

PART TWO

CONTROLLING
RATES OF CRIME

CHAPTER FOUR

Should Conviction Rates Be Controlled?

MEASURING CONVICTION RATE NUMERATORS

One issue regarding any measure is, how *reliable* is the measure (see Lin, 1976; 176–181)? A measure is reliable if different people, or even the same people at different times, record the same event the same way. If different people witnessing the same event all reported that a conviction of first degree robbery had occurred, that measure could be considered reliable. If some people reported no conviction, some a conviction for assault, some a conviction for second degree robbery, and the rest a conviction for first degree robbery, one would have to conclude that the measure of the conviction was unreliable.

Fortunately for our purposes, it can be assumed that official records reliably measure convictions of crimes. One can at least expect most criminal courts to keep files on the cases heard there, in which convictions and offenses are recorded. Researchers or planners may have to tabulate these convictions, which can be costly and time consuming. Tabulation errors can easily occur. But if researchers or planners take time and care, they will have reliable data from which to work.

Serious problems do arise in developing a refined numerator to reflect differences in *kinds* of convictions. It is relatively simple to ascertain how the number of all convictions in one court changes from one time period to the next. But suppose someone wants to focus attention on changes in the number of serious offenses alone? Attempting to separate serious from trivial crimes presents difficulties. Should the criterion be the maximum sentence for a particular offense? Suppose many people convicted of that offense receive far less than the maximum sentence? Should the criterion be the actual sentence imposed in each case? If so, why? Since judges impose different sentences in different cases, the sentence may depend on factors other than what the defendant has done (see, e.g., Hagan, 1975). Length of sentence may even depend on the judge's mood at the moment. Does one simply distinguish offenses by name and not try to rank them in order of seriousness? What if a person is arrested for one offense and convicted for another? And what if that difference occurs because a defendant pleads guilty—based as much on prior record and social status as on the current charge—in exchange for leniency (see Sudnow, 1965)? These are typical issues in trying to classify offenses by seriousness.

Suppose one decided to divide convictions into *groups* by seriousness. Sellin and Wolfgang (1964) developed a scale for measuring seriousness. Rossi et al. (1974) found that people rate seriousness of offenses in pretty much the same way regardless of their class, race, or sex. And yet, one might use legal categories, such as felonies, gross misdemeanors, and misdemeanors instead. This would create a problem in the state of Minnesota. Regardless of the crime, the conviction is considered a felony if the sentence is more than a year of confinement, a gross misdemeanor if the sentence is from more than ninety days to a year of confinement or a fine of more than $300, and a misdemeanor if the sentence is for confinement of up to ninety days or a fine of up to $300 (Minnesota Statutes, 1971). This leads us back to the issue of whether the criterion should be the offense for which a defendant is convicted or the length of the sentence imposed. To complicate matters further, defendants can be sentenced to receive sanctions other than confinement. Is a sentence of a year on probation more or less serious than a sentence of thirty days in jail (see Zimmerman, 1976: 144–185)? There are no clear answers.

Another problem arises in deciding whose convictions to include in the numerator. An increased conviction rate before one judge or in one court may sometimes be linked to a decreased conviction rate before another judge or in another court. It has been claimed, but never demonstrated publicly, that when one judge or court or jurisdiction reacts severely to an offense like prostitution or selling drugs, the offenders will go elsewhere. Thus, they will appear before other judges or in other courts if charged simultaneously by more than one jurisdiction. This is the problem some scholars call "defining system boundaries." Deciding which judges' and which courts' convictions belong in one group is especially problematic when numbers or rates of convictions are changing. No social scientist can agree precisely how system boundaries should be drawn.

In sum, the crime control planner has many choices as to which categories of convictions should be controlled. And any choice will be arbitrary.

MEASURING CONVICTION RATE DENOMINATORS

If choosing the numerator of a crime rate is complex, choosing a denominator is mind boggling. For one thing, there are so many more possible denominators. Recall from Chapter 3 that choosing a denominator implies determining a population at risk. Which population is most appropriate? Is it all those who reside in the jurisdiction from which the numerator is drawn? What about people who work in the jurisdiction but live elsewhere? How are people who are born or who die, or who move into or out of the jurisdiction during the period being measured, to be counted?

Should children under the age of seven, who generally cannot be adjudicated delinquent in juvenile or family courts, be included in the population at risk? If criminal convictions but not adjudications of delinquency are included in the numerator, then perhaps delinquents should also be excluded from the denominator. In those states which permit family or juvenile courts to bind over cases to the adult criminal courts when the persons charged are at least fourteen or fifteen years of age, should this age group be included in the denominator?

One can change the method of selecting a denominator if one is interested in changing the probability of conviction for those already brought before the courts. One might want to lower this probability in the name of pretrial diversion from the criminal justice system (see National Pretrial Intervention Service Center,

1973) or to raise the probability in the name of deterrence (J. Wilson, 1977). Does the population then include all those arrested or summoned to court? What if they are never brought before a judge or magistrate? Suppose a private citizen files a criminal complaint but no arrest or summons results? What if a person appears initially but charges are then dropped before a preliminary hearing? What if, after a preliminary felony hearing, the prosecutor decides not to take a case to a grand jury for indictment? What if a grand jury hears a case and fails to return an indictment (though such cases are rare)? Following an indictment, a defendant may be asked to enter a plea of guilty before the trial judge, as the judge sets a time for trial, in a procedure called "arraignment." What of defendants who are never arraigned, possibly because they cannot be found? And what if cases that get through all the other stages never come to trial? If a defendant is tried and convicted of another offense from that charged, how, if at all, should this be reflected in the denominator (let alone the numerator)?

Since a denominator has been chosen, many of the measures of the denominator pose problems of reliability. Records of cases that have not gone through trial can be hard to find or simply disappear. Prosecutors may take possession of files on pending cases, and files have been known to get lost. Arrest data may be incomplete. Unprocessed criminal complaints may be discarded. There is some margin for error in census data about the population of any jurisdiction. Such errors may be assumed to be minimal unless one is trying to make refined measurements of changes in the population, especially during as short a period as a year. Of course, the greater the change in a conviction rate from one period to the next, the less concerned one will be about the possibility of reliability error. This is part of the issue of deciding how large a change in a conviction rate is required to show that a crime control strategy is working.

This issue is especially troublesome if one wants to use a measure of crime rates in a jurisdiction as the denominator, as has been done in deterrence research (Palmer, 1977). Conviction rates will be much lower if one uses victim survey reports instead of police reports in the denominator. The smaller the denominator, the greater the change in conviction rates that will result from a change in number of convictions. The greater the change in conviction rates, the more substantial the success or failure of crime control will appear to be.

We have already seen that choosing which crime rate to change is a major problem for the planner. It is now clear that choosing which conviction rate to change poses a similar problem. No matter how narrowly the problem of crime control is defined, the problems are many and complex. It is as difficult to imagine changing all kinds of crime rates at once, as it is to imagine changing all conviction rates simultaneously. This will become clear later in this chapter.

CURRENT TRENDS

Two relevant tables appear each year in the national figures published by the Federal Bureau of Investigation: (1) "Disposition of Persons Formally Charged by the Police" and (2) "Offenses Known, Cleared; Persons Arrested, Charged and Disposed of." These tables indicate relatively small, up-and-down changes, from 1968 to 1975, in (a) percentage of offenses cleared by arrests, (b) arrests as a percentage of offenses known, (c) persons charged as a percentage of offenses known, (d) conviction of same and lesser charges as a percentage of offenses known, and (e) percentage of persons charged convicted of same and lesser charges. These rates have nearly remained constant. On the other hand, the rate of offenses known to the police has increased—a 40 percent increase for the seven index offenses. Also (given the comparability of patterns for disposition of persons charged with index offenses and other offenses), there is presumably a lesser, but still consistent, increase for other offenses. In other words, U.S. police are filing offense reports faster than the population is increasing. But thereafter, arrests are made for the same percentage of offenses known, the same percentage of charges result from offense reports and arrests, and the same percentage of persons charged for each offense are convicted both of the same offense and of lesser offenses. In still other words, arrests, charges, and convictions are increasing at practically the same rate as police "offenses known."

If we define success in controlling crime as fewer convictions, then the relevant conviction rates (convictions per inhabitants) indicate that crime is getting worse. If we presume that success in crime control requires holding inhabitants more responsible for crime, then we may take comfort from these figures. If we presume that figures for convictions per offenses known, arrests, and charges brought indicate the quality of those reports, arrests and charges; or indicate how well judges and juries help police and prosecutors control crime; or indicate deterrence value (the probability of sanction following commission of an offense), then these conviction rates indicate no change in the quality of U.S. crime control. Likewise, if we presume that the best the courts can do is divert those arrested and charged from the criminal justice system before unduly stigmatizing and debilitating defendants, or costing taxpayers the expense of taking care of convicts, then these conviction rates indicate no change in the quality of crime control by the courts.

From a practical standpoint, current U.S. trends indicate that conviction rates of all kinds covary with police activity. There are only two known exceptions to this rule. One is that proportions of arrests and charges for particular offenses resulting in convictions (a) *increase* as legislatures *lower* the penalties prescribed for those offenses and (b) *decrease* as legislatures *raise* the penalties. The other exception is a qualification of the first. Offenses, like murder—which most people believe to be especially serious—once reported to police, are highly likely to be followed by arrest, prosecution, and conviction. Thus, if police dealt only with very serious offenses, the proportion of convictions to offenses known, arrests, and charges would increase, while the proportion of convictions to number of inhabitants would decrease. These exceptions are considered in the next section. As we consider approaches to changing conviction rates, you should bear in mind that any of the strategies that change police-produced rates of crime (see Chapter 5) will probably indirectly change conviction rates by population, too.

EVALUATING CHANCES OF CONTROLLING CONVICTION RATES

One can imagine rewarding prosecutors, jurors, or judges for arranging lower conviction rates in their jurisdictions. In theory, such strategies could be expected to reduce conviction rates effectively. This may actually occur in jurisdictions where bribery is widespread (Pepinsky, 1976: 120–121). However, the political resistance to such a strategy is so obvious that we cannot give it serious consideration.

On the other hand, granting some kind of assistance to defense lawyers may be worthwhile. Consider the pretrial diversion projects which were started in several communities in the late sixties with funding from the U.S. Department of Labor. Representatives of these programs work with defendants and their lawyers to arrange programs of employment, education, or counseling for the defendants. With this aid, the defense counsel can approach the trial judge and propose the program.

The criminal procedure law in a number of jurisdictions permits a trial judge to "continue" or "adjourn" a case for some period to see whether a defendant can remain at liberty without getting into further trouble. Then, unless the judge decides that the defendant should not be left at liberty, the charges against the defendant are dismissed. The conviction is then taken off the defendant's record. It has been shown that such procedures significantly lower conviction rates for minor offenses, provided the denominator of the rates is the number of people arrested or charged (National Pretrial Intervention Service Center, 1973).

If pretrial diversion lowers conviction rates, and if the denominator of the rates is a measure of some larger segment of the community population, the conviction rates will probably soon rise to their old level. If this kind of help is available, many people will probably come before the courts who previously would not have been charged. The group using the program may consist of people who would otherwise not have become defendants, while the traditional defendants become as likely to be convicted as before.

There are several indications that diversion only temporarily diverts people from the criminal justice system. Eventually the system has as many clients as ever, if not more, and the diversion programs merely add new groups of defendants to the old. After probation and parole programs were instituted at the turn of the century to divert prison convicts back into the community, rates of imprisonment soon returned to their former level. Probationers and parolees were generally those who previously would have had no formal supervision (Rothman, 1975). Later, in the 1960s, reflecting the spirit of the Great Society, community corrections programs became popular (see the President's Commission on Law Enforcement and Administration of Justice, 1967). Accordingly, prison populations dropped, but began climbing again in 1970, reaching record levels by 1976 (R. Wilson, 1977). Following implementation of juvenile diversion programs, juvenile training school populations began dropping in 1971, only to start climbing again in 1975 (Komisar, 1978).

Much the same set of possibilities can be projected for an alternative approach to lowering conviction rates: that of arranging a higher rate of release from jail of pretrial defendants. It has been found that such defendants who are free on bail or on recognizance have a significantly lower chance of being convicted than those who await trial in jail. (However, this might be because those who are released have the least serious cases to begin with, Bottomley, 1973: 88–93.) Since pretrial release does give defendants a chance (a) to help prepare their defense, (b) to appear in court without the stigma of a jail uniform and shackles, and (c) to delay trial without suffering the discomforts of jail, there is a better than even chance that pretrial release would lower the likelihood of conviction.

On the other hand, a higher rate of pretrial release would give the police more good candidates for arrest. If arrest rates thus rose, there would be more defendants awaiting trial even as the probability of conviction lessened. A greater likelihood of arrest, plus a lower likelihood of conviction, could cause convictions per population to be as high as or higher than before.

Today in the United States, most cases that result in conviction involve no trial. Instead, defendants plead guilty to some charge, generally as a consequence of what is known as a "plea bargain." For example, 84 percent of convicted defendants in federal courts in 1974 pleaded guilty (Hindelang et al., 1977: 599). In a plea bargain, the prosecutor or judge (depending on the jurisdiction) offers the defendant one or more of the following: One or more charges will be dropped; the defendant will be permitted to plead guilty to a lesser offense; or a certain kind of sentence (such as probation) will be recommended or imposed. One can imagine that if defendants who now plead "guilty" pleaded "not guilty" instead, at least a few of them would be acquitted. Hence, conviction rates would probably be lowered by implementing a recommendation of the National Advisory Commission on Criminal Justice Standards and Goals (1973: 46). This states that plea bargaining should be ended in all U.S. jurisdictions by 1978, and that defendants be permitted to plead guilty only to the charges as against them, without promise of special consideration in sentencing (as is the practice in England; Bottomley, 1973: 114–115). However, no one, including the Commission, has figured out how prosecutors and defense counsel could be made to implement the change, unless the law were changed to forbid guilty pleas.

If the law of a jurisdiction were changed to require a trial before any defendant could be convicted, judges might well compensate by imposing heavier sentences on defendants whose cases were seriously, carefully presented, so that defense counsel would have an incentive to act as though their clients' guilt was a foregone conclusion, allowing cases to proceed to disposition in short order. Or judges could impose stiffer sentences on convicted defendants whose cases had been heard by juries rather than by the judge alone, while convicting at a higher rate in "bench trials" (that is, trials in which the judge rather than a jury determines guilt or innocence) than juries are inclined to do. It is therefore possible that making trials mandatory would not affect any conviction rate. If the rate of convictions per trial decreased anyway, the decrease would probably be temporary. As in England, one could expect police and prosecutors to be more selective, processing cases with a good chance of conviction. This outcome is to be expected from use of a computerized system in the United States—called the Prosecutor's Management Information System—which tells prosecutors and police which cases to concentrate on for arrest and prosecution. These cases are most likely to yield convictions and severe sentences (Scopetta, 1978). Hence, with any denominator consisting only of a group brought into the court system—as by arrest, arraignment, or any further procedure—conviction rates would probably show no change some time after trials had been made mandatory. In fact, some of the rates might even increase as officials overcompensate for the change in procedure.

An inverse relationship between severity of punishment and

likelihood of conviction is well documented (Ross, 1976; J. Wilson, 1977). The recent change in New York State law, which made a life sentence mandatory for conviction for the sale or distribution of certain drugs, illustrates the point. This temporary change in the law led police in many cases to charge defendants with lesser offenses than sale or distribution (such as possession of a drug). And in other cases, prosecutors offered to reduce charges (before indictment, to comply with the law) in plea bargaining. Defendants facing a possible mandatory life sentence were unlikely to plead guilty to the charge(s) against them. Thus, by any denominator, the conviction rates for the sale of these drugs in New York State declined, though some other conviction rates for other offenses may have increased accordingly (*New York Times*, 1976). (In addition, it appears that the law had no impact on drug use in New York; see Joint Committee on Drug Use Evaluation, 1977.)

On the other hand, Galliher et al. (1974) report that conviction of marihuana possession was facilitated by reducing the penalty in Nebraska. Data thus far indicate that substantially increasing penalties is a good way to lower conviction rates, while substantially decreasing them is a good way to raise conviction rates for particular offenses. It is hard to imagine legislatures raising or lowering penalties for all or even many offenses at once. This strategy is suited to changing only a few conviction rates.

One other proposal for controlling convictions (see, e.g., Schur, 1965, and Morris and Hawkins, 1970) is to "decriminalize" certain offenses. The idea is to have legislatures take certain crimes off the statute books—notably so-called "crimes without victims," such as drug offenses, gambling, sale and distribution of pornography to consenting adults, and sexual acts (like those known as "prostitution," "sodomy," or "fornication") between consenting adults. Because the parties to these crimes are willing participants, laws against them are notoriously difficult to enforce—like the distribution of liquor during Prohibition. Whatever enforcement does occur involves such unsavory practices as police undercover work in which officials themselves may engage in illegal activities like buying drugs, and in the use of informants—often paid for their services—who themselves engage regularly in the illegal activity.

The legalization of such acts would obviously reduce conviction rates for *those offenses* by population. It is less obvious that decriminalization would lower overall conviction rates by population for long. Monkkonen's (1977) research on U.S. arrest rates between 1860 and 1920 indicates a longstanding shift by police from making arrests on their own initiative—like public order arrests—to using citizen complainants to generate information for more and more arrests for crimes *with* victims. Given the recurrent pattern whereby the criminal justice system's gains back all its old clientele some years after the use of diversion measures, it is likely that after decriminalization, the police would provide more than enough defendants to make up for the loss of crimes without victims. And since the rate of conviction by arrest and prosecution for crimes without victims is generally as high as, if not higher than, for other crimes (F.B.I., 1978: 215–216), the courts' performance in maintaining the probability of conviction by arrest and prosecution would likely suffer (to say nothing of by offenses known, since complaints of crimes without victims usually involved arrest). On the whole, decriminalization does not seem a promising way of controlling conviction rates.

The problem of changing conviction rates shows how difficult it is to find a strategy reasonably capable of changing all rates as desired at once. It also shows that many promising strategies can easily be undermined over a long period of time. Finally, it indicates that good strategies might be found to reduce particular rates over the long term if the purpose is narrowly defined.

Another note of caution is in order. Criminologists are prone to make flat pronouncements. However, in predicting the outcome of an attempt to control crime, nothing is definite. Our data on the outcomes of attempts to control crime are extremely limited, and the educated guesses based on these data fallible indeed. An educated guess is better than a wild guess, but it can still prove wrong. Thus, when I state, for instance, that stiffer penalties for crimes will decrease conviction rates, this is only an honest appraisal of the data I have so far. Someday, you or I or someone else may discover a situation in which penalties are increased and conviction rates either remain the same or rise. My statements are designed to spur you to further inquiry. Therefore, be skeptical. Any theories or general pronouncements about the "facts" are guesses, not gospel.

SIDE EFFECTS OF CONTROLLING CONVICTION RATES

To some extent, the side effects of changing conviction rates can be expected to depend on the strategy used. Strategies which make trials of defendants, rather than guilty pleas, more likely can easily worsen court congestion and lengthen the backlog of cases on the court calendar. This has led some groups, like the American Bar Association (1971), to conclude that plea bargaining must be recognized as a legitimate court practice. Periodically, throughout the United States, congestion leads to moves to provide more judges and courts. This would obviously increase the expense of running court systems. In fact, any of the strategies outlined above would add to someone's expense, with the possible exception of less of pretrial detention.

If defendants detained pending trial were released from jail, the risk of their committing new crimes before trial would increase. However, so would the chance of their contributing to productive work in the outside world.

It is much easier to rechannel pressure to place people under formal supervision than to resist the pressure altogether. If a strategy makes the conviction of some defendants less likely, other kinds of supervision may increase. An increased rate of supervision in pretrial diversion programs has already been mentioned. Involuntary commitment to mental institutions (as Rothman, 1975, implies) is another possibility. The problem of supervision would be extended to the decriminalization of such acts as sale and possession of drugs.

If a strategy seems effective and one or more conviction rates are included, this success may carry consequences of its own. A lower conviction rate may imply that the people who *are* convicted are worse criminals than ever. The stigma on them can become stronger, as can the popular belief in the legitimacy of conviction for crimes. For better or worse, one consequence of a lower conviction rate is that fewer people will wonder whether the court is doing right in convicting the remainder.

A secondary consequence might be severer sentences for those still convicted of crime. The notion that they are more deserving of conviction can be extended to several other notions: They deserve stronger punishment; they need more treatment; society needs more protection from them. In sum, one must weigh the humanity of treatment of those convicted of crimes against the humanity of reluctance to convict in the first place. The two kinds of humanity or compassion seem to be antithetical (Pepinsky, 1977).

Researchers have found repeatedly that the wealthier people are, the more likely they are to avoid getting into trouble with the criminal justice system (Quinney, 1970). One can thus infer that rich defendants are more likely than poor ones to be able to take advantage of new ways of avoiding conviction. If conviction rates go down, the average income of those convicted may also decline, and any class bias in the process leading to conviction may become stronger.

While lowering conviction rates may keep productive people from wasting away in jail, and may increase the credibility of those convictions that do take place and enhance the legitimacy of the court process, it may also (a) cost people money, (b) increase the risk of crime, (c) worsen the treatment of those still convicted, and (d) increase the class bias in the court process. Planners are damned if they do, and damned if they don't. This adds substance to the issue of whether to reduce the risk of type I treatment error (by reducing conviction rates) or to avoid increasing type II treatment error (by leaving conviction rates alone, or perhaps even lowering penalties for some offenses in order to increase conviction rates).

POLITICAL CONSIDERATIONS

The prospect of change can easily frighten people. If things have been done one way for some time, people are apt to believe that the *status quo* is the least possible evil. They know they can live with the system as it currently works. After all, they have been doing so. The attraction of possible gains from social change are apt to be outweighed by fears of the risky unknown.

This is especially true of proposed structural changes in people's work situations. A proposal for change can connote criticism that they have not been doing their jobs too well. Court system personnel are apt to see a proposal to control conviction rates in this way. To them, it implies that they have been working to convict people undeservedly. Their resistance can consist of defending the way they have been doing their jobs (Pepinsky, 1976: 13–71).

Court system personnel may also resist the implication that proposal may lessen their power. For example, prosecutors may believe they possess unique competence to decide which conviction and which sentences defendants should receive. Thus, they might strongly resist any attempt to restrict plea bargaining.

Some people might see their jobs threatened by a proposal to control conviction rates. For instance, probation officers who prepare presentence reports might foresee fewer jobs for them with lower conviction rates.

How can one hope to overcome such obstacles? The problems suggest that the planner must reassure officials that they need not fear the consequences of a proposal. The proposal can stress the ways in which the special competence of officials can be better utilized. It can emphasize the responsibilities and powers which would be retained by officials. It can describe new responsibilities which could be given to those with reduced workloads. For instance, a proposal for a program of pretrial diversion might suggest that probation officers who previously had prepared presentence reports could be trained for and assigned to the preparation of diversion programs for defendants. This kind of approach would not necessarily overcome all official resistance to a proposal, but it could help.

A proposal to reduce conviction rates would also be resisted by the general public or by elected officials guessing about the attitudes of their constituents. Some can be expected to oppose a higher rate of pretrial release and lower conviction rates on the ground that this would represent "coddling criminals." Others might simply believe that criminals deserve to be punished, or that they should not be set free possibly to hurt other people.

Feelings of retribution are difficult to overcome. One can question whether the retribution is worth the expense to taxpayers of keeping people in jail or in prison. One can ask whether retribution could be satisfied by demanding that defendants make special efforts not to be convicted, as in diversion programs. As to the risk posed by setting more defendants free, one could suggest that it might be worth taking—as against the certain public expense of carrying defendants to conviction and beyond.

Some might argue that lower conviction rates imply that it costs more per defendant convicted to maintain the court system. To this, one might suggest alternative kinds of cost accounting (see Chapter 12).

Still others might believe that it would be wrong to treat those convicted more severely and with greater discrimination. One could respond to this challenge by asking why convicted people would merit special consideration, and whether such sympathy for them was consistent with advocating that conviction rates be kept as high as possible.

Thus, in trying to overcome political obstacles to proposals for reducing conviction rates, a variety of appeals can be made. Such attempts at persuasion seem necessary in getting a proposal adopted; whether they would prove sufficient remains to be seen.

ETHICAL ISSUES

A number of ethical issues are implied in the above discussion. These issues can be subsumed under a larger one: is it worse to convict people unnecessarily (type I treatment error) or to let guilty people go free?

Obviously, lowering conviction rates raises the probability that offenders will escape the punishment which the law declares they deserve. But judges and juries are not foolproof arbiters of guilt or innocence under any circumstances. They do not personally witness crimes being committed, and like researchers, they cannot escape making guesses about what has happened. The problem of determining guilt or innocence is illustrated by the case of George Whitmore, Jr. In June 1964, in New York City, Whitmore confessed to the murders of Janice Wylie and Emily Hoffert in a sixty-page statement which included a detailed map of the scene of the crime. Four months later, someone else confessed to the crime, and it was decided that Whitmore was innocent (Zimbardo, 1967: 18–19). Judges and jurors may often *feel* certain that they know whether defendants are guilty or innocent, but they may also be wrong. And so, we may conclude that higher conviction rates imply a greater probability that innocent defendants are found guilty. Do we want to maximize the chances that innocent people remain at liberty, or that people who deserve conviction receive it? Where do we draw the line? Which direction do we take at any given time? Such questions are far easier to ask than to answer.

Is it desirable that defendants awaiting trial be released from jail? In theory, the Eighth Amendment to the U.S. Constitution prescribes that the only legitimate reason to detain defendants in jail is to guarantee their appearance at trial. The risk of released defendants' escaping trial by flight has been found to be minimal, but should any such risk be tolerated?

Despite the theory, defendants are often held in jail to minimize the risk that they will commit new offenses before their guilt or innocence is determined (see, e.g., Vera Institute of Justice, 1972). Should we subscribe so completely to a classical presumption of innocence that we conclude that no one should be detained for this reason? If not, how great a risk of new crimes being committed can we tolerate? Conversely, how willing are we to tolerate the disruption of outside relations, such as those of the family and employment, that detention may produce? How much money is it worth to hold defendants in jail?

If reduced conviction rates indicate less crime, and higher conviction rates increased deterrence of crime, are we more inclined to use the indicator of crime control that risks people's getting hurt *without* state protection, or the one that risks people's getting hurt *by* state intervention?

If decreased conviction rates lead to increased class discrimination in conviction and sentencing, should we tolerate this stronger class bias? Is it better to have less class bias enforced at a greater rate, or more class bias enforced at a lesser rate? Does it make any difference if we assume that lower-class people are more likely to commit crimes than upper-class people (though some of the data from self-report studies—reviewed in Chapter 9—weaken this assumption)?

If reduced conviction rates lead to worse treatment of those still convicted, is such a result consistent with our principles of humanity? Does the result imply that we are giving up on some people who might otherwise have become valued members of society?

Is greater legitimacy being given to a court system whose very existence might be oppressive? Conversely, is greater legitimacy for the court system, or a greater respect for the "rule of law," desirable?

To those who believe in the need to punish people more, since higher conviction rates appear antithetical to more severe sentences: Which is more important, punishing more people, or punishing people more?

There are other issues as well. Is the expense of diversion programs justifiable? If the expense of running a court system remains constant and a conviction rate declines, since it is then arguable that the expense of each conviction increases: Is a greater expense for obtaining any one conviction justifiable? And how can various expenses be balanced one against the other? In many cases, in order to justify financial expense, that expense must be related to things which have no fixed financial value. For instance, how much is it worth for defendants awaiting trial to spend evenings at home with their families? Again, these cost-benefit issues are more fully addressed in Chapter 12.

These are only a few of the issues a planner must resolve. Try putting yourself in the position of a planner, and ask how you would handle these problems.

CONCLUSION

In trying to reduce conviction rates, planners must face many issues which have not been covered here. Full coverage is impossible. If you think of issues which are not covered as you read this and later chapters, it is both understandable and commendable. It indicates that you are contributing ideas to the task of crime control planning. The issues raised here are intended to stimulate you to think for yourself. There is no pretense of telling you everything the beginning student of criminology needs to know.

If you have not thought of other issues, review the chapter to see whether you can create some. The new issues will raise new implications; consider these too. Learning about crime control planning has no end. One can scarcely aspire to know all there is to know about it. But that is part of the excitement; strange and wonderful new ideas about crime control always remain to be discovered.

Approaches to changing conviction rates also show how attempts to change one kind of crime rate might have implications for other kinds of rates as well. For example, increased pretrial release of defendants, while reducing some conviction rates, might also lead to increases in police and victim survey rates of crime, and in recidivism rates as well. Such possibilities are considered and reviewed in Chapters 7 and 11 to 13, but you can begin now to consider some of these implications for yourself. As you read the chapters of this book, consider the interrelationships among them. By the time you reach the last chapter, you may find that you have already arrived at many of the ideas presented there. This task should be relatively easy in moving from this chapter to the next, which considers how to change police-produced rates of crime. The challenge of relating chapters will become far greater later on.

REFERENCES

American Bar Association. 1971. *Standards Relating to the Prosecution Function and the Defense Function*. New York: Institute of Judicial Administration.

Bottomley, A. Keith. 1973. *Decisions in the Penal Process*. South Hackensack, N.J.: Rothman.

Federal Bureau of Investigation. Annual. *Crime in the United States: Uniform Crime Reports*. Washington, D.C.: United States Government Printing Office.

Galliher, John F., James F. McCartney, and Barbara Baum. 1974. "Nebraska's marihuana law: a case of unexpected legislative innovation." *Law and Society Review* 8 (Spring): 441–445.

Hagan, John. 1975. "The social and legal construction of criminal justice: a study of the pre-sentencing process." *Social Problems* 22 (June): 620–637.

Hindelang, Michael J., Michael R. Gottfredson, Christopher S. Dunn, and Nicollette Parisi. 1977. *Sourcebook of Criminal Justice Statistics— 1976*. Washington, D.C.: United States Government Printing Office.

Joint Committee on Drug Use Evaluation. 1977. *The Nation's Toughest Drug Law: Evaluating the New York Experience—Final Report*. Washington, D.C. United States Government Printing Office.

Komisar, Lucy. 1978. "Putting Johnny in jail: how real is the juvenile crime scare?" *Juris Doctor* 8 (June–July): 16–27.

Lin, Nan. 1976. *Foundations of Social Research.* New York: McGraw-Hill.

Minnesota Statutes. 1971. "Convictions of felony or gross misdemeanor; when deemed misdemeanor or gross misdemeanor." *Minnesota Statutes Annotated*, Sec. 609.13.

Monkkonen, Eric. 1977. "Labelling theory and crime: a time series analysis." Paper presented at Social Science History Association Meeting, Ann Arbor, Mich. (October 23).

Morris, Norval, and Gordon Hawkins. 1970. *The Honest Politician's Guide to Crime Control.* Chicago: University of Chicago.

National Advisory Commission on Criminal Justice Standards and Goals. 1973. *Courts.* Washington, D.C.: United States Government Printing Office.

National Pretrial Intervention Service Center. 1973. *Diversion from the Criminal Justice System: Technical Assistance Handbook in Practical Intervention Techniques and Action Programs.* Washington, D.C.: National Pretrial Intervention Service Center.

New York Times. 1976. "U.S. study backs critics of New York's Drug Law." *New York Times* (September 5): 1, 40.

Palmer, Jan. 1977. "Economic analyses of the deterrent effect of punishment: a review." *Journal of Research in Crime and Delinquency* 14 (January): 4–21.

Pepinsky, Harold E. 1976. *Crime and Conflict: A Study of Law and Society.* New York: Academic Press.

———. 1977. "Despotism in the quest for valid U.S. crime statistics: historical and comparative perspectives." Pp. 69–82, in Robert F. Meier (ed.), *Theory in Criminology: Contemporary Views.* Beverly Hills, Calif.: Sage.

President's Commission on Law Enforcement and Administration of Justice. 1967. *Task Force Report: Corrections.* Washington, D.C.: United States Government Printing Office.

Quinney, Richard. 1970. *The Social Reality of Crime.* Boston: Little, Brown.

Ross, H. Laurence. 1976. "The neutralization of severe penalties: some traffic law studies." *Law and Society Review* 10 (Spring): 403–413. Cliffs, N.J.: Prentice-Hall.

Rossi, Peter H., Emily Waite, Christine E. Bose, and Richard E. Berk. 1974. "The seriousness of crimes: normative structure and individual differences." *American Sociological Review* 39 (April): 224–237.

Rothman, David J. 1975. "Behavior modification in total institutions." *Hastings Center Report* 5 (February): 17–24.

Schur, Edwin M. 1965. *Crimes Without Victims: Deviant Behavior and Public Policy—Abortion, Homosexuality, Drug Addiction.* Englewood Cliffs, N.J.: Prentice-Hall.

Scopetta, Nicholas. 1978. "Getting away with murder: our disastrous court system." *Saturday Review* (June 10): 10–13.

Sellin, Thorsten, and Marvin E. Wolfgang. 1964. *The Measurement of Delinquency.* New York: Wiley.

Sudnow, David. 1965. "Normal crimes: sociological features of the penal code in a public defender's office." *Social Problems* 12 (Winter): 255–276.

Vera Institute of Justice. 1972. *Preventive Detention in the District of Columbia: The First Ten Months.* New York: Vera Institute.

Wilson, James Q. 1977. *Thinking About Crime.* New York: Vintage Books.

Wilson, Robert. 1977. "U.S. prison population again hits new high." *Corrections Magazine* 3 (March): 3–22.

Zimbardo, Philip G. 1967. "The psychology of police confessions." *Psychology Today* 1 (June): 17–20, 25–27.

Zimmerman, Sherwood Edwin. 1976. *Sentencing Councils: A Study By Simulation.* Albany, NY: State University of New York (dissertation).

FOOD FOR THOUGHT

1. Imagine that you are on the staff of a member of the U.S. Congress, whose constituents tend to be very critical of the courts. The Congressperson asks you to look over current trends in U.S. conviction statistics, to pick out those which show U.S. courts in the worst light, and to outline an argument to go with the trend figures. Try constructing arguments that show (a) the failure of change in probability of conviction, given police offense reports, arrests, and charges or (b) the increase in conviction rates per inhabitants, indicating a failure of the courts, and work out a rationale for the stronger argument.

2. Now, put yourself in the position of counsel for a group interested in using U.S. trend figures to defend the courts. What are your arguments, and which one is stronger?

3. You are on the staff of a state legislative committee considering a bill to increase the number of criminal court judges in the state substantially. What would be the impact of this proposal on various conviction rates?

4. Try to figure out a strategy for making various conviction rate trends indicate simultaneously that courts are deterring crime and that less crime is occurring.

5. Imagine that you are a prison inmate evaluating the crime control strategies outlined in this chapter, with the thought that you might be rearrested after your release. How would you evaluate each strategy?

6. Is plea bargaining unjust? If so, how could it be discouraged so as to rectify the injustice?

CHAPTER FIVE

Should Police-Produced Rates of Crime Be Controlled?

MEASURING POLICE-PRODUCED RATE NUMERATORS

Imagine yourself a patrol officer told to report offenses "fully and fairly." This could prove to be a tough assignment. Generally speaking, you would have to balance the disadvantages of two kinds of risk: the risk of "crying wolf" (type I measurement error) and the risk of failing to report as serious a crime as had really taken place (or type II measurement error).

Most police offense reporting is reactive (Black, 1970; Pepinsky, 1976c). That is, instead of finding offenses by themselves, the police make reports based on citizens' complaints. Typically, a citizen will call the police dispatcher, who will send patrol officers to decide whether to make a report. More rarely, a citizen complainant will find police on the street. Reactive police decisions on whether to report offenses are based on how seriously they consider the complaint. Do the police assume that things are as bad as citizens allege, or do they presume that citizens exaggerate the seriousness of events?

It has been suggested that as officers gain experience, they tend to become cynical about citizens' complaints. Experienced officers become more inclined not to report allegations (Pepinsky, 1976c) or to ignore citizen complainants when they are called (Reiss, 1971). The police may come to ignore certain chronic complainers, like the wife who periodically asks to have her husband arrested for assaulting her. They may decide that the wife is lying. Or they may have found on prior occasions that she will not cooperate in prosecuting her husband, making offense reporting and arrest a wasted effort (Pepinsky, 1976c). The police may learn to treat some categories of complainants as unreliable. The complaints of the elderly are especially likely to be dismissed (Pepinsky, 1976c), as are certain kinds of complaints by some racial or ethnic groups (e.g., complaints of assault by blacks against blacks; LaFave, 1962, confirmed by Skolnick, 1966: 171). Motives of complainants may be particularly suspect in some kinds of cases, as in reporting welfare checks stolen to justify replacement checks, or reporting inventory losses to justify collecting insurance. Whether to gain attention, to collect insurance, or to vent anger at a known suspect, the complainant may also exaggerate the amount of loss or harm done.

Patrol officers may also find it difficult to decide whether to treat certain kinds of conflicts as crimes. When acquaintances, such as family members, neighbors, or landlords and tenants are quarreling, the police may well decide that reporting an offense will make the quarrel worse, not better. (This premise underlies the night prosecutor program in Columbus, Ohio—see National Institute of Law Enforcement and Criminal Justice, 1975b—in which quarreling parties are encouraged to work out their differences without resort to offense reporting, arrest, and prosecution.)

On the other hand, police who sympathize with complainants can encourage citizens to report offenses more readily than ever by getting to know the citizens in their districts and displaying a willingness to take complaints seriously.

In sum, the number of offenses reported by the police will vary as the police become more or less willing to take citizen complaints seriously.

In addition, the police report some offenses on their own initiative, or proactively. Because the police personally can see little of their territory at once, the number of offenses—particularly serious offenses—they can discover by themselves is severely limited. But to some extent, the police can report more offenses by investigating suspicious circumstances aggressively, and in doubtful cases reporting offenses (e.g., reporting a breaking and entry— opening access to premises and moving through the access without authorization—based on finding an open window, for which the owner cannot account, into an otherwise locked business after business hours).

Knowing how much discretion is involved in filing offense

reports, a researcher can read and evaluate these reports to try to estimate the likelihood of over- or under-reporting. The researcher may conclude, for instance, that a reduction in the number of burglaries reported from one year to the next is simply a matter of tougher police reporting standards. This is the task some police statisticians and the Federal Bureau of Investigation (President's Commission on Law Enforcement and Administration of Justice, 1967b: 211) take on in reviewing the reports and figures they receive. If, as is rumored (see Chapter 2), reporting ambiguities give statisticians a pretext for adjusting the figures upward or downward for political purposes, it should also be recognized that the ambiguities are inevitable. Thus, there is bound to be room for honest disagreement as to whether offense reports exaggerate or understate the crime brought to police attention.

There are also ambiguities in deciding how to count offenses for which arrests are made. It is common for arresting officers to charge suspects with many offenses at once. For instance, a person caught taking a television set out of someone else's home might simultaneously be charged with grand theft, burglary, possession of burglar's tools, and resisting arrest. The police may believe that the suspect should ultimately be found guilty of all these offenses. Also, the police may be consciously playing their part in the game of plea bargaining (see D. Newman, 1966). If the complaint accompanying the arrest states a number of offenses, the prosecutor has leverage in getting the defendant to plead guilty without trial. In exchange, the prosecutor can offer to drop some of the charges— let us say, to accept a plea of guilty to burglary in exchange for dropping the charges of grand theft, possession of burglar's tools, and resisting arrest. Multiple charges reduce the pressure on the plea-bargaining prosecutor either to reduce charges (e.g., reduce a charge of burglary to one of criminal trespass—being on another's premises without permission) or to recommend special consideration in sentencing (e.g., probation instead of incarceration) in exchange for the guilty plea.

Which, and how many, offenses are to be counted for each arrest? The Federal Bureau of Investigation (annual) counts only one offense—that considered most serious—per arrest. Instead, one could record in arrest rate numerators every offense charged in each arrest. Or, if a person were arrested once for offenses committed at different times (e.g., three burglaries over a three-week period), one offense might be recorded in arrest rate numerators for each occasion.

Going a step further, one might also include in the numerator offenses cleared by arrest for which no charges were made. A traditional measure of police success is the "clearance rate by arrest." In theory, this is the percentage of offenses known to the police that results in arrest. The higher the percentage, the better the police are doing at law enforcement. In order to raise the percentages, U.S. police attempt to get suspects arrested for one offense to confess to others in police files. Whether the suspects actually committed these offenses may be questionable. The suspects have nothing to lose by confessing, and their cooperation with police may gain them lenient treatment (see Skolnick, 1966).

The offenses cleared might be included in arrest rate numerators together with multiple offenses charged in each arrest. As a measure of crime, arrest figures occupy a middle ground between offenses known and convictions. Identification of a suspect in an arrest provides corroboration that an offense "known" to the police has in fact occurred. At the same time, it is a more inclusive measure than conviction.

In every jurisdiction, police make arrests based on differing standards. During the 600 hours I spent riding with patrol officers in the high crime area of Minneapolis (Pepinsky, 1976c), the most common basis for arrest was a warrant for failure to pay a $3 parking ticket. (The drivers could get out of jail as soon as they posted $25 bonds.) Elsewhere (see American Bar Association, 1968: 1–4, 31–42), police may write summonses to appear in court without arresting the suspects. For this reason, arrest rate numerators for less serious offenses may not be comparable among jurisdictions.

The Federal Bureau of Investigation annually includes in its arrest numerators juveniles taken into custody. In theory, in the U.S., acts of juveniles below a certain age may be "delinquent acts" (would be crimes if committed by adults) or "status offenses" (like truancy), but not "crimes" (see Chapter 2), and these children cannot accumulate public arrest records like adults. Perhaps, then, it is wrong to include juvenile arrests in measures of crime.

A final issue in measuring arrest rate numerators is this: To what extent should arrests by different law enforcement agencies be combined? In a U.S. city, arrests may be made by county sheriff's deputies, city police, state police, or federal agents. The arrests made by any one of these agencies is an incomplete basis for measuring the arrest rate in the area. It may also be difficult to determine how many of the arrests made outside as well as inside the city are allocable to the city itself.

MEASURING POLICE-PRODUCED RATE DENOMINATORS

The clearance rate by arrest has already been described; its denominator is straightforward: the number of incidents reported as offenses by the police. The only major ambiguity about clearance rate denominators occurs when one police agency reports the offense and another makes the arrest. Normally, if the reporting agency were notified of the arrest, it would credit the clearance to itself. The arresting agency would normally add an offense to its own records and count the clearance, too. (Everybody wants a clearance.) It could be argued that only one of the agencies—perhaps the agency that made the arrest—should include both the arrest and the reported offense in its clearance rate figures.

If arrest rate denominators are to be based on inhabitants of jurisdictions, a basic choice remains: whether to have the rates measure the risk of *committing* crime or of *being victimized* by crime. The distinction is clear in the case of measuring arrest rates for rape. Normally, men alone can commit rape. (I know of but one exception to this rule. A friend of mine, while a Manhattan prosecutor, got a woman convicted of rape. She was found guilty of the offense by reason of having been an accessory before the fact. She had arranged for the rape to take place in her apartment.) It would therefore make sense to include only male inhabitants in the rate denominators if the rates were to be measures of risk of committing rape. In fact, the denominator might well be limited to male inhabitants at or above the normal age of onset of puberty, if not at the legal age for criminal prosecution as adults. On the other hand, women alone can be rape victims, and the risk of victimization would therefore more appropriately be measured by limiting rate denominators to numbers of women, including young girls.

Needless to say, the problem of computing aggregate measures of risk or of victimization is compounded as offenses are combined. Perhaps that is why the common practice is simply to include all inhabitants in arrest rate denominators, ignoring further subtleties (as annually by the Federal Bureau of Investigation).

CURRENT TRENDS

Generally speaking, U.S. police-produced crime rates have been increasing since the mid 1940s (President's Commission on Law Enforcement and Administration of Justice, 1967b: 19–41; Federal Bureau of Investigation, annual). The rates have dropped or changed only sporadically. Increases in property crimes, such as burglary, were greater than those of crimes against the person, such as murder, until about 1963, when they suddenly zoomed. Until the mid 1960s, increases in arrests for index crimes, especially property crimes, lagged behind increases in offenses known to the police. Since then, arrests and offenses cleared by arrest have remained roughly a constant percentage of offenses known.

Until the 1970s, the biggest increases in police-produced crime rates occurred in cities, especially large cities. In the last decade, the trends in large cities have started to level off, while climbing dramatically in suburbs and rural areas.

All trends took a sharp upward turn in the 1960s. The index "offenses known" rates, as reported by the Federal Bureau of Investigation, climbed 157 percent between 1960 and 1974 (Hindelang et al., 1977: 443).

It is worth noting that rising police-produced rates are not a worldwide phenomenon. A notable contrast to the United States is provided by Japan, where police-produced rates generally rose during the Great Depression, then dropped back to pre-Depression levels during World War II, climbed again during the U.S. Occupation (offenses known to Depression levels, arrests to a lesser extent), and have once again fallen back to pre-Depression and pre-war levels (Bayley, 1976b; Clifford, 1976; Lunden, 1976). In Japan, there seems to be a homeostatic mechanism which forces police-produced rates back to prior levels after short-lived domestic upheavals, while in the United States, rates have until recently risen to unprecedented levels.

Although arrest rates have continued to rise, police "offenses known" rates declined from 1976 to 1978. Overall, index offense rates nationwide declined 0.3 percent from 1975 to 1976, due to declines in rates of murder (down 8.3 percent), robbery (down 10.3 percent), burglary (down 5.7 percent) and auto theft (down 5 percent) (Federal Bureau of Investigation, 1977). In 1977, the overall decrease was 4 percent, with declines largest in large cities and smallest in rural areas (*New York Times*, 1978a). Again, in the first quarter of 1978 compared to the same period in 1977, index crime rates overall were down another 4 percent. Only rape (up 4 percent) and aggravated assault (up 1 percent) climbed during this period (*New York Times*, 1978c).

How can these declines be explained? One clue, I think, lies in a shift in policy by the Law Enforcement Assistance Administration (L.E.A.A.), the agency responsible for dispensing federal crime funds. At this time, L.E.A.A. has shifted from funding technological development for the police to crime prevention projects. For instance, $7,000,000 of the L.E.A.A. budget for fiscal year 1979 (which begins October 1) was earmarked for community anti-crime programs (*Criminal Justice Newsletter*, 1978a: 2). In one week alone, it was announced that the cities of Virginia Beach, Va., San Francisco, Salt Lake City, Nashville, University City, Mo., Fort Worth, Colorado Springs, Colo., and Jackson, Miss., had been given a total of more than $2,000,000 for "Integrated Criminal Apprehension Programs" (*Criminal Justice Newsletter*, 1978b: 7). Data must be collected and reported back to the funding agency as an evaluation of the results of all federal crime funding. The primary measure of police success in crime prevention projects is changes in "offenses known" rates. Thus, in effect, the police across the country have been paid by L.E.A.A. to report less crime. This is close to a crime control proposal I have made to pay officials for filing fewer reports (Pepinsky, 1976a: 120–123), and is similar to an experimental procedure used in Orange, Calif. (Greiner, 1974).

The F.B.I.'s (1977) figures for 1976 give an early indication that declines in robbery and burglary rates are attributable to changes in police reporting practices. The rate of reported theft climbed 116.5 per 100,000 population, while rates of burglary and robbery declined 108.9 per 100,000. Early crime prevention projects concentrated on burglary and robbery. A friend of mine was on a large East Coast urban police force. For the sake of good appearance in a burglary prevention project, he had been instructed by his sergeant not to report burglaries with minor losses. It is quite possible that police departments reported some cases of robbery and burglary as cases of theft instead.

One example is the politics of crime reporting in Chicago. There, Police Superintendent O'Grady reported that all index crime rates had declined an average of 8.8 percent in the first six and a half months of 1978 from the same period in 1977 (*Chicago Tribune*, 1978a). The next day, the *Chicago Tribune* (1978b) noted the superintendent's pleasure in reporting the declines, but cautioned that the report might be too optimistic because of problems of underreporting offenses to the police. Soon after, the decrease was again discussed in a report evaluating the Chicago Police Department's "Beat Rep" program, in which the Illinois Law Enforcement Commission (I.L.E.C., the state funnel for L.E.A.A. funding) had paid the police to organize 3,500 volunteers in 10 districts to watch out for suspicious activity. Although the decreases in offense rates had been lower in the funded districts than in the remainder of the city (attributed, ironically, to increased reporting activity by the volunteers), the program was deemed successful enough for the I.L.E.C. to give the police an additional $100,000 to set up storefront offices in the 10 districts. A police representative claimed that the police had not publicized the project in the past because they were not out for publicity (*Chicago Tribune*, 1978c).

Consistent with attributing the drop in crime to police politicking and fund raising is the fact that rape has been an exception to the nationwide crime rate declines. The police have recently come under intense criticism from women's groups for taking rape complaints too lightly, and reporting more rapes is the better part of political wisdom. The chief anomaly is the steady decline in murder and voluntary manslaughter (wrongful killing in the heat of passion) rates. In some cases of deaths in fights, for example, police, coroners, and prosecutors can decide to mark deaths as accidental rather than pursue the matter as criminal. However, the 2 percent decline in the rate between the first quarter of 1977 and that of 1978 (*New York Times*, 1978b) is a little large to be wholly explained in these terms. It may also be that more people are staying near home during this inflationary period rather than going to such places as bars, providing fewer opportunities for murders outside the home. This is reflected in recent figures for New York City, which indicate a disproportionate rise in the murder rate among family members (*New York Times*, 1978b).

It is also possible that a self-fulfilling prophecy is at work. There are indications that the decline in official crime rates has decreased the fear of crime among Americans. In a University of Dayton study, 94 percent of Dayton residents reported being unafraid to walk the streets after dark in 1976, as compared to only 68 percent in 1974. As Jacobs (1961) reports, with more people on the streets, neighborhoods are less vulnerable to street crime. In addition, the reported decline in crime may be responsible for persons moving back into urban neighborhoods and revitalizing them, and for rejuvenation of downtown areas, which would help insulate urban areas from street crime. Meanwhile, the possibility that crime rate declines are attributable to a decline in numbers of Americans in the "crime-prone" ages (16–25) is remote. As Zimring points out, crime rates have declined in Chicago neighborhoods where the young population has remained stable (*New York Times*, 1978a: 36).

It remains to be seen whether the decline in U.S. crime rates will be sustained. It is notable that the crime index rates also declined between 1971 and 1972, only to climb somewhat in 1973 and then to rise sharply in 1974 and 1975. The current preference of U.S. law enforcement to emphasize the crime problem is reflected in the way the F.B.I. (1977) presented its figures for 1976. Percentage comparisons were given only to 1975 and then to 1972, just *after* the preceding decline. This was designed to show that over a period of years, crime was still a growing problem. Are U.S. police and funding agencies especially cautious about reporting crime around the time of Presidential elections (1972, 1976), pending possible shifts in federal funding policy? How long can the police go on reporting declines in offense rates before the public decides that it no longer needs to pay so much for police services, driving the police to make the public afraid of crime once again? These questions remain to be answered by future events.*

---

* As this book went into production, the F.B.I. announced that index "offenses known" rates increased 5 percent overall in 1978.

EVALUATING CHANCES OF CONTROLLING
POLICE-PRODUCED TRENDS

Perhaps the strength of family and work bonds among small groups of individuals is vital to sustained control of police-produced crime rates. This thesis has been presented by Bayley (1976a; 1976b) and is reflected in Clifford's (1976) studies of crime control in Japan. The social position of a Japanese is likely to be far more stable than that of an American. At home and at work in Japan, reciprocity is well established: one defers to the authority of one's superiors and accepts responsibility for the well-being of one's inferiors. A disgrace of one person is the disgrace of all in the group. To illustrate, employees of large businesses in Japan commonly remain with the firm for their full careers. Striking against the employer is virtually unthinkable. In return, almost never is a worker laid off. Thus, Japan has negligible unemployment by comparison with western countries. The supervisor may even be obligated to act on behalf of the employee in such matters as arranging marriages for the employee's children.

By contrast, as Farber (1973) describes American trends, Americans are likely to treat one another at work with expediency. This tendency is generalized to the family, so that law and customs make it easier and more likely that spouses, children, and guardians are acquired and discarded like other investments as needed.

In many studies, geographical mobility has been found to be associated with increased crime. Samaha (1974) found movement away from communities to be associated with rising crime in Elizabethan England. Hay et al. (1975) reported the same phenomenon for eighteenth-century England. McKenzie (1921: 165–166), Glueck and Glueck (1950), Sullenger (1950), Reiss (1951), and Friday and Haye (1976) have all found that as juveniles change residence, they are more likely to become delinquent. This trend has even been reported in the Netherlands, a country with an extraordinarily small crime problem (Buikhuisen and Timmerman, 1970). Change of residence has also been found to be associated with adult criminality (Carpenter and Haenszel, 1930). Cohen and Felson (1978) have found that property crime increases as people who move freely leave their property unprotected. Also, they report that violent crime increases with the likelihood that people encounter one another as strangers.

Consider, now, the matter of supply and demand for police services. The Japanese who runs into trouble is more likely (a) to turn to someone other than the police and (b) to hesitate to involve outsiders, including the police, in affairs that may affect the reputation or autonomy of the family or work group. In addition, since it is much harder for the Japanese than for the American to leave a family or job and yet maintain social acceptance, the Japanese tends to be more restrained than the American about fighting with other group members or about incurring their disapproval. Hence, Japanese are less likely than Americans either to ask for police help or to give the police a reason for law enforcement.

On the other hand, since Japanese police, too, are more secure on the job than U.S. workers, they have less cause to sell their services than do U.S. police. The irony is that although police are supposed to be hired and paid for *preventing* crime, their importance is likely to be seen as a measure of how many offenses they report or arrests they make. Since social support for U.S. police is quite weak (Clark, 1965), the police have unusual incentive to publicize their work. They show that they are needed by encouraging citizens to report offenses and by trying to make as many arrests as possible. Hence, U.S. police are more likely than their Japanese counterparts to facilitate offense reporting and arrest, as Americans become more prone to lean on police for assistance (Pepinsky, 1977b).

Generally speaking, law enforcement becomes more likely as the propensity of citizens to change jobs, families and residences increases (Pepinsky, 1975b). It looks as though any measures which do not serve to lower these geographical mobility (movement) rates can succeed no more than temporarily in lowering police produced crime rates. With any lesser measures, like changes in police patrol patterns, the remaining pressure of the citizenry for police protection and of the police for job security will probably become too great to restrain police reporting activity.

As Wilson (1977: 89–108) has recently reported, apart from changes in police reporting practices, the police have done little to reduce the rates they produce for extended periods. Experiments that were conducted in New York City indicate that "offenses known" rates for crimes like robbery—which take place on the street—may be reduced by beefing up the foot patrols. (Meanwhile, naturally, arrests increase.) There are sporadic reports of similar success in sending marked squad cars into areas with many auto thefts (as by the Law Enforcement Assistance Administration, 1977). However, in a major experimental study, the Kansas City Police failed to change either "offenses known" or arrest rates by varying levels of motorized patrol in adjoining sectors of the city (Kelling et al., 1974). The remarkable feature of these "successes" is that none of them has continued. The experiments have been short-lived, and so have their effects on crime rates.

Still less do efforts to refine law enforcement technology (see, e.g., Massey, 1975; National Institute of Law Enforcement and Criminal Justice, 1975a) have any apparent effect on police-produced crime rates.

One limited approach to reducing "offenses known" rates, not yet tried, might be successful. The importance of clearance rates could be further emphasized. For example, salary increases for a police department might be tied, as an incentive, to increases in clearance rates. This would make officers more reluctant to file reports in cases where arrest was unlikely. Arrest rates for many offenses would probably increase, while "offenses known" rates would decrease. The measure could be rationalized as rewarding the police for concentrating their efforts, both at record keeping and at detection, on cases in which they could do something: arrest people. The police would once again be able to produce statistics indicating success rather than failure. This might give them enough respectability to keep them from having to sell their services as they now do.

The trouble with such a measure is its short lifespan. Police would eventually become very efficient at reporting only offenses likely to lead to arrest, or they would be pressed to make more and more questionable arrests. In a few years, the police would work themselves down in offense reporting to a point at which they practically had to report every citizen complaint or work themselves upward in arrests until public outcry forced them to desist. They would either be reporting offenses like murder or other offenses by identified suspects, in which arrest was almost certain, or reporting crimes like armed robbery that were serious enough for police inaction to be intolerable. At a certain point, if "offenses known" rates were to be further decreased, citizens would have to live with fewer police services. Control of police-produced crime rates then requires that citizens become more self-sufficient—supporting and restraining one another more at home and at work without official intervention and protection. If police-produced crime rates are to be reduced or held stable for an extended period, citizens must learn how to restrain themselves from changing families and jobs.

Reducing family and job mobility would be unprecedented. Americans are so accustomed to the idea that the freedom to move is desirable that they have scarcely even begun to think about restricting it. Instead of liberalizing divorce laws, tax credits might be given to couples for the numbers of years they remain married. Similar tax incentives might be given to employers and employees to remain together (Pepinsky, 1976a: 125–131). The freedom from capital gains tax given those who sell one residence and purchase a new one might be reconsidered. Programs offering tenants the chance to apply rent to purchase of premises might be expanded. In general, measures that encourage people to stay together in the same families, jobs, and neighborhoods might be encouraged, while measures that facilitate mobility might be abandoned.

With an increased commitment to ongoing, supportive relationships, Americans might also move to emphasize shared responsibility to prevent wrongdoing. Like the French, Americans might impose civil and criminal liability for failure to act to prevent crimes (called *misprision*) or for failure to play the role of the Good Samaritan. Neighbors and coworkers might be legally enjoined to compensate victims of crime, and might be fined or otherwise penalized for having had offenders in their midst (see Pepinsky, 1976a: 133–143).

If Americans wanted to try to restrict family and job mobility, many promising experiments should be easy to conceive and try. As a result, eventual sustained progress in controlling police-produced crime rates could be anticipated.

SIDE EFFECTS OF CONTROLLING
POLICE-PRODUCED CRIME RATES

One result of a sustained decrease in "offenses known" rates could be a job loss for law enforcement personnel. If the public's demand for police services fell, fewer police would be needed. In the United States, this problem could be particularly serious. In October 1975, 60 percent of all criminal justice employees—669,518 persons—were employed in law enforcement. This was a 16 percent increase in only four years (Law Enforcement Assistance Administration and Bureau of the Census, 1977: 18). In a society in which unemployment is a growing problem, it is not clear how ex-police personnel could earn a living. As it is, U.S. patrol officers mostly perform services—such as taking people to the hospital, looking for lost children, and getting cats out of trees—rather than enforce the law (Pepinsky, 1975a). Many of them have complained about this, and it would be a challenge to find things other than law enforcement for police officers to do. Perhaps we need to have crime reported so that police can earn a living.

In addition to police-produced crime rates, many other personal factors vary with changes in jobs, families, and residences (Pepinsky, 1975b; 1977a). The less the mobility, the fewer secrets people can and do keep from one another. Personal privacy becomes more important as people move more and encounter others who are strangers and hence less trustworthy. Thus, long-term reductions in police-produced crime rates may cost citizens some of their privacy, but perhaps that is, in part, because people would need less of the protection privacy affords. The need for protection of privacy, which is taken for granted in contemporary U.S. literature (see, e.g., Rule, 1974), exists particularly where people do not know each other very well in the first place.

Increased social mobility, and the higher police-produced crime rates that go with it, tend to blur the distinction between strangers and acquaintances. On the one hand, a high level of mobility implies that new persons are as welcome in a community as their predecessors. The stranger can walk boldly in a neighborhood in which people are often on the move; can more easily acquire housing and a job; and will probably feel "at home" more quickly. Police protection for enjoying the same rights as any other inhabitant will be greatest in a community with high mobility. By contrast, in a community in which family and business membership are stable, strangers are more apt to stand out, to encounter suspicion even from police, and to be isolated even if they move into a neighborhood or get a job (Jeffery, 1971; O. Newman, 1972).

Perhaps you have noticed differences when encountering people in mobile and stable communities. I have. For instance, when I go to a large city, if I try to say hello to people on the street, they will look away. However, if I crash a party, no one is likely to notice that I am uninvited. When I am in a small town, people routinely smile and greet me on the street, but it may take a year or more before I get over being the somewhat uncomfortable newcomer at parties where people are gossiping about mutual acquaintances. Many Europeans have told me how warm and friendly Americans are, but then confess how hard it is to become friends with them. In general, as mobility increases, people more readily feel at home, while the feeling of being at home becomes more remote. Strangers are easily tolerated because tolerance no longer requires intimacy. People are quickly welcomed because welcoming no longer implies special ties or obligations. Strangers have the same rights and police protection as inhabitants because inhabitants are strangers to one another.

Thus, if people's home and work relationships become stable—if they feel more secure in familiar surroundings and have less call for law enforcement services—then they run greater risks of intolerance and even brutality when they move to a new place. And when the police do act—when people are brought into the criminal justice system—police and other officials will be less inclined to act mercifully and tolerantly toward the wrongdoers (Pepinsky, 1977a). As mobility decreases and the distinction between outsiders and insiders becomes clearer, the deviant becomes a less sympathetic figure. When the police become less likely to treat citizens as criminal suspects, the remaining suspects become more suspicious, more clearly deviant, and less forgivable than ever.

The choice can be summarized this way: Mobility makes people kinder to strangers but strangers to their own kind. If we reduce police-produced crime rates by stabilizing people's relationships at home and at work, we can expect to encounter rising intolerance of outsiders and less freedom to move about in outside communities.

One possible way out of the dilemma is to arrange to have several tightly knit communities mix and intermingle (see Parnell and Pepinsky, 1978: 21–30). Anthropologists state that if each individual belongs to many partially competing interest groups, the loyalty to these groups and their members will help to restrain the individual from carrying out aggression. Murphy's (1957: 1034) hypothesis to this effect was found by Van Velzen and Van Wetering (1960) to be consistent with behavior across societies. By dividing loyalties, various peoples avoided the violence that Gluckman (1959) associated with close-knit social ties.

The crossing of close social ties accounts for the happier, safer U.S. urban neighborhoods studied by Jacobs (1961). To Jacobs, one essential feature of these neighborhoods was that they were not one-purpose neighborhoods, such as residential or commercial. Instead, different kinds of activities were simultaneously carried out. Thus, different people with varying but close social ties constantly intermingled. The streets of these neighborhoods were never abandoned (e.g., when residents were asleep, customers circulated among bars). Many of those circulating through the neighborhoods knew others well enough to count on their assistance if they were in trouble, and outsiders were interested enough in the peace of the neighborhood to intervene when violence threatened. As a barrier to crime, diversifying activity within any small neighborhood is consistent with Brantingham and Brantingham's (1975) finding that the borders of Tallahassee neighborhoods were more vulnerable to burglary than the interiors. That is, where the variation in such characteristics as average rent or characteristics of residents from block to block was least, the risk of burglary was lower. One way to minimize this variation, to blur boundaries between neighborhoods, is to maximize diversity within each block. Then, the average difference between one block and another can be minimized throughout a city.

This kind of arrangement runs counter to the American propensity to put things, including people, each in its own special place. Zoning laws, which regulate where different activities can be located, minimize rather than maximize neighborhood diversity. On the other hand, Americans are accustomed to being tied to diverse groups—living here, working there, socializing with others, belonging to voluntary associations like Kiwanis, and so forth. If Americans could capitalize on this way of life, changing it only by staying with each of the groups they join, and all of them together, then perhaps they could simultaneously become kinder to strangers and to each other.

U.S. law enforcement technology and personnel have increased so much that in the largest cities, police can arrive at the scene of any emergency within several minutes. While the chance of their aborting a crime or apprehending a criminal remains minuscule (for crimes typically occur quickly, too, and the police can maintain surveillance over very little of their districts at a time), Americans can get police assistance promptly once trouble has occurred. If police-produced crime rates fell and police service were therefore reduced, more people who needed immediate police assistance might not receive it in time. In sum, police would probably lose jobs, and citizens privacy, freedom of movement, and police protection, if the conditions necessary for sustained reduction of police-produced crime rates were met.

POLITICAL CONSIDERATIONS

In the United States, concern for police security has so dominated law enforcement policy as to make concern for crime control almost impossible. This is represented by two highly publicized attempts to set standards and goals for U.S. law enforcement: one by the President's Commission on Law Enforcement and Administration of Justice (1967a) and the other by the National Advisory Commission on Criminal Justice Standards and Goals (1973). In both documents, the logic of crime control is practically lost in the long list of standards—which cover such issues as whether the police should have college degrees, how complaints against the police should be handled, and what technology the police should use.

The underlying purpose of these and most other recent recommendations for U.S. police is apparently to create work other than crime control. I myself have participated in this enterprise with a proposal that citizens be enlisted to help police figure out how to fill their time with alternate duties (Pepinsky, 1976b). If the make-work is not for the police themselves, it is for others, such as producers of equipment, psychological or legal counselors, and social science consultants. I am aware that increased crime control implies less police work. My own actions have been motivated by sympathy with the many police officers I know who want to do something worthwhile. It is no small political problem to make police officers accept the idea that the only real way for them to demonstrate success in crime control is to make their services obsolete.

We who aim to help police are in a double bind. If we create more work for them and help police forces to grow and prosper, if we increase the number of services and protection the police offer to the community, we can expect "offenses known" rates and arrest rates to rise and can anticipate less progress in clearing offenses by arrest (Pepinsky, 1977b). For police forces to grow and prosper, we must help police to show that their crime control performance is worsening.

One spokesman, former Boston Police Commissioner and until recently Montgomery County, Maryland, Police Chief DiGrazia, has taken the position (in speeches and guest appearances around the country) that the public should accept police as providers of emergency services who are incapable of crime control. This implies that we ought to continue to support the growth of police *because* police figures show that they are failing to control crime in the first place. Given the chance that police-produced crime rates could be reduced by less police activity, DiGrazia comes very close to implying that more crime is an acceptable price to pay for having more police protection.

To motivate police to help reduce the crime rates they produce, and to increase their clearance rate, we must show police that they would still have respected work and decent livelihoods if they succeeded. You, the reader, are invited to consider how this might be done. The issue has not been addressed in police research or policy literature.

Two general approaches can be imagined. One involves making current police officers secure in their jobs. The other is to increase the nation's job supply sufficiently to compete effectively with police recruitment.

Using the first approach, police might be given lifetime guarantees against being laid off (in the manner of federal judges) and guarantees that salary increases and the *per capita* budget for overhead would more than keep pace with the cost of living (Pepinsky, 1978). Control over police budgets would be maintained only by restrictive hiring of new personnel. Hence, existing personnel would be secure and would be likely to gain social status as entry into the profession became more selective. Police might move beyond feeling a need to sell more of their services to the public. Instead, they might help to make it possible for the crime rates they produce to drop.

Using the second approach, enough attractive jobs might be created in other sectors of the economy so that police need not worry about job security. Obviously, this would be no mean feat today, when policy makers—with economists' advice—try in vain to lower unemployment. It remains to be seen whether an economy as materially and technologically rich as the U.S. economy can provide enough useful things to keep a growing population occupied. Elsewhere (Pepinsky, 1976a: 125–131), I have proposed a tax and subsidy designed to give employers incentive to hire more workers without paying them less, as a means of crime control. Schumacher (1975) considered how to make modern economies more labor intensive—to make people more useful. However, the thinking on this issue is so new that you, the reader, can contribute greatly by coming up with new ideas. The political challenge of reducing police-produced crime rates may be formidable, but it is open to inspired thinking.

ETHICAL ISSUES

The contrasting experience of the Japanese and Americans suggests that loyalty competes with impartiality in a society. As police-produced crime rates increase, impartiality prevails. The police symbolize the right of all to receive equal protection regardless of affiliation with those they meet. By contrast, loyalty implies an obligation to discriminate between "them" and "us." Loyalty to brothers or sisters demands that they be defended against strangers regardless of other merits of the case. In conflicts between them and us, loyalty requires us to treat *them* as wrong.

The competition between impartiality and loyalty has been considered by other writers in other terms. Parsons (1951), one prominent American sociologist, refers to relationships based on impartiality as "universalistic" and those based on loyalty as "particularistic." Tocqueville (1945, originally published in 1835 and 1840), the brilliant, prophetic young Frenchman who toured the United States in the mid nineteenth century, described impartiality as a passion for equality and loyalty as knowing one's place in the social order (e.g., as a born aristocrat would). As Americans pursued their passion for equality, Tocqueville foresaw that they would become more selfish, more egoistic. They would care less for each other and for affairs of state, would be concerned primarily with increasing their personal well-being, and would prefer to have others, like the police, manage their problems for them.

Durkheim (1951, originally published in 1897), the French sociologist, inferred from suicide patterns that some social orders, notably armies, demanded such loyalty that people would kill themselves "altruistically" in defense of comrades and country. Other social orders, notably in places where Protestantism predominated, equalized each person's status (in the eyes of God), so that people killed themselves egoistically, in the despair of isolation.

The trouble with impartiality—with owing the same duty to everyone—is that no special duty is owed to anyone in particular. Being close to someone, like a spouse, can intensify feelings of hostility. At the same time, as impartiality becomes an accepted principle of life, the special restraint and consideration owed to near ones loses force. As in the United States today (National Commission on the Causes and Prevention of Violence, 1969: 25–26), the risk of bodily violence is high among those closest to us, not from our enemies. In the anonymity of the impartial social order, it becomes easier to steal without being detected (who notices how Joe Jones got his television set?), and the threat of bringing dishonor upon one's in-group (when each person is judged individually) no longer restrains one from wrongdoing. In the impartial social order, where everyone acts autonomously, the claim that "it's none of your business" legitimizes acting without regard for even close relatives and colleagues. Upholding a principle comes dangerously close to taking the law into your own hands. In this amoral world, the police can find a lot of crime to report and a lot of public acceptance, if not eagerness, for the police to manage interpersonal problems.

Loyalty, on the other hand, justifies discrimination, bigotry, and intolerance. Each person belongs in his or her place. The wife belongs in the home. Children must adopt the beliefs of their elders. Outcasts would not feel comfortable sharing our bounty even if they were given the chance—which they do not deserve because they are outcasts. Vengeance is a sacred obligation, under the principle of "death before dishonor." To call in outsiders, including the police, entails a loss of face not only for oneself but for one's group. Belonging to the in-group is so critical that the police will be reluctant to swell their own ranks. Instead, they will be highly selective in recruiting and prolonged in training and initiation rituals (Bayley, 1976a). The police survive more by defending their integrity than by producing growing crime rates and pressing for expansion.

The capacity to treat every human being as special has been ascribed to Christ. It appears that human limitations require the rest of us to choose where to concentrate our favorable attention at the expense of intolerance elsewhere. Should we treat outsiders equally and be intolerant of those who are close, or should we treat insiders specially and outsiders intolerantly? The choice is between having a little compassion for many people or a lot of compassion for a few. For each of us, this ethical dilemma lies at the root of deciding whether to favor the growth or the decline of police-produced crime rates.

CONCLUSION

The police are the criminal justice officials most closely linked to the public. Unlike others in the system, most police officers spend their time in the community. They have the primary responsibility for bringing cases into the criminal justice system. The amounts of crime and criminality reported in police figures exceed those reported by any other officials. Thus, sustained changes in police-produced crime rates probably requires greater changes in society than would sustained changes in conviction rates.

Criminological literature has largely ignored ideas for such fundamental changes as those considered here. It may well seem grandiose to criminologists to think in such radical terms. You, the reader, may share this belief. But whether or not we want the radical kind of change involved, this chapter is intended to show that the change is imaginable and perhaps even attainable.

REFERENCES

American Bar Association. 1968. *Standards Relating to Pretrial Release.* New York: Institute of Judicial Administration.

Bayley, David M. 1976a. *Forces of Order: Police Behavior in Japan and the United States.* Berkeley, Calif.: University of California Press.

———. 1976b. "Learning about crime: the Japanese experience." *Public Interest* 44 (Summer): 55–68.

Black, Donald J. 1970. "Production of crime rates." *American Sociological Review* 35 (August): 733–747.

Brantingham, Patricia L., and Paul J. Brantingham. 1975. "Residential burglary and urban form": *Urban Studies* 12 (October): 273–284.

Buikhuisen, W., and H. Timmerman. 1970. "Verhuizing en criminaliteit" ("Moving and criminality"). *Nederlands Tijdscrift voor Criminologie* 12 (March): 34–39.

Carpenter, Niles, and William M. Haenszel. 1930. "Migratoriness and criminality in Buffalo." *Social Forces* 9 (December): 254–255.

Chicago Tribune. 1978a. "Major crime declines 8.8% in city." July 26, sec. 1, p. 1.

———. 1978b. "Good news about local crime." July 27, sec. 3, p. 2.

———. 1978c. "Civilian crime watch saluted by police." August 28, sec. 4, p. 1.

Clark, John P. 1965. "Isolation of the police: a comparison of the British and American situations." *Journal of Criminal Law, Criminology, and Police Science* 56 (September 1965): 307–319.

Clifford, William. 1976. *Crime Control in Japan.* Lexington, Mass.: Lexington.

Cohen, Lawrence E., and Marcus Felson. 1978. "Social change and crime rate trends: a routine activity approach." Paper presented at Academy of Criminal Justice Sciences Meeting, New Orleans (March 9).

Criminal Justice Newsletter. 1978a. "LEAA to get $646.5 million in FY 1979." September 25, p. 2.

———. 1978b. "LEAA grants." October 9, p. 7.

Durkheim, Emile (John A. Spaulding and George Simpson, trans.). 1951. *Suicide.* New York: Free Press.

Farber, Bernard. 1973. *Family and Kinship in Modern Society.* Glenview, Ill.: Scott, Foresman.

Federal Bureau of Investigation. Annual. *Crime in the United States:*

Uniform Crime Reports. Washington, D.C.: United States Government Printing Office.

Friday, Paul C., and Jerald Haye. 1976. "Youth crime in postindustrial societies: an integrated perspective." *Criminology* 14 (November): 347–368.

Gluckman, Max. 1959. *Custom and Conflict in Africa.* Glencoe, Ill.: Free Press of Glencoe.

Glueck, Sheldon, and Eleanor T. Glueck. 1950. *Unraveling juvenile delinquency.* Cambridge, Mass.: Harvard University Press.

Greiner, John M. 1974. *Tying City Pay to Performance: Early Reports on Orange, California, and Flint, Michigan.* Washington, D.C.: Labor Management Relations Service of the National League of Cities, National Association of Counties, United States Conference of Mayors.

Hay, Douglas, Peter Linebaugh, John G. Rule, E. P. Thompson, and Cal Winslow. 1975. *Albion's Fatal Tree: Crime and Society in Eighteenth-Century England.* New York: Pantheon.

Hindelang, Michael J., Michael R. Gottfredson, Christopher S. Dunn, and Nicolette Parisi. 1977. *Sourcebook of Criminal Justice Statistics—1976.* Washington, D.C.: United States Government Printing Office.

Jacobs, Jane. 1961. *The Death and Life of Great American Cities.* New York: Random House.

Jeffery, Clarence Ray. 1971. *Crime Prevention Through Environmental Design.* Beverly Hills, Calif.: Sage.

Kelling, George L., Tony Pate, Duane Dieckman, and Charles E. Brown. 1974. *The Kansas City Preventive Patrol Experiment.* Washington, D.C.: Police Foundation.

LaFave, Wayne R. 1962. "The police and non-enforcement of the law." *Wisconsin Law Review* 5 (no. 1): 104–137.

Law Enforcement Assistance Administration. 1977. "New Haven patrols sniff out criminals." *LEAA Newsletter* 6 (August): 6.

——— and Bureau of the Census. 1977. *Trends in Expenditure and Employment Data for the Criminal Justice System: 1971–1975.* Washington, D.C.: United States Government Printing Office.

Lunden, Walter A. 1976. "Violent crimes in Japan in War and Peace, 1933–1974." *International Journal of Criminology and Penology* 4 (November): 349–363.

McKenzie, R. D. 1921. "The neighborhood: a study of local life in Columbus, Ohio." *American Journal of Sociology* 27 (September): 145–168.

Massey, R. G. 1975. *The Police Patrol Car: State of the Art.* Washington, D.C.: United States Government Printing Office.

Murphy, Robert F. 1957. "Intergroup hostility and social cohesion." *American Anthropologist* 59 (December): 1018–1035.

National Advisory Commission on Criminal Justice Standards and Goals. 1973. *Police.* Washington, D.C.: United States Government Printing Office.

National Commission on the Causes and Prevention of Violence. 1969. *To Establish Justice, To Insure Domestic Tranquility*. Washington, D.C.: United States Government Printing Office.

National Institute of Law Enforcement and Criminal Justice. 1975a. *Active Night Vision Devices*. Washington, D.C.: United States Government Printing Office.

————. 1975b. *Citizen Dispute Settlement Program* ("Night Prosecutor"), Columbus, Ohio: *An Exemplary Project*. Washington, D.C.: United States Government Printing Office.

Newman, Donald J. 1966. *Conviction: The Determination of Guilt or Innocence Without Trial*. Boston: Little, Brown.

Newman, Oscar. 1972. *Defensible Space: Crime Prevention Through Environmental Design*. New York: Macmillan.

New York Times. 1978a. "Decline in crime rate is reported; may aid renewal of central cities." June 25, pp. 1, 36.

————. 1978b. "Murder increasing." June 25, p. 36.

————. 1978c. "Serious crime rate down in first quarter of '78." July 2, sec. 1, p. 13.

Parnell, Phil, and Pepinsky, Harold E. 1978. "A case for treating aggression and violence socially rather than biologically." Paper presented at American Society of Criminology Meeting, Dallas (November 11).

Parsons, Talcott. 1951. *The Social System*. New York: Free Press.

Pepinsky, Harold E. 1975a. "Police decision-making." Pp. 21–52, in Don M. Gottfredson (ed.), *Decision-Making in the Criminal Justice System: Reviews and Essays*. Washington, D.C.: United States Government Printing Office.

————. 1975b. "Reliance on formal written law and freedom and social control, in the United States and the People's Republic of China." *British Journal of Sociology* 26 (September): 330–342.

————. 1976a. *Crime and Conflict: A Study of Law and Society*. New York: Academic.

————. 1976b. "Goal definition for police patrolmen." Pp. 33–47, in Robert Cohen, Robert P. Sprafkin, Sidney Oglesby and William L. Claiborn (eds.), *Working With Police Agencies*. New York: Human Sciences.

————. 1976c. "Police offense-reporting behavior." *Journal of Research in Crime and Delinquency* 13 (January): 33–47.

————. 1977a. "Despotism in the quest for valid U.S. crime statistics: historical and comparative perspectives." Pp. 68–82, in Robert F. Meier (ed.), *Theory in Criminology: Contemporary Views*. Beverly Hills, Calif.: Sage.

————. 1977b. "Stereotyping as a force for increasing crime rates." *Law and Human Behavior* 1 (September): 290–308.

————. 1978. "Communist anarchism as an alternative to the rule of criminal law." *Contemporary Crises* 2 (July): 315–327.

President's Commission on Law Enforcement and Administration of Justice. 1967a. *The Challenge of Crime in a Free Society*. Washington, D.C.: United States Government Printing Office.

————. 1967b. *Task Force Report: Crime and Its Impact—An Assessment*. Washington, D.C.: United States Government Printing Office.

Reiss, Albert J. Jr. 1951. "The accuracy, efficiency, and validity of a prediction instrument." *American Journal of Sociology* 56 (May): 552–561.

————. 1971. *The Police and Their Many Publics*. New Haven, Conn.: Yale University.

Rule, James B. 1974. *Private Lives and Public Surveillance: Social Control in the Computer Age*. New York: Schocken.

Samaha, Joel. 1974. *Law and Order in Historical Perspective: The case of Elizabethan England*. New York: Academic.

Schumacher, E. F. 1975. *Small Is Beautiful: Economics As If People Mattered*. New York: Harper & Row.

Skolnick, Jerome H. 1966. *Justice Without Trial: Law Enforcement in a Democratic Society*. New York: Wiley.

Sullenger, T. Earl. 1950. "The social significance of mobility: an Omaha study." *American Journal of Sociology* 55 (May): 559–564.

Tocqueville, Alexis de (Richard D. Heffner, ed.). 1945. *Democracy in America*. New York: New American Library.

Van Velzen, H. U. E. T., and W. Van Wetering. 1960. "Residence, power groups, and intra-societal aggression: an enquiry into the conditions leading to peacefulness within non-stratified societies." *International Archives of Ethnography* 49: 169–200.

Wilson, James Q. 1977. *Thinking About Crime*. New York: Vintage Books.

FOOD FOR THOUGHT

1. Would you be more inclined to give your police department money to hire more personnel if (a) the offense rate fell while the clearance rate by arrest rose, or (b) the clearance rate by arrest fell while the offense rate rose? Why?

2. Large U.S. cities have more than 3.5 police personnel per 1,000 inhabitants, while smaller towns have fewer than 2. What, if anything, do you imagine a higher concentration of police indicates about the quality of life for the inhabitants?

3. You are hired by the police department of a U.S. city with several hundred thousand inhabitants. In general, "offenses

known" and arrest rates are rising, and clearance rates by arrest are slightly declining. You are asked to draft grant proposals for obtaining federal funding. The chief asks you to outline some ideas on ways to spend federal crime control money. What ideas do you suggest?

4. If current U.S. police practices were to remain unchanged until the year 2000, what would the lack of change imply about the quality of life?

5. Should police officers be encouraged or discouraged from fraternizing with people in the communities they patrol?

6. Would Americans be better off letting "offenses known" rates continue to rise?

CHAPTER SIX

Should Victimization Rates Be Controlled?

MEASURING VICTIMIZATION RATE NUMERATORS

In two of the three earliest victim surveys (Biderman et al., 1967; Ennis, 1967b; Reiss, 1967), there was much ambiguity in what the figures meant. Ennis (1967b: 87–93) had four "experts" review respondents' descriptions of alleged offenses. The experts could agree only 65 percent of the time on whether the respondents had actually described crimes according to law. Reiss (1967: 150) surveyed a sample of people whom he knew had reported offenses to the police in the preceding *month*. He found that 20 percent of the alleged offenses were not reported to his interviewers.

Unknown factors may affect victimization rate numerators in many ways. Victim survey respondents are typically asked to recall all occasions when they themselves—and sometimes other members of their household or business—have been victimized during the preceding six or twelve months. They are asked to give this information to an uninvited interviewer for free. The interviewer is apt to be low paid and scarcely trained in criminal investigation, with little incentive for carefully eliciting and recording information. Instead of trickling in for evaluation and transcription, the interviews from a survey come in in large batches. This increases the chance that errors will go undetected and uncorrected. Responses are usually obtained from random samples rather than from all inhabitants. Thus, the difference between rates for all inhabitants and those for respondents might be greater at any one point in time than the changes from one time to the next. Victim reports never carry a case further into the legal process to be tested against evidentiary standards, in order to decide what action should be taken.

If Reiss shows that 20 percent of offenses reported to police can be forgotten or otherwise not mentioned within a month, imagine how much the percentage might increase six months or a year later—especially when respondents are reporting on behalf of others as well as themselves. (Household members do this in current victim surveys for burglary, theft, and motor vehicle theft, and business representatives did so for their companies.) And what goes one way could go the other. If offenses can be forgotten or ignored, they can also be imagined or fabricated. Levine (1976), backed up by a wealth of literature on problems of interviewing, has discussed the many possibilities that victim survey figures are inflated indicators of crime. Let us review some of these possibilities.

It is not hard to make up a plausible description of an offense and embellish upon it as the interviewer probes further. One might simply report having come home to find the stereo missing (maybe in fact it had been repossessed), or a broken window pane in the door (maybe one of the children had broken it accidentally), or Johnny's jacket taken from his high school locker. The interviewer cannot be expected to separate fact from fiction, since (a) the interviewer has only the word of respondents to go on, (b) respondents may be quite unaware that they are embellishing on their memories, and (c) if the interviewer were too skeptical and reported a suspicion that many data were inaccurate, he or she would be liable to dismissal as being ineffective ("How come you're having so much trouble when all our other interviewers report getting mostly accurate responses?"). The ability to detect fabrication is even more remote in the (roughly) 25 percent of current national victimization interviews conducted by telephone.

Interviewers are not closely supervised in large studies like the national victim surveys. Some of them are tempted to fabricate data themselves, especially in the direction of exaggerating the numbers, since their employers are looking for evidence of underreporting in police figures (Levine, 1976: 321–324). It is, after all, much quicker and easier to fill out forms without relying exclusively on interviews. (During the 1970 census, an experienced interviewer regaled me with accounts of how easy it was to fabricate data with minimal risk of getting caught. Since he had a set quota of interviews to complete each day, this gave him a lot of paid time off.) There are ways to detect this kind of cheating. The Bureau of the Census, under the auspices of the National Criminal Justice Information and Statistics Service (the N.C.J.I.S.S., 1977: 43) has had supervisors and senior interviewers reinterview 4 or 5 percent of respondents, reconciling differences in discussions with the original interviewers. These reinterviewers, more experienced than the average initial interviewer, told respondents that they were checking on whether initial interviews were correct. Thus, respondents were forewarned to remain as consistent as possible. Not surprisingly, then, discrepancies between the initial and repeat interviews occurred for only 1 or 2 percent of the items checked (Hindelang et al., 1978: 231–233).

Leslie T. Wilkins, a statistician currently on the faculty of the State University of New York at Albany, describes one simple, almost foolproof technique for detecting cheating that was used in research he directed for the British Home Office. One begins by looking at the data from all interviewers to discover variables that are closely related. For instance, one might find a strong relationship between the age of female victims and the chances of their having their purses snatched. The strength of this relationship can be expressed statistically as a measure of *correlation*. Here, no relationship is expressed as .00, a perfect positive relationship (for every increase in the value of one variable there is a corresponding increase in the value of the other) is expressed as 1.00, and a perfect negative relationship (one value decreases as the other increases) is expressed as −1.00.

It is almost impossible to fabricate data to yield a correlation of a particular value. It is also extremely improbable in random samples that correlations among several unrelated pairs of variables in one interviewer's data will all deviate far from high correlations for the same pairs in the data from other interviewers, as a matter of chance alone. Under the assumption that most interviewers are honest, the comparison of correlations will uncover serious cheaters. Victim surveyors have not followed such a procedure.

Honest sloppiness would be much harder to detect, let alone correct, except sporadically.

Victim surveyors are usually thorough in collecting data. Data collection is expensive, and to justify the expense, a mound of data is gathered at each interview. For instance, the N.C.J.I.S.S. (e.g., 1976c: 139–162) reports using an interview form that is eighteen pages long with about twenty items per page, *plus* an extra six pages for recording a description of each incident the respondent reports. When so many data come in from a large number of interviews to be reviewed for errors, it is safe to guess that a lot of detail will be overlooked. Furthermore, the data have to be transcribed, ultimately to computer tapes, for analysis. The sheer mass of the data may make it impossible to verify that the data have been transcribed accurately.

(If you think the problems of accuracy in victim surveys are imposing, consider the potential problems in an enormous survey like the U.S. decennial census. The problems posed here are not unique to victim surveys.)

Although the random samples recently drawn for the N.C.J.I.S.S. (e.g., 1976a, 1976b, 1976c, 1977) are substantial, carefully designed, and probably more precise in estimating population figures than most survey samples, they are not precise enough to detect shifts in victimization rate trends for populations reliably. For instance, sample N.C.J.I.S.S. (1976c: 168) figures indicate that the rate of aggravated assault in St. Louis was 15 percent higher in 1974–1975 than in 1971–1972. Allowing for random error alone, if the population rate had not changed for this period, chances would be better than even that the sample rate would still go up or down by 3.5 percent. This is a substantial figure if one is looking for changes in trends. If the aggravated assault rate had risen 18 percent in the three-year period up to 1971–1972, and fallen only 3 percent in the next three years because of a crime prevention measure, the trend would have been reduced a sixth of the way to the point of no growth in the rate—a lot of progress overlooked because of sampling error.

Victimization reports cannot be tested legally. By contrast, the prospect of legal test may lead citizens to exercise caution in reporting crime officially. The Bureau of the Census (N.C.J.I.S.S., 1977: 37–51) has tried partial corroboration of victimization reports, but acknowledges that systematic biases in their data may have gone undeterred and undetected.

Respondents remain largely free to make reporting errors without fear of detection and without prospect of correction.

Even if victimization is reported just as it occurred, the N.C.J.I.S.S. (1977: 39–41) has discovered a phenomenon it calls "telescoping": a tendency for respondents to report incidents as having occurred more recently than they did. To correct for this, respondents in recent nationwide surveys have been reinterviewed once every six months for three years. The first interview establishes which incidents have already occurred. Then, if the same incident is described in subsequent interviews, it can be deleted from the later data.

The N.C.J.I.S.S. (1977: 41) has distinguished "incidents" from "victimizations." More than one person may be victimized— that is, more than one victimization—per incident. Rates in these data for households and for businesses contain incidents in the numerator, while rates for persons or individuals contain victimizations. This inflates victimization rates in comparison to "offenses known" rates. For instance, if an incident appearing in both police and victim survey rates had two victims (e.g., a couple allegedly robbed on the street), it would count as one additional offense known to police per 100,000 inhabitants but as two additional victimizations per 1,000 persons.

For all the problems and vagaries of victim reporting, much effort and expense have gone into refining the technique since its first use more than a decade ago. The care that goes into some victim surveys, particularly one that concentrates on one locale—like the survey in Pueblo, Colorado, reported by Inciardi (1976: 186– 188)—is impressive. If I dwell on problems in measuring victimization rate numerators, it is to compensate for the unguarded enthusiasm of some of today's crime measurement specialists, who see the victim survey as the tool which, more than any other measure, tells us how much crime there *really* is. To know which of two measures of crime is closer to reality, you have to know whether one is more overreported or underreported than the other. Thus far, no absolute criterion—as opposed to a political or an ethical one—is available. U.S. crime measurement specialists historically have assumed that each successive measure underreports more than it overreports (Pepinsky, 1976b). To illustrate, the most comprehensive methodological study of the U.S. national victim surveys to date—sponsored by the National Academy of Sciences (Penick and Owens, 1976)—exhaustively reviews the potential for underreporting in victim surveys and makes repeated recommendations for attacking this problem; however, it does not mention the possibility of overreporting. By contrast, there has been no government investigation like Levine's (1976) of the possibly substantial overreporting in the most inclusive crime measures. Can Levine be so wrong? Regardless of politics or ethics, are victimization figures closer than any others to defining *the* reality of the American crime problem?

In criminology, such a dramatic breakthrough is bound to be too good to be true.

MEASURING VICTIMIZATION RATE DENOMINATORS

One issue of measuring victimization rate denominators is the same as for police-produced rates: that of selecting the population at risk (see Chapter 5). Again, if the rate is to measure the risk of victimization, only possible victims should be included in the denominator. For instance, by legal definition, men cannot be raped; thus, they might well be excluded from rape denominators (although this is not the current practice).

The victimization rates calculated for the N.C.J.I.S.S. (1976a, 1976b, 1976c, 1977) have limited denominators to populations at risk. The numerators for commercial robberies and burglaries have been divided by thousands of businesses. For victimizations of private persons, they are divided either by thousands of persons or thousands of households (as when tabulating rates of victimization by income of heads of households).

The new problem introduced by victimization rate measurement is that of comparing denominators with those for police-produced rates. The N.C.J.I.S.S.'s rates for commercial robberies and burglaries have been separately computed, using different denominators, from those for personal robberies and burglaries. In contrast, the F.B.I.'s (annual) national "offenses known" and arrest figures indicate only combined burglary and robbery rates per inhabitants. To make the N.C.J.I.S.S. rates comparable to F.B.I. rates, commercial and personal victimization numerators for each offense could be added together, using hundreds of thousands of inhabitants in the denominator.

CURRENT TRENDS

A few sets of victimization trend data have appeared. The N.C.J.I.S.S. has published a comparison of 1972 and 1974 findings of victim surveys in Chicago, Detroit, Los Angeles, New York, and Philadelphia (1976b), a comparison of 1971–1972 and 1974–1975 findings in Atlanta, Baltimore, Cleveland, Dallas, Denver, Newark, Portland, and St. Louis (1976c), and a national survey with figures published for three consecutive years, 1973–1975 (1976a, 1977).

   Trends in these data are as yet unclear. For one thing, sampling error is thought to be large enough for the surveyors to conclude that many of the changes are too small to be statistically significant. That is, there is a good chance that changes as large as those found in the samples would occur even if the rates in the larger populations had not changed. For instance, the surveyors (1977: 9) conclude that the following changes, from 1974 to 1975, in U.S. victimization rates per 1,000 persons age twelve and over, are too small to generalize to the total U.S. population: −7.1 percent for rape, −5.6 percent for robbery and attempted robbery, −9.0 percent for robbery and attempted robbery with injury, −5.3 percent for robbery and attempted robbery with injury from a serious assualt, −13.7 percent from robbery and attempted robbery with injury from minor assault, −4.0 percent for robbery and attempted robbery without injury, +1.5 percent for assault, −1.8 percent for aggravated assault with injury, +5.0 percent for attempted assault without a weapon, +1.0 percent for crimes of theft, −1.0 percent for personal larceny with contact, +16.1 percent for purse snatching, −8.3 percent for pocket picking, and +1.0 percent for personal larceny (theft) without contact.

   Statistical significance is a combination of the size of the percentage change and the number of reported offenses. For personal crimes in the national survey, 1974–1975, only these offenses had a combination of enough reports and high enough percentage changes to be considered significant: −7.4 percent for aggravated assault (with a 90 percent chance that a change this great would not have occurred unless the overall U.S. population rate had in fact changed), −10.0 percent change for assault with a deadly weapon, +7.8 percent change for simple assault, and +16.4 percent for simple assault (with a 95 percent chance that changes this great would not have occurred unless the population rates had changed). That is, for the 1974–1975 national comparisons of victimization rates for personal crimes, most of the changes were not considered statistically significant.

Let us cite two examples. According to the surveyors' criteria for minimal significance. In order to conclude confidently that the population rape rate had changed even slightly, the sample rate would have had to change 21.3 percent from one period to the next. Also, to conclude confidently that the population purse-snatching rate had even slightly changed, the sample rate would have had to change at least 25.9 percent. Meanwhile, by comparison, the U.S. police "offenses known" rate for rape, which has increased dramatically and steadily in recent years—174 percent from 1960 to 1975—continued the increase in 1974–1975. It climbed all of 0.4 percent (F.B.I., 1976: 49).

Meanwhile, too, in the N.C.J.I.S.S. (1976b, 1976c), studies of cities at two different times, rates have been found to go up, down, and remain stable in a pattern too complex to unravel.

Given the imprecision of the victimization trend data, interpretable patterns of trends must take many years to emerge. Even if increases or decreases from one time to another are too small to be considered statistically significant, if they continue for a prolonged period they become significant. For instance, a 3 percent increase in robbery victimization rates from survey samples might not mean much if it occurred between 1973 and 1974 but if such small increases continued steadily until 1983, (a) the pattern would be so stable as practically to rule out chance in samples and (b) in a ten-year period of 3 percent increases each year, the total increase would be close to 40 percent, which is quite significant.

The prospects for such long-term figures are problematic. The N.C.J.I.S.S. surveys were temporarily suspended in 1977 (Ostrow, 1977), and the commercial surveys have not been resumed. The main obstacle to continuing the surveys for a long period is expense. The N.C.J.I.S.S. has already encountered problems justifying the $5.6 million it had spent annually on surveys to 1977, or the total $53 million that collecting and analyzing the data had cost over five years.

Despite the imprecision of the N.C.J.I.S.S. figures, some remarkable patterns in the trend data have already emerged. These patterns suggest that the way interviewers and respondents interact may affect the data. One pattern, in the N.C.J.I.S.S. (1977: 2) national sample, is that the rates generally increased from 1973 to 1974, and barely changed or decreased from 1974 to 1975. Since the same respondents were interviewed repeatedly over the period, the figures suggest that respondents might have gotten tired of answering questions (six extra pages per incident reported) and, in cases which they might earlier have reported, kept silent instead. The other pattern, in the same data, is that young men reported fewer incidents as time went by, while young women reported more incidents (N.C.J.I.S.S., 1977: 3–4). Could it be that young women had more time on their hands, and hence thought more about upcoming interviews and reported incidents more fully? Victimization data are a product of the interaction between interviewers and respondents. This interaction may take place in many "legitimate" ways. Some early patterns in the data may reveal features of this interaction. Respondent-interviewer interaction takes place much closer to the survey report than to an alleged incident. Thus, the interaction has the more direct influence over the survey data.

EVALUATING CHANCES OF CONTROLLING VICTIMIZATION RATES

If changes in allocation of police personnel or technology show no sign of changing police-produced crime rates permanently (Chapter 5), there is no reason to believe that these changes would control victimization rates either. As suggested elsewhere (Pepinsky, 1977b), once victimization rates have been measured long enough to reveal trends, these rates may change as police offenses known rates change. One indication of the likely parallel is this: Just as police-produced rates may increase as people become strangers to one another, so Hindelang et al. (1978: 260–262) find that the risk of victimization increases with the amount of time spent with nonfamily members. In addition, if police maintain the growth of "offenses known" rates, they will have to convince the public that their problems are increasing, since the police have difficulty finding offenses by themselves and depend heavily on citizen complaints. Conversely, as indicated by the University of Dayton survey revealing reduced fear of crime with declining police offense rates (*New York Times*, 1978: 36; see Chapter 5), citizens who are aware that police figures are declining will be less likely to perceive themselves as victims. Thus, changes in police-produced rates can be expected to imply changes in victimization rates. Conversely, if victimization rates continue to rise, police may be under more pressure to report more offenses. Police are already being criticized for reporting only a fraction of what is reported in victim surveys (e.g., *Chicago Tribune*, 1978). Thus, although adequate data are still needed, changes in victimization rates should imply changes in police-produced rates. This close relationship between police-produced and victimization rates is explored at length in Chapter 7. For now, note that strategies found ineffective for changing police-produced rates (Chapter 5) stand little chance of affecting victimization rates either.

Can people be deterred by the threat of penal sanctions? It has recently become popular among Americans to recall the virtues of deterrence theory (see, e.g., Van den Haag, 1975; Wilson, 1977). The theory, articulated more than two centuries ago by Beccaria (1968), stated that if penal sanctions are imposed swiftly, surely, and severely enough, people will no longer commit crimes. It is a matter of controlling recidivism (to be considered in Chapter 10) to deter those who have already committed crimes from doing so again. Here, however, we are considering general rather than specific deterrence—whether the prospect of penal sanctions can be made swift, sure, and severe enough to keep people from committing their first crime. If this can be arranged, then victim survey respondents will have less occasion to report incidents and victimization rates should decline.

Is the theory of deterrence valid? (For a review of literature on the subject, see Palmer, 1977.) That issue need not be resolved in order to evaluate deterrence as a strategy of crime control. According to the theory, conditions must be such that deterrence is practically unnecessary. If crime is prevalent, penal sanctions that are swift, and severe cannot be simultaneously imposed.

1. As discussed in Chapter 4, criminal justice officials who are called on to invoke a *more severe* punishment for a common crime will do so *less surely*.
2. As sanctions become more severe, criminal justice proceedings become more elaborate and time consuming. Consider the difference between the week or so it may take to settle an alleged parking violation versus the months or years it may take for the trial, appeals, and final judgment in a capital case (one in which the defendant may be executed). The *more severe* the prospective punishment, especially for a common crime, the less swiftly it is imposed.
3. Speed implies error. The *swifter* the punishment, the *less sure* the relationship between conduct and punishment.

Hence, the three elements of deterrence are like the south poles of three magnets (see Pepinsky, 1978, for a more detailed development of this analogy). Increase the force of the field of the south pole of any one magnet and it will push the south poles of the other magnets farther away. The only way to keep the south poles of the three magnets together is to weaken the force of each field. Similarly, the only way to bring together swiftness, sureness, and severity of penal sanctions is to weaken the force with which the criminal justice system tries to accomplish any of these ends. The less criminal justice apparatus devoted to reacting against an offense, the better deterrence works. This, of course, implies—if punishment is to be sure—that the offense seldom occurs in the first place.

Just as the south poles of the strong magnets might temporarily be pushed together before one slips away, a "crackdown" may deter temporarily. Two examples are campaigns of traffic enforcement and the concentrated police foot patrols mentioned in Chapter 5. Otherwise, if an offense occurs so seldom that deterrence scarcely seems needed, then and only then will deterrence work well and lastingly. Even Wilson (1977: 186), the deterrence advocate, acknowledges "the grim irony" that as crime increases, the chances of punishment go down. If most people are behaving properly in the first place, a strategy of deterrence may keep them that way. For serious crimes that seldom occur, like multiple murders of strangers, swift, sure, severe sanctions can be expected. When a serious crime rarely occurs, public intolerance and special attention to the unique case unite to make punishment occur as a deterrence theorist would have it do. But if improper behavior is widespread, deterrence cannot even in theory be made to work.

The findings of deterrence researchers—that the probability of sanction, and sometimes the severity of sanctions, increase as crime rates go down—is consistent with the idea that deterrence works better in areas that need less crime control in the first place (Blumstein et al., 1978: 25–53).

It seems absurd to try to make deterrence work by increasing the rate or severity of punishment in any case, for in deterrence terms, the more deterrence is accomplished, the less occasion there is to punish. If more people have to be imprisoned for longer periods for the sake of deterrence, then deterrence is not working.

Hence, at the present time, it appears pointless to argue whether deterrence theory is valid. If it is valid, it cannot be used except as a temporary expedient or when it is not needed. If it is not valid, it could only appear to work when it is not needed. Either way, deterrence theory opens no avenue to controlling crime that is not well controlled in the first place.

If victimization rates cannot be controlled by a deterrence strategy, then perhaps they can still be controlled by imprisoning people to render them socially harmless. Wilson (1977: 225) argues that crime would decrease substantially if we put all those convicted of serious offenses in prison. Criminals would then be off the streets for the duration of their sentence, when otherwise they would be major contributors to crime. On its face, this strategy of *incapacitation* seems plausible. But think further. First, this strategy would require that criminal justice officials keep punishment sure while making it more severe—which no one yet knows how to accomplish. Second, even greater incapacitation could only temporarily lower crime rates. Were this strategy established, progress in crime control would cease. And at what cost? If Americans managed to make their criminal justice officials more punitive than before, so that they might keep punishing as often as before and more severely, it would probably require a greater atmosphere of fear and distrust than Americans have ever known. This would predispose people to rely more heavily on police and to prey more on one another (to hurt them first), which would probably help increase "offenses known" and victimization rates. Higher and higher proportions of the population would have to be incapacitated, or else the strategy of incapacitation would break down. In the short run, this strategy might lower both "offenses known" and victimization rates. In the long run, it is bound to be self-defeating. A criminogenic social order is like a patient whose cancer has metastasized: removing diseased parts cannot bring order and stability to the whole organism, and surgery may even make the patient sicker. At best, removing parts is a temporary expedient to prolong a failing life.

There is no agreement that incapacitation could even temporarily reduce crime rates much. Van Dine et al. (1977) estimate that serious violent offenses in Franklin County, Ohio, would have been reduced by only 4 percent had all those indicted for the offenses and convicted of any offense been sentenced to five years in prison.

Boland (1978), and Palmer and Salimbrene (1978), take issue with Van Dine et al.'s estimate. They argue that incapacitation would have reduced violence in Franklin County by as much as 18 percent. The debate is still on, but as Van Dine et al. (1978) point out in rebuttal, even if the 18 percent figure were correct, a substantial increase in incarceration of even first-time offenders would still leave more than 80 percent of future violence untouched. Acknowledging the limitations of simulation studies, Blumstein et al. (1978: 75) also conclude that "the percentage of crimes [that can be] averted through incapacitation is not very large in high-crime-rate jurisdictions." Incapacitation is further considered in Chapter 10.

Deterrence and incapacitation, then, illustrate the problem (see Chapter 1) of cures that would probably be worse than the disease. In part, this is because these cures are designed to stop bad behavior without encouraging other behavior in its place.

Suppose that, instead of looking to technology, deterrence, or incapacitation, we consider selection of victim surveyors as a means of controlling victimization rates. What might happen if the N.C.J.I.S.S. continue to dominate victim surveying in the

United States? To begin with, as indicated by the general rise in 1973–1974 and the drop in 1974–1975 national trend figures, we can anticipate an initial surge in victimization rates as interviewers and respondents are introduced to the survey, and then a fall as the survey loses its novelty. A 1924 experiment in a series (called the Hawthorne Studies) on worker productivity at the Western Electric Company showed how effective novelty can be in increasing worker productivity. Productivity increased, as expected, when artificial lighting was increased; However, it also increased for a control group with unchanged lighting conditions. Productivity again increased for both groups when natural lighting was blacked out. A third group was placed in a room with *decreased* lighting. Its productivity, too, increased (Roethlisberger and Dickson, 1964). You can probably recall from your own experience that when you are given a new or newly restructured task to perform, you begin working with a burst of enthusiasm. However, if you continue for long, you slack off as tedium sets in. Similarly, in victim surveys, one may expect the early enthusiasm of interviewers and respondents to be reflected in greater recall and more conscientious recording of incidents, until tedium sets in and the decline in reporting activity follows.

As the N.C.J.I.S.S. continues its victim surveys beyond the initial enthusiasm and tedium, it is likely to have the same stake in encouraging increased reporting rates as U.S. police departments have in reporting more offenses. As Levine (1976) suggests, this would be true of any organization whose survival largely depended on showing the importance of continuous victim surveys. It is harder to convince people that steady or declining victimization rates are important than if the figures increase. Indeed, the N.C.J.I.S.S. may have temporarily lost its survey mandate because its early figures failed to indicate an upturn in victimization rates. If one is interested in generating long-term *increases* in victimization rates, hiring a survey organization would be a good way to do it.

Better yet, the job of victim surveying might be given to the police. This is not such a strange idea. Twice yearly, Japanese patrol officers survey all the residences in Japan—inventorying property, obtaining demographic data, and generally inquiring about what is happening in the neighborhood (Bayley, 1976: 84). U.S.

patrol officers usually have plenty of free time (Pepinsky, 1975: 25), and could certainly use it to interview representatives even of *every* household and business in their patrol districts. Besides obtaining victimization data, the patrol officers could learn a lot more about their communities than they do from the suspects and complainants they are accustomed to meeting.

If U.S. police have generated steadily increasing "offenses known" rates in recent years, they could probably do the same with victimization rates. And these increases would further support the growth of police work.

Finally, high and growing victimization could be generated if the data were published by victim compensation agencies. Victim compensation programs have been instituted in various countries, such as Australia and New Zealand, and in some U.S. states, such as New York. These plans compensate for losses due to physical injuries caused by crimes, set ceilings on amounts available, and require that someone be convicted of the crime. The plans have been criticized for giving too little too grudgingly. No government plan provides compensation for property loss or damage; these matters are left to private insurance companies. (For a review of victim compensation programs, see Edelhertz and Geis, 1974.)

If the government were to insure the public against all substantial losses from crime, making it as easy as insurance companies often do to file and collect small claims, people would be encouraged to report crimes. Thus, data would be available which would probably push victimization rates to record heights. It has been proposed that insurance premium charges be used as a check on crime measures (Price, 1966). But why not go further to check on insurance claims records? Nationalizing insurance for all crimes would make people eligible to report incidents without first paying insurance premiums, and would logically extend the principle of protecting the victim. If one aim of controlling victimization rates is to get as much crime reported and socially visible as possible, making the victim surveyor the crime insurer would be a good method. It would give respondents strong incentive to report as many incidents as they could. This would be the ultimate control mechanism for making "hidden" crime visible.

Suppose, instead, that we wish to reduce victimization rates.

It then makes sense to turn over victim surveying to an agency whose interest lies in providing an alternative to persons treating one another as victims and criminals. The night prosecutor program (Law Enforcement Assistance Agency, 1975), described in Chapter 5, is a step in this direction. Going further, the state might provide mediation services offering extralegal assistance in resolving personal conflicts. Such services have been proposed and described elsewhere (Pepinsky, 1976a: 123–125). To encourage people to deal with one another directly, without the third-party intervention provided by the criminal justice system, mediation services would be prohibited from serving as parties to legal actions, from keeping client information files not already in the public domain, from structuring client contact, and even from taking any action on a client's behalf outside of the client's presence. The idea would be to support and encourage citizens to resolve their problems with others personally.

In teaching people to get along without the criminal justice system, this is one possible alternative. To control victimization rates, such a service would be asked to conduct victim surveys. The service's budget, perhaps even the salaries of employees, could be geared to the service's success in reducing crime in its community. Given this incentive, the service would be in a position to initiate a self-fulfilling prophecy: that victim surveys corroborate the service's success in helping community residents to protect themselves against victimization. As people were made to feel safer and stronger about protecting themselves from crime, they might well act stronger. Thus, reduced victimization rates might be more than mere statistical artifacts. If motivated police can paint a convincing picture of growing crime, then another agency should be able to succeed in decreasing victimization.

SIDE EFFECTS OF CONTROLLING VICTIMIZATION RATES

The side effects of controlling victimization rates are much like those of police "offenses known" rates. The higher the rates rose, the more citizens would depend on police to manage their problems with one another. Social mobility would be encouraged, and distinctions between strangers and intimates would blur further.

The lower the rates, the greater the level of community intolerance toward outsiders would be. Violence, both in and out of the criminal justice system, would become less common, but less restrained once it did break out (Pepinsky, 1977a). This could be neutralized (as outlined in Chapter 5) by sufficient diversity of cross-cutting and yet close-knit ties established within a community (Parnell and Pepinsky, 1978: 21–30).

The unique side effect in controlling U.S. victimization rates—unless police were given the job of victim surveying—would be that a major source of police power would be neutralized. For the last half century, American police have enjoyed a virtual monopoly in describing the size of the crime problem. Take this monopoly away from the police, and they lose a major instrument for persuading the public to support them. U.S. police would be particularly hard pressed to justify requests for increased support if victimization rates were steadily declining, which brings us to consider . . .

POLITICAL CONSIDERATIONS

U.S. police would have few complaints about victimization data as long as rates climbed. If the rates declined, the police would need the measures to protect their job security described in Chapter 5 just as badly as if "offenses known" rates were going down. Worse yet, if victimization rates declined and victim surveys were done by outsiders, the police would also feel the impotence of players sitting on the sideline. They would probably criticize victim surveys strongly. Their objections to the surveys, and indeed, such political objections from any source, would probably be: (a) the cost of the surveys and (b) the invalid nature of victimization figures.

As the experience of the N.C.J.I.S.S. shows, victim surveys are costly. Gathering data from people who take no initiative in coming to you is the most expensive procedure of all. That cost distinguishes victimization data from police-produced and conviction data. The costs are even greater in periodic rather than regular surveys. Periodic surveys mean repeated reorganization and other inefficiencies of small-scale enterprise, such as the added cost of employing and training temporary workers rather than career employees. It is plausible for political opponents of victimization rates and their control to conclude that proponents must show that the extraordinary cost of this crime measurement technique is justified.

The original justification of victim surveys was the promise that these data would—as never before—show the true shape, size, and direction of U.S. crime. If we show that we can change victimization rates at will, the sacred victim surveys will lose importance. Measures which people can manipulate to suit their social purposes will likely not be seen as true measures of crime, for they gauge more than the behavior of criminals. Any crime measure that is manipulated for a special purpose is liable to be presumed invalid. The justification of the expense of victim surveys will be refuted, and it becomes much easier to show why they should be dropped.

One response to this line of reasoning is that victim surveys depend not on measurement validity but on the principle of democratizing and diversifying official crime control services. To the classic liberal democrat (in American parlance, the conservative), government expense is justified only if it creates diversity of view and experience. Thus, government spending to collect and disseminate information is justified because the money is spent to diversify sources of information.

Even though classical liberal democracy is part of the American tradition (Lippman, 1965), the current view is the opposite: We are justified in collecting and disseminating information about crime if we deliver the truth. Americans will not control victimization rates unless or until this current view gives way to its liberal predecessor.

ETHICAL ISSUES

The chance to contribute to a victim survey is seductive, and yet it carries a price. It offers the hope of having public policy shaped to fit one's own problems. It is like the questionnaires I used to receive from a legislator who belonged to a committee reviewing proposed appropriations for military funding. There would be a question like: "Do you support continued funding for development of the B-X bomber?" One could check the answer corresponding to one's preference: "_____Yes, I support funding for the B-X bomber." "_____No, I don't think deterring a foreign threat is worth the expense." If you accepted the legislator's offers to consider your views in making policy, and if you are limited to answering questions of his choice, then you risked the possibility that the information would be used against your wishes.

Suppose you have a problem with a neighbor's children who dig up your flower garden, and you welcome the opportunity for help—official help, if that is all that is offered—in deciding how to respond. If, then, you report the incident to a victim survey interviewer, the higher crime rate you helped report provides the rationale for employing extra police labor to cover the time needed to send patrol officers to your home to offer to arrest any vandals. The only problem is that the patrol officers go first to your neighbor, who has you arrested before you can be interviewed. The situation might be a bit whimsical, but it does show the problem involved in having the government take care of your problems for you. Ironically, making government decisions more democratic gives the government the authority to make people's decisions for them (Pepinsky, 1977a).

One possible resolution of this issue is to hold that crime control policy should rest only on the problems of those who report crime to the police or the courts. Regarding problems that are not reported, people should be left officially alone. Critics of this position argue that people may be too weak, too intimidated, or too poorly served to ask officials for help (the critics' position being that of the classic conservative—the American liberal democrat). Hence, they say, we need to "reach out to" (or more recently, to "have outreach to") the victims of our social order to let us help them. This message is implicit in the way Ennis (1967a) categorized his respondents' reasons for not reporting offenses to police.

Another kind of ethical issue is posed by rejecting deterrence and incapacitation strategies. If these are ruled out, the use of punishment in crime control can be justified on only two other grounds: rehabilitation or retribution. As we shall see in Chapters 8 through 11, rehabilitation of criminals is practically inconceivable even if desirable. Whether or not rehabilitation is a viable strategy for controlling criminality, one might advocate giving the victim the satisfaction of having the offender suffer. This is the basis of retribution: to satisfy our craving for vengeance by making those who have caused us to suffer share our burden. Newman (1978) argues that this is the only adequate moral justification for punishing others.

The legitimacy of retribution involves a further moral issue: Should injured parties be allowed to exert retribution? Or should they be restrained by having relatively disinterested officials punish for them without anger, under the law? Those left to act out their own retribution will be more restrained than officials by bonds of affection and interdependence. However, they have no duty to be restrained about hurting strangers—enemies—who hurt them. If victimization rates rise, retribution can be expected to become more prevalent as it is placed in the hands of officials. If victimization rates decline, retribution can be expected to become more violent as it becomes restricted to clear-cut enemies. To favor retribution is still to be left to choose whether it is morally preferable to raise or lower victimization rates.

CONCLUSION

The control of victimization rates raises the most fundamental, profound political and moral issues about which kind of order and conflict is preferable to those not treated as criminals in the social system. Chapter 7 explores the extent to which other crime rates—those of conviction and those produced by police—can be controlled while avoiding such serious issues. Going a step further, the possibilities of radical social change, which would be needed to control the various rates of crime simultaneously, will be considered. In particular, we will consider whether Americans can afford higher crime rates.

REFERENCES

Bayley, David H. 1976. *Forces of Order: Police Behavior in Japan and the United States*. Berkeley, Calif.: University of California Press.

Beccaria, Cesare (Henry Paolucci, trans.). 1968. *On Crimes and Punishments.* Indianapolis: Bobbs-Merrill.

Biderman, Albert D., Louise A. Johnson, Jennie McIntyre, and Adrienne W. Weir. 1967. "Incidence of crime victimization." Chap. 2, pp. 26–118, in President's Commission on Law Enforcement and Administration of Justice, *Field Surveys I: Report on a Pilot Study in the District of Columbia on Victimazation and Attitudes Toward Law Enforcement.* Washington, D.C.: United States Government Printing Office.

Blumstein, Alfred, Jacqueline Cohen, and Daniel Nagin (eds.). 1978. *Deterrence and Incapacitation: Estimating the Effects of Criminal Sanctions on Crime Rates.* Washington, D.C.: National Academy of Sciences.

Boland, Barbara. 1978. "Incapacitation of the dangerous offender: the arithmetic is not so simple." *Journal of Research in Crime and Delinquency* 15 (January): 126–129.

Chicago Tribune. 1978. "Good news about local crime." July 27, sec. 3, p. 2.

Edelhertz, Herbert, and Gilbert Geis. 1974. *Public Compensation to Victims of Crime.* New York: Praeger.

Ennis, Philip H. 1967a. "Crime, victims and the police." *Trans-action* (June): 36–44.

——. 1967b. "Crime victimization in the United States: report on a national survey." In President's Commission on Law Enforcement and Administration of Justice, *Field Surveys II.* Washington, D.C.: United States Government Printing Office.

Federal Bureau of Investigation (F.B.I.). Annual. *Crime in the United States: Uniform Crime Reports.* Washington, D.C.: United States Government Printing Office.

Hindelang, Michael J., Michael R. Gottfredson, and James Garofalo. 1978. *Victims of Personal Crime: An Empirical Foundation for a Theory of Personal Victimization.* Cambridge, Mass.: Ballinger.

Inciardi, James A. 1976. "Criminal statistics and victim survey research for effective law enforcement planning." Pp. 177–189, in Emilio C. Viano (ed.), *Victims and Society.* Washington, D.C.: Visage Press.

Law Enforcement Assistance Administration (National Institute of Law Enforcement and Criminal Justice). 1975. *Citizen Dispute Settlement Program ("Night Prosecutor"), Columbus, Ohio: An Exemplary Project.* Washington, D.C.: National Criminal Justice Reference Service.

Levine, David P. 1976. "The potential for overreporting in criminal victimization surveys." *Criminology* 14 (November): 307–330.

Lippman, Walter. 1965. *Public Opinion.* New York: Free Press.

National Criminal Justice Information and Statistics Service (N.C.J.-I.S.S.). 1976a. *Criminal Victimization in the United States: A Comparison of 1973 and 1974 Findings.* Washington, D.C.: United States Government Printing Office.

———. 1976b. *Criminal Victimization Surveys in Chicago, Detroit, Los Angeles, New York and Philadelphia: A Comparison of 1972 and 1974 Findings*. Washington, D.C.: United States Government Printing Office.

———. 1976c. *Criminal Victimization Surveys in Eight American Cities—National Crime Surveys in Atlanta, Baltimore, Cleveland, Dallas, Denver, Newark, Portland and St. Louis: A Comparison of 1971/72 and 1974/75 Findings*. Washington, D.C.: United States Government Printing Office.

———. 1977. *Criminal Victimization in the United States: A Comparison of 1974 and 1975 Findings*. Washington, D.C.: United States Government Printing Office.

New York Times. 1978. "Decline in crime rate is reported; may aid renewal of central cities." June 25, pp. 1, 36.

Newman, Graeme R. 1978. *The Punishment Response*. Philadelphia: Lippincott.

Ostrow, Ronald P. 1977. "Survey gauging impact of crime is suspended." Louisville Courier-Journal (September 23): A16.

Palmer, Jan. 1977. "Economic analyses of the deterrent effect of punishment: a review." *Journal of Research in Crime and Delinquency* 14 (January): 4–21.

———, and John Salimbrene. 1978. "The incapacitation of the dangerous offender: a second look." *Journal of Research in Crime and Delinquency* 15 (January): 130–134.

Parnell, Phil, and Harold E. Pepinsky. 1978. "A case for treating violence and aggression socially rather than biologically." Paper presented at American Society of Criminology Meeting, Dallas (November 11).

Penick, Bettye, K. Eidson, and Maurice B. Owens III. 1976. *Surveying Crime*. Washington, D.C.: National Academy of Sciences.

Pepinsky, Harold E. 1975. "Police decision-making." Pp. 21–52, in Don M. Gottfredson (ed.), *Decision-Making in the Criminal Justice System: Reviews and Essays*. Washington, D.C.: United States Government Printing Office.

———. 1976a. *Crime and Conflict: A Study of Law and Society*. New York: Academic.

———. 1976b. "The growth of crime in the United States." *Annals of the American Academy of Political and Social Science* 423 (January): 23–30.

———. 1977a. "Despotism in the quest for valid U.S. crime statistics: historical and comparative perspectives." Pp. 69–82, in Robert F. Meier (ed.), *Theories in Criminology: Contemporary Views*. Beverly Hills, Calif.: Sage.

———. 1977b. "Stereotyping as a force for increasing crime rates." *Law and Human Behavior* 1 (September): 299–308.

———. 1978. "Communist anarchism as an alternative to the rule of criminal law." *Contemporary Crises* 2 (July): 315–327.

Price, James E. 1966. "A test of the accuracy of crime statistics." *Social Problems* 14 (Fall): 214–221.

Reiss, Albert J. Jr. 1967. "Measurement of the nature and amount of crime." Vol. 1, pp. 1–183, in President's Commission on Law Enforcement and Administration of Justice, *Field Surveys III: Studies in Crime and Law Enforcement in Major Metropolitan Areas*. Washington, D.C.: United States Government Printing Office.

Roethlisberger, Fritz Jules, and William J. Dickson. 1964. *Management and the Worker*. Cambridge, Mass.: Harvard University Press.

Van den Haag, Ernest. 1975. *Punishing Criminals: Concerning a Very Old and Painful Subject*. New York: Basic Books.

Van Dine, Stephan, Simon Dinitz and John Conrad. 1977. "The incapacitation of the dangerous offender: a statistical experiment." *Journal of Research in Crime and Delinquency* 14 (January): 22–34.

———. 1978. "Response to our critics." *Journal of Research in Crime and Delinquency* 15 (January): 135–139.

Wilson, James Q. 1977. *Thinking About Crime*. New York: Vintage Books.

FOOD FOR THOUGHT

1. In doing victim surveys, how would you rank police, survey agencies, victim compensation agencies, and mediation services as surveyors in order of desirability?

2. Why do you think deterrence and incapacitation theories are so popular even if they are so impractical?

3. If all measures of crime are so difficult to validate, what qualities make one measure better than another?

4. Should government officials keep crime victims from taking revenge? To what extent should government officials carry out retribution on their behalf?

5. Is it reasonable to belive that victimization rates could or should be controlled in the United States?

6. On balance, is it better to assume that current American victim survey figures overstate or understate the size of the American crime problem? Why do you think so?

CHAPTER SEVEN

Controlling Crime Rates: A Review

CONVENTIONALLY DESIRED CHANGES

There are basically two kinds of denominators for crime rates: measures of population and measures of official action. With a measure of population, political convention prefers that the rate be reduced. With official action, political convention prefers that the rate be raised.

With crime rates by population, the problems of controlling convictions were examined in Chapter 4. Usually, we want these rates to decrease. A high conviction rate is a poor reflection on the society. Confidence that conviction rates are true, real, or valid measures of crime is not vital to the belief that rising conviction rates are bad. It is bad enough that society must increase its conviction rate, regardless of the justification. If conviction rates are rising because people are more inclined to hurt one another by committing crimes, then the situation calls for remedy. If conviction rates are rising faster than the actual increase in crime, then it is because people are growing more punitive toward one another without greater cause. That situation, too, calls for remedy.

On the other hand, conviction itself is supposed to be a remedy for crime. The use of the law to punish criminals is a form of homeopathic medicine; we use an agent of sickness as a cure for the disease. When, therefore, we homeopaths use reports of incidents—representations of sickness or disease—as denominators in our conviction rates, we want the disease—convictions—to grow in greater proportion in the numerator. When convictions rise in proportion to prosecutions, arrests, offenses known, or victimizations, we typically conclude that society is being helped. These increases supposedly indicate that the criminal justice system is reacting as it should to a higher proportion of crimes committed. This is taken to mean that the system is more effective as a deterrent or agent of retribution.

Apparently, criminal justice officials should try to get more convictions over time. But suppose prosecutors and police discover that the courts are more disposed to convict than before. This tells them that there is more reason than before to bring cases to trial. If courts convict a larger percentage of those arrested and prosecuted, then police will probably be more willing to arrest (and to file offense reports) and prosecutors more willing to charge. If the percentage of offense reports, arrests, and prosecutions resulting in conviction remains the same—let alone climbing further—then conviction rates per inhabitants are bound to climb, too. Make the conviction remedy more available, and the disease of crime will appear to grow.

You can see how contradictory demands are placed on the criminal justice system. The more officials convict those arrested and prosecuted, the higher the conviction rate by population. And the higher this rate, the more difficult it will be to maintain conviction rates by reports of incidents. As we saw in Chapter 4, the U.S. ratio of convictions to other official reports of incidents— through offenses known to the police—has remained relatively stable in recent years, but this stability cannot be expected to endure. Consider the extremes. In a society in which crime is rarely reported, when people do call on officials, the event reported as a crime will probably be unusual and especially outrageous. There should be strong community support for apprehending and punishing the criminal. Officials, undistracted by high crime caseloads, can do a thorough, rapid job of bringing the criminal to justice.

At the other extreme, where reports of crime are commonplace, victims and their neighbors and friends will be blasé about pursuing the case through court. Where reporting crime is commonplace, reports are likely to seem trivial. As in the United States, when reporting is routine, most of the reports concern property offenses. For instance, among the F.B.I.'s (1975: 55) index offenses, property offenses in recent years have been about ten times as great as offenses against the person. If property offenses are so commonplace, community ties must be loose enough for thieves to be able to transport and sell stolen property in relative obscurity. It is hard for many victims and other community members to help officials bring criminals to justice, even if they are so inclined. Meanwhile, officials have so many cases that most of them can receive only perfunctory attention. It is hard to find suspects. Once found, for trivial matters, for cases in which evidence is minimal and where action, for busy officials, seems more trouble than it is worth, arrests, prosecutions, and convictions are not obtained. It is something of a miracle that U.S. conviction rates per prosecutions, arrests, and offenses known have remained stable for the past decade. It is too much to expect these rates to increase as convictions per inhabitants increase, and even the stability of the rates probably cannot last much longer.

It is bad enough that we ask officials to perform well in contradictory ways. In addition, the worse officials appear to be doing, the better they are paid and supported. A society that is losing the game of crime control is like a gambler using a losing system. The greater the loss, the more desperate the gambler is to invest more money in hopes of breaking even. Think of yourself as a court administrator trying to convince a legislator that you need more courts, more judges and other court personnel, and higher pay and logistic support. Do you tell the legislator that the courts are doing well? You had better not. Your strongest argument is that the courts are failing to carry the increased load being placed on them. Ideally, your data will show that conviction rates by inhabitants are increasing (indicating that court personnel are working harder than ever), while conviction rates by prosecutions, arrests, and offenses known are dropping (indicating that the personnel are falling behind in their struggle to fight crime). Officials are rewarded for failing to control crime, and if instead they succeed too well, they risk jeopardizing their jobs. This problem is particularly acute in the United States, where responsibility for crime control falls more on officials than on private citizens. As we saw in Chapter 5, in Japan crime control is more successful where support for officials is generally taken for granted, and where responsibility for crime control falls more on families, neighbors, and co-workers.

In sum, when we tell criminal justice officials that we are

looking at their crime rate data to evaluate how well they are doing, we tell them:

1. Prevent crime by,
2. enforcing the law more vigorously,
3. which will show that there is more crime to control,
4. which will show that you are too burdened with cases to enforce the law in each case vigorously,
5. which will show that you need more support.

These contradictory demands apply not only to conviction rates but to police-produced crime rates as well. If arrest rates per inhabitants rise, the crime problem is worsening. Nonetheless, police are supposed to increase their clearance rates of offenses known. Police were the first U.S. officials to learn to show that they needed more money because their workload of arrests was increasing. This occurred in the mid-nineteenth century in New York City (Costello, 1885, as found in Inciardi, 1976: 179–180).

As citizens refer more problems than the police can handle, the more offense reports the police file, the worse the prognosis for arrest. But if police show that they are arresting suspects for a larger proportion of complaints, citizens are encouraged to report still more offenses. U.S. police arrest rates now indicate that:

1. Crime threatens to get worse.
2. Police are hard put just to keep arrests in proportion to crime.
3. Therefore, police need more support.

Thus, increased support for officials feeds the cycle. More support carries the expectation of more arrests, which creates room for more offense reporting. This makes it harder to maintain clearance rates by arrest, which implies a greater need to support police and other criminal justice officials.

Now that victim surveys have begun to reveal discrepancies between victimization and offenses known to police, officials have further problems. Police, it is believed, should reduce this discrepancy by encouraging citizens to report offenses more readily than ever. These additional reports are likely to be more trivial, more confused, and harder to follow up, increasing the problems of arrest, prosecution, and conviction. "Offenses known" rates rise indicating that the crime problem is worsening. And citizens, encouraged that police are more willing than ever to respond to their injuries, may be more eager than ever to regard incidents as crimes instead of cases of unpleasantness or inconvenience. Although it is too early to know how much more citizens will complain to victim survey interviewers, those who are encouraged to report crimes should be able to dream up incidents for interviewers faster than police can gather the information for their "offenses known" figures. Offenses known per victimizations would probably decrease as police labored to make these rates rise, while rises in offenses known to police per 100,000 population would indicate that the crime problem was getting worse.

Were police and victim surveyors independently to report crime for a long time, each would probably become more successful in gathering complaints that had not been reported to the other. Thus, both rates of offenses known per victimizations and rates of victimizations per offenses known would decrease. Just as Reiss (1967: 150, replicated by National Institute of Law Enforcement and Criminal Justice, 1972) found that 20 percent of those who had reported incidents to police failed to report them to his interviewers, victim surveyors would probably find a substantial, growing percentage complaints that were not mentioned in victim surveys. Pressure on citizens to report more crime is apt to make discrepancies between police and victim survey figures grow rather than diminish.

To sum up: Those who produce numerators of crime are asked: (a) to increase the numerators (in proportion to preceding numerators) to indicate that they are responsive to crime, (b) to decrease the numerators (in proportion to population) to indicate that their response is controlling crime, and (c) to increase the numerators (in proportion to population) to indicate that the public needs them more than ever, which (d) decreases the numerators in proportion to preceding official crime control action.

The ultimate issue of controlling crime rates is how and whether all of these changes can be arranged simultaneously. Let us leave aside issues of job security for the time being. Let us assume that officials would relinquish their jobs if their services were no longer needed. In this situation, how could rate figures be made to show that officials are more responsible for crime *and* that crime is being contained? Once this is determined, we can try to figure out how crime control might be made palatable to officials who would have less of a problem to which to be paid and empowered to respond.

RESPONSIVENESS TO CRIME AND CONTAINMENT OF CRIME

Failure of crime control leads people to overlook a simple truth: the less official means of crime control are used, the better they work. As we have just seen, if officials beginning at the court level try to *pull* more convictions or arrests into their caseloads, enough new cases will probably keep conviction and arrest rates from rising. The gap between offenses known to the police and victimizations will probably widen, too.

On the other hand, as we saw in Chapters 5 and 6, it is self-defeating for officials to try to *push* more cases into the criminal justice system. The more the police succeed in getting crimes reported to them, the greater their problem in maintaining their clearance rate by arrest, and the harder it will be to obtain convictions. And again, as the police stir public fear and imagination by more offense reporting, victimization rates will grow faster than "offenses known" rates (assuming that the police are not conducting the victim surveys themselves).

Legislatures cannot make officials enforce the law both more often and more severely. As we saw in Chapter 4, the more severely officials are told to enforce the law, the less surely they will do so. The criminal justice process is not as mechanical as Beccaria (1968) and other utilitarians believed. Between the formula for enforcing the law and its implementation are human beings (officials) who have to decide what value to place on other human beings (suspects and defendants). It would be one thing for a legislature to enact an *ex post facto* ("after the fact") law or bill of attainder (a law making people liable to punishment for who they are rather than what they do), making all those who have ever been convicted (or, as in Nazi Germany, all Jews) subject to extermination (though *ex post facto* laws and bills of attainder are commonly forbidden today, as in the U.S. Constitution, art. 1, sec. 9, para. 3). Under these circumstances, the law would order officials to punish or kill those identified as enemies without determining whether the treatment was deserved.

Instead, the criminal law requires officials to weigh the evidence about a person's conduct before deciding about arrest, prosecution, or conviction. Conscience is crucial, and no way has been found to remove it. There is evidence that many officials are prone to soothe their conscience by acting as though they are simply following orders (Pepinsky, 1977). For instance, a prosecutor and defense attorney who are plea bargaining may agree that a certain bargain is practically dictated by information in police arrest reports and the defendant's prior record (Sudnow, 1965). Court officials can easily tell themselves that they are just doing what the police indicate. To a lesser extent, the police can say that their decisions to report offenses and make arrests are dictated by the implicit instructions of complainants, radio dispatchers, and other police officers (Pepinsky, 1975: 33–34, 39–43). These rationalizations are vital to officials, who otherwise would find it hard to live with themselves for confining and otherwise punishing suspects and defendants day after day. Perhaps we should take comfort from the fact that few criminal justice officials are out-and-out sadists.

Rationalizations about "following orders" can enable officials to maintain decision-making routines—including those that draw more and more cases into the criminal justice system (Pepinsky, 1977)—but when the routines suddenly change, the rationalizations are no longer tenable. If, for instance, the legislature radically changes the penalties for crimes (and probably redefines many crimes, as in Indiana, 1977), police have no guidelines for deciding whether and for what to arrest; prosecutors for deciding what to charge and whether to pursue conviction; and judges for deciding how to treat cases at trial. If officials aim to keep on following implicit orders from others, they are bound to assume that these others have not suddenly changed their desire for punishment. In addition, officials give implicit orders to other officials about future cases. Thus, they are likely to try to adapt legal language to indicate the seriousness of current cases compared to past cases. Thus, when the New York state legislature suddenly made the sale of narcotics a crime serious enough to merit life imprisonment, police began charging pushers (sellers) they would formerly have arrested for sale with possession. Prosecutors proved unwilling to indict as many drug pushers for sale, and judges and juries proved unwilling to return as many convictions. Officials generally were reluctant to apply the more punitive new law to suspects and defendants. By changing penalty schedules, legislatures may move officials to change the provisions of the law they apply to cases, but they cannot make officials more or less punitive or sadistic. Not, at least, without identifying particular individuals who are to be punished without regard to official assessments of their acts.

Criminal justice officials have not yet succeeded in raising these probabilities: (a) that what victims report to victim surveyors will be reported to and by police; (b) that what is reported as offenses known to the police will be followed by arrest; or (c) that arrest will be followed by conviction, by pushing or pulling more cases into the criminal justice system, with or without legislative orders. The more active officials become in reporting offenses, arresting or convicting, the less surely they will do so.

If more official activity produces undesirable changes in response rates to crime, should officials do less? Should prosecutors and other court officials obtain fewer convictions? Initially, the probability of convictions following arrest and offense reporting would decline. Let us assume that decisions to prosecute continued to be based largely on how persuasive the evidence was. Then, if police stopped making arrests or reporting offenses for the kinds of cases no longer being prosecuted, prosecutors would probably obtain conviction following offense reporting and arrest. At the same time, rates of conviction, arrest, and offense reporting per inhabitants would decline. To this extent, rate figures would indicate progress in both containment and official responsiveness to crime.

However, the disparity between offenses known to the police and victimization rates would probably grow. Even if citizens learned to manage their affairs with less official intervention or protection, and reported fewer incidents to victim surveyors, these changes would probably lag behind official changes. Based on victimization rates, official responsiveness to crime would be decreasing. The only conceivable way to overcome this problem is to put crime control in the hands of citizens rather than criminal justice officials.

Another problem is this: For complete success in crime control, the recent tendency of crime rate measures to vary in the same way must be changed. One measure of official action can rise in proportion to a preceding crime measure, while both measures decline in proportion to population, in only one way: the larger, preceding crime measure must decrease by a larger percentage than its successor. To illustrate, suppose that over a period of time the conviction rate for burglary declines in a particular jurisdiction from 10 per 100,000 population per year to 8, a decrease of 20 percent. Suppose further that the earlier victimization rate for burglary in the jurisdiction is 100 per 100,000 population, making the initial rate of convictions to victimizations 1 : 10. For the later rate of convictions to victimizations to be greater than 1 : 10, burglary victimization per 100,000 population must drop below 80— that is, more than 20 percent. (Since the population denominators are the same for convictions and victimizations at each point in time, this means that burglary victimizations must decline by a greater percentage than burglary convictions.)

Thus, if all indices of the crime problem are simultaneously to change in a desirable direction, reductions in probabilities of victimization have to lead reductions in police "offenses known." These reductions, in turn, must lead those of arrests, which would mean fewer convictions. This, too, makes it inconceivable that the impetus for crime control can come from officials. Instead, it must come from citizens who are becoming socially reorganized, at least in part, on their own.

As we saw in considering current police "offenses known" trends (Chapter 5), it is possible, if improbable, that law enforcement can lead to a sustained drop in crime rates by population alone. If drops in "offenses known" rates lead citizens to fear their neighbors less, neighborhood ties could be strengthened, and citizens could in turn take the lead in crime control. Thus, the self-fulfilling prophecy that citizens can control crime would occur. I believe that U.S. police will be motivated to generate new fear of rising crime rates before this process occurs. As noted in Chapter 5, the proposition that the police can only temporarily reduce crime rates by population remains to be tested.

Suppose citizens do initiate the change for criminal justice officials, rather than the reverse. For now, let us leave aside the question of how citizens might change their own perceptions of the crime problem. If they did so, what would happen? First, they would be less likely to report incidents to victim surveyors, and victimization rates would drop. Fewer offenses would be reported to police, and "offenses known" rates would drop. Let us assume that the incidents no longer reported to victim surveyors or police are only borderline crimes. In other words, if citizen reporting decreased, the incidents involved would be those *least likely* to be reported *both* to the police and to victim surveyors. Accordingly, the disparity between victimization rates and "offenses known" rates would decrease. Incidents still reported to police would be more likely to result in arrest, prosecution, and conviction. By keeping cases out of the criminal justice system, citizens would succeed in bringing down rates of arrest and conviction per inhabitants.

Thus, for the greatest containment and responsiveness to crime, criminal justice officials may have to wait for citizens to take the lead. Also, officials who follow that lead will do less—*not* more. To repeat: the less official crime control measures are used, the better they work.

If citizens become more reluctant to treat incidents as crime, and if the rates of crime and of response to crime change as expected, then according to our criteria, deterrence is working. The probability of sanctions (rates of response) will increase, while rates of crime decrease. Most of the cases remaining in the criminal justice system should be more serious than those no longer treated as crimes, and those convicted of crimes should be treated as more unusual and culpable than before. Hence, more severe sanctions can be expected. A criminal justice system with fewer cases can devote more attention to each. Hence, conviction and punishment should be swifter than before. Swifter, severer, surer imposition of sanctions, along with lower crime rates, is exactly what deterrence theory predicts. The irony is that citizens have to learn to do without criminal justice protection and intervention before apparent progress toward deterrence can be achieved. Regarding deterrence theory, too: the less official crime control measures are used, the better they work.

This is not as strange as it may seem. According to deterrence theory, if the criminal justice system imposes sanctions swiftly, surely, and severely enough, people will commit almost no crimes and punishment will almost never be imposed. Furthermore, it is consistent with deterrence theory to argue that officials could receive community support and encouragement to punish criminals swiftly, surely, and severely only if crime were practically unthinkable and thus considered intolerable and unforgivable. Although, as argued in Chapter 6, deterrence theory may not be a viable means of crime control, it may accurately predict how the criminal justice system would operate if crime control had already been achieved. Changes in crime rates and response to crime are desirable from the point of view of deterrence, among others.

Even if social ties within communities became strengthened, crime rates might change in undesirable ways. One group might charge members of another group with offenses—a kind of intergroup warfare—so that victimization rates and police "offenses known" rates would continue to rise. Officials who felt their jobs or status threatened by increased public self-sufficiency might increase their proactive law enforcement in retaliation—as today, in areas like prostitution, drugs, gambling, and organized crime. Thus, "offenses known," arrest, and conviction rates by population would increase. Officials who had fewer cases referred to them might become lackadaisical; thus, the probability of arrests or convictions would fall. Although, in theory, the strengthening of communities is *necessary* for simultaneous success in controlling the various crime rates, it could prove to be *insufficient* in many ways. In this reason, the crime control analyst should carefully monitor trends in each of the rates to see just how crime control fails as a particular strategy is implemented.

WHAT DOES A MEASURE OF CRIME MEASURE? A REASSESSMENT

Let us suppose that our wildest dreams are realized. We manage sustained reductions in victimization, offenses known, arrests, and convictions by population, and sustained increases in arrests by offenses known and convictions by arrests—all at once. What would we have accomplished?

As explained in Chapter 5, progress in crime control would imply that people were becoming kinder to their own kind and stranger to strangers. Progress in crime control implies that people who regularly live and work together wrong one another less and help and support one another more. It implies that family, neighbors, and co-workers are more successful in preventing and defending against attack and predation by outsiders. It implies greater bigotry toward outsiders. It implies that physical violence among the population—including official punishment—is rarer but generally more severe when it does occur. It implies that people move around less, knowing fewer people but more intimate with those they do know. It implies little privacy among intimates but greater anonymity among strangers.

Does success in crime control imply a better life? Does it imply that people are, on the whole, hurt less? Not necessarily. A Chinese person once vividly recounted childhood memories of the relationship between her mother and her paternal grandmother to me. In the traditional Chinese family, the family of the eldest son remains with his parents. When the son's father dies, the son becomes head of the family. But in the day-to-day affairs of running the household, his mother rules his wife (Levy, 1963). As my friend described her childhood at home, her mother was miserable at the hands of a despotic grandmother. The mother could hardly wait for the grandmother to die. However, mother and grandmother fulfilled their respective roles of helping maintain the family with no thought of alternatives, without physically assaulting one another and without stealing or vandalizing one another's possessions. Had either been threatened by a stranger, by illness, or by other privation, the other would have rallied to her support and defense without hesitation.

Who can say whether, in the final analysis, the strains of intimacy are more or less painful than the strains of isolation?

The more we discover about measuring how much people are hurting one another, the more elusive such a measure becomes. We can determine whether the average life expectancy of a society is increasing, but whether people are to be blamed for one another's death is a highly ambiguous issue. Suppose, for instance, that the death rate from gunshot wounds drops as the death rate by cirrhosis of the liver increases. We could decide that people were killing each other more by repressing their physical violence toward one another. We know that everyone is certain to die of something, and that under other social conditions, each death could conceivably be prevented (only to have the person die of something else). Short, then, of deciding that the level of physical violence declines as average life expectancy increases, how can the total level of violence in a society meaningfully be assessed? Even if we focus on homicide, people commonly concede that many homicides are justifiable, even excusable—from acts of war to accidents. The state may even commit homicide, as in war, capital punishment, or shooting a fleeing felon, and some homicides may be defined as acts of mercy. Without human discretion, wrongful homicides cannot be determined.

The problems of assessing absolute levels of property offenses are knottier still. If it is decided that bicycles belong to individuals, and the wrong individual takes a bicycle home, we may call the act a theft. But if all the bicycles in a town are considered community property, there is no way that riding a bicycle can be considered theft. Under some circumstances, we may decide that changing the form of property entails damage, under other circumstances, not. If a group of citizens decide that a building should be torn down, parts taken away to be used again, and the site turned into a park, we may conclude (a) that destruction—a crime—has taken place if some people blow up the vacant structure or (b) that among those responsible are city council members, whose participation makes the explosion an act of construction. Apart from cultural values, which can change from place to place and from time to time, there is no absolute difference between right and wrong in the form and location of property. It therefore becomes nonsense to decide whether the level of property crime has changed when people alter their values and ways of life sufficiently to cause major changes in *measures* of crime.

Of course changes in perceptions of crime are unlikely to be sudden and dramatic. As U.S. crime rates increase, any changes in perceptions are probably subtle. These changes should be most visible in terms of reporting. Is a garbage can missing? Once considered a prank, today it might be reported as a theft. Did the bully wrestle Johnny to the ground during school recess? Where once it was considered that Johnny had to learn how to stand up for himself, today it might become a problem of juvenile delinquency. Did a neighbor's child throw a rock through the window? Last year, you went to his parents, but today you call the police and report vandalism. Are you splitting up with a girlfriend or boyfriend who takes your favorite vase from the apartment? Yesterday it might have been just more evidence that the split was justified, but today it becomes a theft report. Do you come home and find the side door ajar, but nothing missing? Once you might have wondered whether you yourself had left the door open, or whether someone had come in and been scared off. You might have joked about the incident with friends. Today you report a burglary. Does someone get angry with you at work and shout, "You'll be sorry!" Yesterday, you might have shrugged it off, but today you report a threat. Does a teenager accost you on the street and demand money? Once you might have told the person to get lost and perhaps reported an incident of disorderly conduct. Today, you give the teenager money and report a robbery.

Historians of crime measurement have not attempted the painstaking work that would be necessary to uncover such subtle changes. For myself, when I started riding with patrol officers, I was struck by the contrast between how neighborhood problems had been handled privately as I grew up and the trivial matters reported to the police today. Many people reported their neighbors for such things as playing stereos too loudly, damaging plants in the garden, or parking more than seventy-two hours in front of their homes (in violation of a city ordinance)—knowing quite well who the neighbors were—without having approached them first.

Whether or not any of these changes has actually occurred, the point is this: Crime rates can rise and fall because of such small shifts in perception. That is, what was once no offense can be considered a minor offense, and a minor offense can become a serious offense. It is these small changes that are apt to underlie crime rates trends—the moving boundary between matters of private and public concern.

In the final analysis, whether we define an act as a crime is arbitrary. The decision has political significance, to be sure. To call something a crime implies that government officials should take into custody a person accused of offending another. The political implications of calling a matter a crime are further explored in Chapter 9. There, I argue that the poor in any social system are more likely than any other group to be considered criminals. Each of us must decide, personally, whether the conventional notion of progress toward crime control is good, but none of us can show that such progress is objectively right or wrong, real or unreal.

CRIME AND AFFLUENCE

How have Americans, on the average, managed to become so prosperous? This topic in itself could fill a library. But some conditions underlying the growth in American prosperity are fairly obvious. We have advanced far beyond the time when the Englishman Adam Smith (1937: 4–11, originally published in 1776) described how three people working together could produce far more needles than each could by working alone. Machines turn out goods and services at incredible rates with little human intervention. Transport technology permits the rapid shipment of goods and services, too, so that residents of New York can buy California tomatoes cheaply, and in a few hours, a line of credit can be opened for a merchant halfway around the world.

It follows that in order to compete, producers of goods and services must increase the scale of their production. The larger the scale, the better the producer can afford machines and the more it can control and organize production from raw materials to distribution of the finished product. The more production is consolidated, the more small producers get squeezed out of the market. The larger the scale of production and the more technology used, the less human labor is needed. Although advertisers continually try to persuade Americans that they need more goods and services than ever before, the need for human labor still lags behind the increasing size of the available work force. It was once thought that the leisure accompanying growing prosperity would be an unmixed blessing. Now, Americans are learning that a lot of leisure can be a burden, and are more inclined to talk of the problems of unemployment than the joys of leisure. As affluent Americans on the average absorb goods and services far beyond the subsistence level that economists like Smith (1937, as originally published in 1776) saw people trying to overcome, their capacity to produce has outstripped their ability to employ their work force. The overall American unemployment rate is half again as high as those of England, France, and the Federal Republic of Germany, and four times that of Japan, even though unemployment in those countries has reached unprecedented heights in recent years (Ruby, 1977: 89). The level of unemployment among American teenagers is foreboding: it is approaching 20 percent for all teenagers and has reached 40 percent for black teenagers (Nicholson, 1977: 88). Americans are at the frontier of a new economy, in which everyone on the average is becoming richer and more than ever is being produced and bought, but where everyone contributes less to production. Human labor is becoming superfluous to production in the American economy.

Durkheim (1951: 241–276) stated in 1897 that prosperity got people into trouble. Of particular interest to him was that suicide rates increased along with the overall wealth in societies. He attributed the additional suicide to what he called "anomie," which in its Greek origin means "unregulated." To Durkheim, anomie was the hopelessness that people suffered when they had no sense of achieving worthwhile goals in life. Anomie arose in times of prosperity because people achieved the economic goals they had set for themselves and could not figure out what else was worth working for. To this I would add that anomie comes of discovering that other people no longer need what one can produce by one's labor. This opens the door to despair that one has nothing worthwhile to do with one's life—that one's life is purposeless and that life itself has no value. Not only is the value of one's own life degraded, as reflected in increased suicide rates, but the same is true of others. They, too, cease to offer goods and services, or to feeling and display gratitude and need for one's actions. Why, then, restrain one's frustration? Why not do violence to others? When labor is superfluous to existence, the value of life itself is degraded, and more common violence is apt to be reflected in crime rate figures.

Every middle-class American child for the last generation or so has heard of the dangers of becoming spoiled. If the child gets whatever he or she asks for, the child is said to become insatiable and to learn to expect something for nothing. Panhandling has become a way of life for middle-class American youths in many parts of the country in the last decade or so. Perhaps much of this panhandling is something of a declaration of outrage that so many adult Americans have superfluous cash. When well-nourished youths beg for money for no cause but themselves, and for no labor but the asking, here, too, is a sign of anomie. Why not get what you can take? What you get is not worth much in such an affluent society. If you happen to be among the American poor, the wealth you see around you must appear outrageously extravagant. The thought that others could scarcely be hurt by what little one takes is bound to grow. If restraints against predation are falling for this reason, and because Americans are becoming strangers to those closest to them, then increased reports of property offenses are also to be expected.

The desire of U.S. police to create a need for their services has already been described, especially in Chapter 5. This need can be seen as one aspect of the societal problem of anomie. With the growth of prosperity and the saturation of the market for goods, more jobs are created to provide services. The proportion of Americans employed in service occupations is growing (Aronowitz, 1973: 79–80, 291–322). Just as criminal justice bureaucracies are increasing and getting involved in more of people's affairs, other service bureaucracies are creating and expanding markets for other services, such as health care, child care, vocational and marriage counseling, and credit services. The list of services available to Americans seems almost unending and is getting longer. If Americans can be persuaded that they need "professional" help—that they now have more problems than ever before—the job market can be expanded.

Consider the way of life that is created by this proliferation of service jobs and the declining use for human labor in production. If this process were carried to its logical extreme, everyone would relate to others only as client or as professional. No one would have ongoing personal ties. Children would be cared for professionally from birth. After divorce rates had risen high enough, marriage itself would become a relic of the past as women and men met only for brief sexual liaisons and then parted. In fact, some women might specialize in professional childbearing as civil servants, while some men specialized as procreators. People would seldom sleep in the same place from one night to the next, and all their meals would be professionally prepared. The most successful in the rush for climbing career ladders would change jobs practically every day. As clients became dissatisfied with the quality of professional service, an elaborate hierarchy of professionals would be available to intervene on clients' behalf. Each person's social life each day would consist of alternating between seeing and working for clients, and seeing professionals. Since professionals would change jobs as frequently as possible, professional-client relations, too, would usually be brief and transitory. Anyone who got depressed or agitated could readily cure the symptoms with medication provided by professionals. Almost everyone would have a lengthy record of at least petty criminal offenses, but few would suffer more than brief periods of probation as criminal justice officials proved unwilling to punish so many people severely. Among the professional services available would be low cost insurance for practically every risk, and so people's attitudes about being victimized repeatedly would consist mainly of annoyance for having to bother with the paperwork of filing insurance claims. By and large, people could be pretty sure that all those with whom they would interact a month or so hence would be strangers today.

This would be the ultimate in limiting one's ties with others to expedience. It would be the ultimate in what Toennies (1957) called *Gesellschaft*—bonds among community members being based on contracts rather than on tradition and personal sentiment (*Gemeinschaft*). It would be the ultimate in what Durkheim (1947) called "organic," as opposed to "mechanical," solidarity of society (i.e., of ties based on contract rather than on normative consensus and tradition). It would be a step beyond the ideal type Farber (1973) describes of a society in which basic ties to family can readily be dissolved and reestablished as it suits the individual's convenience.

Chances are that the progress of American society will change directions many times rather than reach the extremes of mobility and expedience. But envisioning the possible end product of contemporary U.S. society provides a basis for weighing continued progress in one direction as against possible social changes. If this vision of America's future continues to be more attractive than various alternatives, then on balance Americans find that growing rates of crime, and declining rates of response to crime, are worth having.

What do Americans lose by having growing crime rates? Employment opportunities for criminal justice officials expand. In this regard, paying for criminal justice services is not just a cost but a benefit to growing numbers of citizens. On the average, Americans probably have more material wealth *after* property losses due to crime. As prosperity increases, Americans can afford to insure themselves against more risks, and to provide a living for more insurance company employees in the process. The life expectancy of Americans continues to increase, and so on balance the changes that include higher crime rates are better for people's physical well-being.

For all the alarm about crime in the United States, Americans in general have little chance of being seriously victimized. For instance, in a recent National Criminal Justice Information and Statistics Service (N.C.J.I.S.S.) survey (1977: 9), respondents reported robbery or attempted robbery at the rate of 6.7 per 1,000 persons aged twelve and over. At this rate, the average person aged twelve and over can be expected to be a victim of one of these offenses once every 150 years. Based on F.B.I. (1975: 55) figures, the average American can expect to be the victim of murder or nonnegligent manslaughter once every 1,000 years. Victim survey figures indicate that the average American household will have someone at least try to steal its car once every 50 years, and will suffer attempted housebreaking less than once each decade (N.C.J.I.S.S., 1977: 21). And according to N.C.J.I.S.S. (1977: 9) figures, the average American woman over the age of twelve can expect to suffer attempted rape about once every 500 years.

It is true that the risk of being victimized is unevenly distributed. The poor are the most likely to be victimized by street crime. On the other hand, the victimization rates suggest that most middle-class Americans are unlikely to give the poor enough political support so that effective crime control measures can be implemented. Although extreme poverty does exist in the United States, most of the population consists of a relatively affluent and secure middle class that is capable of resisting fundamental social change.

Perhaps even Americans, with their unusually high crime rates, can afford more crime. It is not so clear that they desire more effective crime control.

If crime rates are to be reduced for any length of time, unemployment must be reduced to a minimum, and people must be firmly tied to one another in ongoing interdependent relationships—in family, in neighborhood, and at work. What conditions are necessary to establish such ties? As we saw in Chapter 5, the relationships in Japan grow out of a longstanding tradition of rights and obligations inherent in family membership. Out of this, a model for stable employer-employee relations has grown. Strong, traditional personal ties are one solid foundation upon which crime control can be built.

At best, such traditions are scattered in the United States. If Americans were to strengthen their capacity to do without the criminal justice system, they would have to create binding ties on a basis other than tradition.

Americans *have* had some success in crime control in their own recent past. Police offense rates declined steadily from 1930 to about 1950 (President's Commission on Law Enforcement and Administration of Justice, 1967). The 1930s were dominated by the Great Depression and the 1940s by World War II. In the 1930s, when as much as 25 percent of Americans could not find jobs, destitution rather than prosperity was the national problem. A large part of the population struggled to get enough food and shelter for themselves and their families to survive. Poverty was a common condition—a common enemy. In the 1940s, the enemies were foreign. Young men went to fight. Others worked to provide logistical support for the military. Meat, metal, and gasoline were in short supply. There were chronic violations of wartime regulations (Clinard, 1952), but by and large, reported crime declined markedly.

Conflict theorists such as Coser (1956) assert that having a common enemy brings people together into harmonious, cooperative relations with one another. The idea makes sense. When an external threat makes it obvious to people that their very lives depend on cooperation and mutual support, they band together and take care of each other. Hence, official protection from one another tends to become superfluous. Crime control works better because it is needed less.

Would Americans need to go to war or become destitute in order to strengthen their capacity to control crime? Perhaps so. It is hard to imagine Americans strengthening their personal ties without first having been confronted with a common crisis. Before people can feel they need one another, they must have some valuable labor to perform for one another. And as we have seen, a problem faced by contemporary Americans is that they need each other less and less.

Schumacher (1975) formed an "intermediate technology group" to determine how to make production more labor intensive. He recognized the main problem: the value of what people can give each other has been displaced by machine production. Schumacher found that small groups of people can often produce better, cheaper products by doing by hand much of what is now done by machines. His group designed simple machines and organized production so that the skill and effort of each worker contributed heavily to the product. For instance, the group set up a brickworks in England, operated by three people, which produced bricks as cheaply as those that were imported from a big automated brickworks some distance away. As the title of Schumacher's book—*Small Is Beautiful*—suggests, he considered small-scale production to be a marvel in part because it is easier on our physical environment (e.g., workers' breathing creates less pollution than a smokestack). Also, small-scale production offers dignity and worth to the worker who performs a skilled craft rather than a simpleminded routine on an assembly line or in an office. If intermediate technology can displace large-scale automated production, personal ties of interdependence can be strengthened as persons come to be valued for their skills and as production becomes decentralized so that people work in small groups.

But Schumacher despaired of converting American cities to intermediate technology. Intermediate technology is especially suited to rural life, in which small groups can live and work together. Imagine trying to organize residents of each floor of a Manhattan apartment building to produce bricks or some other needed commodity! The problem of strengthening personal ties in large American cities staggers the imagination.

There are few ideas as to how American's personal ties might be strengthened. If this can be done without war, famine, or pestilence, the method has yet to be conceived. The obvious prerequisite for controlling crime rates is a crisis in which the immediate survival of many if not most Americans is at stake. Whether Americans can evolve subtler bases for interdependence and co-operation remains to be seen.

CONCLUSION

We have considered the potential for controlling crime rates mainly in terms of the contemporary United States. We have come to doubt the fruitfulness of pursuing limited, conventional strategies of crime control, such as giving officials new technology and more power, or trying to make criminal justice officials more active in deterring crime or in capacitating criminals. Indeed, there appears to be little that officials can do except to encourage citizens to fend for themselves. If there are to be consistent, enduring reductions in crime rates and increases in response rates to crime, citizens must organize themselves into stable, mutually supportive, and protective groups—as with families, neighbors, and co-workers. This entails loss of privacy and mobility, and increased bigotry toward outsiders. It may well preclude affluence as well.

Is it desirable to attempt to reduce crime rates in a society like ours? Perhaps Americans gain more wealth and health than they lose as they generate higher crime rates. Perhaps, to Americans, crime is an acceptable cost of doing business. Perhaps, though the possibility is seldom seriously considered, citizens may quite rationally decide that they want higher crime rates and lower rates of response to crime. You, the reader, are in as good a position as anyone to make this choice. On the choice, ultimately, rests the decision as to how to approach the control of crime.

We have yet to consider what might be done to reduce rates of criminality. Rather than determine how a society becomes more or less crime-ridden, much criminological theory tries to distinguish criminals from law-abiding citizens in any society. What makes some individuals more likely than others to commit crimes? What can be done to make the criminals more law abiding? This topic—the control of criminality—is the subject of the next four chapters.

REFERENCES

Aronowitz, Stanley. 1973. *False Promises: The Shaping of American Working Class Consciousness*. New York: McGraw-Hill Paperbacks.

Beccaria, Cesare (Henry Paolucci, trans.). 1968. *On Crimes and Punishments*. Indianapolis: Bobbs-Merrill.

Clinard, Marshall B. 1952. *The Black Market*. New York. Holt, Rinehart and Winston.

Coser, Lewis A. 1956. *The Functions of Social Conflict*. New York: Free Press.

Costello, A. E. 1885. *Our Police Protectors: History of the New York Police from the Earliest Period to the Present Time*. New York: Author's Edition.

Durkheim, Emile (George Simpson, trans.). 1947. *The Division of Labor in Society*. New York: Free Press.

———— (John A. Spaulding and George Simpson, trans., George Simpson, ed.). 1951. *Suicide: A Study in Sociology*. New York: Free Press.

Farber, Bernard. 1973. *Family and Kinship in Modern Society*. Glenview, Ill.: Scott, Foresman.

Federal Bureau of Investigation. 1975. *Crime in the United States— 1974: Uniform Crime Reports*. Washington, D.C.: United States Government Printing Office.

Inciardi, James A. 1976. "Criminal statistics and victim survey research for effective law enforcement planning." Pp. 177–189, in Emilio Viano (ed.), *Victims and Society*. Washington, D.C.: Visage Press.

Indiana, State of. 1977. *Criminal Code*. Title 4.

Levy, Marion. 1963. *The Family Revolution in Modern China*. New York: Octagon.

National Criminal Justice Information and Statistics Service (N.C.J.-I.S.S.). 1977. *Criminal Victimization in the United States: A Comparison of 1974 and 1975 Findings*. Washington, D.C.: United States Government Printing Office.

National Institute of Law Enforcement and Criminal Justice. 1972. *San Jose Methods Test of Known Victims*. Washington, D.C.: United States Government Printing Office.

Nicholson, Tom. 1977. "Labor: a new wage floor?" *Newsweek* (September 19): 88.

Pepinsky, Harold E. 1975. "Police decision-making." Pp. 21–52, in Don M. Gottfredson (ed.), *Decision-Making in the Criminal Justice System: Reviews and Essays*. Washington, D.C.: United States Government Printing Office.

————. 1977. "Stereotyping as a force for increasing crime rates." *Law and Human Behavior* 1 (September): 290–308.

President's Commission on Law Enforcement and Administration of Justice. 1967. *Task Force Report: Crime and Its Impact—An Assess-*

ment. Washington, D.C.: United States Government Printing Office.

Reiss, Albert J. Jr. 1967. "Measurement of the nature and amount of crime." Vol. 1, pp. 1–183, in President's Commission on Law Enforcement and Administration of Justice, *Field Surveys III: Studies in Crime and Law Enforcement in Major Metropolitan Areas*. Washington, D.C.: United States Government Printing Office.

Ruby, Michael. 1977. "Fighting a global lull." *Newsweek* (October 10): 89–90.

Schumacher, E. F. 1975. *Small Is Beautiful: Economics As If People Mattered*. New York: Harper & Row.

Smith, Adam. 1937. *Wealth of Nations*. London: J. M. Dent. (vol. 1 of 2).

Sudnow, David. 1965. "Normal crimes: sociological features of the penal code in a public defender's office." *Social Problems* 12 (Winter): 255–276.

Toennies, Ferdinand (Charles P. Loomis, trans.). 1957. *Community and Society*. East Lansing, Mich.: Michigan State University Press.

FOOD FOR THOUGHT

1. If you were planning crime control and could use only one measure of crime, which would you choose and why? Which two measures? Which three measures? (Be specific, telling which numerator and denominator—if any—you would select.)

2. Imagine yourself being interviewed by the chief of a large U.S. urban police department for a job as director of crime prevention research and planning. The chief asks you what priorities you would recommend for crime prevention experiments by the department. How would you reply?

3. Suppose you were the director of a state planning agency that was responsible for distributing federal crime control funds. What priorities would you set for crime control experiments?

4. How would you respond to the query: Were U.S. crime rates *really* going up in the 1960s, or were U.S. police misleading the public?

5. It has been said that the issue of longer prison terms for repeat offenders involves choosing whether to protect victims or offenders. What are the problems in posing the issue this way?

6. In your own view, is it desirable to reduce U.S. crime rates and to increase rates of response to crime?

7. Do you think you would be happier living in Japan than in the United States, assuming that you could be fully integrated into either culture?

8. Without sacrificing affluence, what new kinds of jobs and bases for strengthening personal ties could be created in the contemporary United States?

9. If you live in or come from another society, how would you compare its problems of crime control with those in Japan and the United States?

PART THREE

CONTROLLING
RATES OF CRIMINALITY

CHAPTER EIGHT

Should Incarceration Rates Be Controlled?

MEASURING INCARCERATION RATE NUMERATORS

The measurement of incarceration rate numerators involves four factors: who, what, where, and when.

Measures of criminality represent persons rather than acts. Ostensibly, criminality figures distinguish personal characteristics of criminals. Separate rate figures can be given for different kinds of people. These figures are used to try to explain what makes people more or less likely to become offenders. For instance, men are generally far more likely to become incarcerated than women. This may be interpreted to mean that sex helps to determine criminality or to indicate that women are more leniently treated than men. This particular controversy has been raging in American criminology since Pollak (1950) argued that sex differences were those of treatment rather than of wrongdoing.

Demographers study characteristics of groups of people. They have established a standard set of distinguishing characteristics. The most common of these demographic variables are sex, age, marital status, race or ethnic group, indicators of class and status such as income level and years of formal schooling, and religion. With the exception of religion, which may have been considered too politically loaded to use, these variables have been applied directly to the world of criminality measurement. To illustrate, the National Criminal Justice Information and Statistics Service (N.C.J.I.S.S., 1976b: 24–25) lists numbers and percentages of inmates sentenced to a maximum of more than a year in state correctional facilities by the categories of sex, race, age, educational level, employment status during most of the month prior to arrest, marital status, personal income for the year prior to arrest, length of time spent on the last job, and occupation during most of the month prior to arrest. Figures are also given for those who did and did not serve in the armed forces.

Whether one breaks down incarceration rate numerators in this manner is largely a matter of ideology. If one believes that criminality can best be controlled by giving individualized treatment to criminals or to those predisposed to crime, then one is interested in who the criminals are. Similarly, if one is searching for evidence of injustice in who is incarcerated, one also looks to categories of inmates for signs of discrimination. If, on the other hand, one is interested in isolating times and places at which people are more or less likely to be caged, the characteristics of inmates may be far less important than overall incarceration rates. For example, if one wonders why people are more likely to be incarcerated on any given day in the United States than in the Netherlands, it matters little whether Dutch inmates, on the average, have more education than American inmates.

Some of the measures of inmates characteristics may be quite unreliable. For one thing, those who have tried to collect data from correctional files commonly report (off the record) that the files are miserably kept. Many data are missing, and many of the rest seem to be so haphazardly recorded that they are scarcely trustworthy. For another thing, data like income level that come uncorroborated from inmates can be misleading. Is an inmate going to report $50,000 in income from burglaries for the prior year? Probably not. And especially for people who work at a variety of odd jobs, it is hard to keep a running total of income for the year. Apart from sex, reporting and recording standards vary greatly.

As with crime rates, the numerators of criminality rates can be divided into categories of offenses. The issues raised in Chapters 4, 5, and 6 need not be repeated. But there is a new problem of categorization that concerns incarceration measures. Inmates may be categorized by the kind of sentence they receive. The differences in categorization can be significant. One change in categorization of U.S. figures has led the N.C.J.I.S.S. (1976b: iii–iv) to conclude that pre-1971 figures cannot be compared to later ones.

Before 1971, the federal government had obtained figures for all *felons* in state and federal institutions. Beginning that year, their figures covered all adult and youthful offenders (i.e., excluding those in juvenile institutions) *sentenced to serve maximum terms of at least a year and a day in prison.* You will recall (see Chapter 4) that felons are generally defined as those who have been convicted of crimes for which they can be (or, in Minneosta, have been) sentenced to serve at least a year and a day in prison. Generally inmates serve terms of a year or less in local jails rather than in state and federal prisons. The new figures should therefore not differ drastically from the old. However, there may be felons serving terms of a year or less in prison and misdemeanants serving longer prison terms as well.

If jails are too crowded, or if a judge feels that a felon can benefit from a special program or facilities at a state institution, a convicted felon (e.g., a burglar) may be sentenced to a term of less than a year and yet be remanded to state rather than local custody. There is a problem, too, in distinguishing jails from prisons. The common U.S. distinction is that prisons are penal institutions run by states, while jails are penal institutions run by local governments—primarily by counties. In the three U.S. states with the smallest land areas—Connecticut, Delaware, and Rhode Island—all jails are run by the state. The N.C.J.I.S.S. excludes figures for these states from its jail census and considers all penal institutions in these states as prisons. Therefore, all felons serving any time anywhere in these states were counted in federal prison censuses prior to 1971, but not necessarily thereafter.

On the other hand, those convicted of more than one misdemeanor may be sentenced to consecutive (as opposed to concurrent) terms of less than a year and a day each, which together add up to at least a year and a day maximum. If these misdemeanants are sent to state or federal institutions, these statistics are included in federal prison censuses *beginning* in 1971. Or a person may serve one misdemeanor sentence in a state or federal prison and then be turned over to another jurisdiction to serve an additional sentence. Arguably, this person could be included in figures after 1971.

Opposed to felons or persons serving maximum sentences are those in jail who are not serving sentences at all. These include persons being held for other authorities (e.g., a soldier, absent without leave, being held for pickup by military police); those arrested but not yet arraigned for trial; those arraigned but not yet tried; and those convicted but awaiting further legal action. Each of these categories is substantial in U.S. jails. As of March 1970, N.C.J.I.S.S. (1971: 10–11) figures indicated that 17 percent of the U.S. jail population were being held for other authorities or not yet arraigned; another 34 percent had been arraigned and were awaiting trial; 5 percent had been convicted and were awaiting further legal action; and 43 percent were serving sentences (more than one-seventh of the sentences were longer than a year). Some, like Blumstein and Cohen (1973), have analyzed incarceration rates and trends using measures only of those in prisons. Others, like Waller and Chan (1974), argue that measures of incarceration should include all those in local jails regardless of whether they have been convicted and are serving sentences.

If we are to measure the rate at which a society locks people up, should we include those in juvenile institutions and persons involuntarily committed to mental institutions? Kittrie (1971) argues that these other forms of confinement are, if anything, more punitive than imprisonment, since these inmates tend to spend more time for less and on vaguer grounds. While inclusion of jail figures would almost double U.S. imprisonment rates (N.C.J.I.S.S., 1971; 1976b), adding those in juvenile institutions would add another 25 percent (Hindelang, et al., 1977: 670), and adding those confined in mental institutions (separate figures for the involuntarily committed being unavailable) would more than double imprisonment figures (Bureau of the Census, 1974: 83). If one looks elsewhere than federal and state prisons, one can find enough people confined in the United States to quadruple the incarceration rate found by Blumstein and Cohen (1973).

Recall that the numerators of crime rates are usually *annual* figures. Most of the crimes included are probably committed in a few minutes. Suppose, instead, that many crimes took a year or so to commit, and many others (like business swindle conspiracies) as much as twenty or thirty years. It is far more important to prevent a twenty-year crime than a three-minute crime. How should the annual crime rate be measured? Should the numerator consist only of crimes commenced during the year? If so, then crimes that have been occurring throughout the year will not be counted. If not, then crimes will be counted more than once from year to year. Should crimes in which people are victimized for several months be equated with those that take an instant? As you can see, once it becomes apparent that there are substantial time differences of events in a rate numerator, the problems of measurement become much more complex.

Measurement of incarceration rates presents these problems. Jail and prison terms vary widely. N.C.J.I.S.S. (1976b: 22–23) 1974 figures for those sentenced to a maximum of at least a year and a day in federal and state institutions illustrate the point. As an incarceration rate numerator, one might use the number of persons admitted to prison during 1974: 167,509. (South Carolina is not included in admissions and departures figures, since it did not submit these data.) But since many people *leave* prison, too, perhaps it would be better to use the excess of admissions over departures: 12,629. There were 49,331 persons in prison at the beginning of 1974 who remained there through the year. Perhaps the excess of admissions over departures should be added to the number remaining in prison throughout the year: 61,960. But this would give those entering prison, and therefore in prison for less than the entire year of 1974, a weight equal to those in prison for the entire year, while those in prison for part of the year who then departed would be subtracted from the figures entirely. To minimize the complexities of weighing admissions and departures, it is conventional to use as a numerator the number of prisoners in custody on a given *day* of the year. It makes little difference which day is chosen. The same day must be used from year to year, so that the intervals remain constant. (You can imagine what the problem would be if the 1974 numerator were from December 31, the 1975 numerator from January 1, and the 1976 numerator from October 1. The first interval would be one day long and the second twenty-one months. If each federal and state institution were permitted to report for any day it chose, there might not be much difference in average intervals for national figures, provided the days chosen were fairly evenly distributed over the year.) The number of prisoners in custody on January 1, 1974 is reported to be 204,211, and on December 31, 1974, 218,205.

A more elaborate version of the measure of prison population for a given day is to obtain the average daily population for the entire year, as is done in New Zealand (Waller and Chan, 1974: 58).

Of course, one can build still larger numerators than these conventional ones by having the numerator represent the total number of persons imprisoned during the year. To obtain this numerator, one would add the number of new admissions for the year to the number of prisoners in custody on January 1. N.C.J.I.S.S. data do not separate new admissions from readmissions, but roughly 100,000 persons entered prison during 1974 who had not been in prison earlier in the year. Hence, this numerator in 1974 would be approximately 300,000.

Do you wish to control the use of or need for any form of confinement? Do you wish to divert people from prison to other forms of supervision and confinement? Do you wish to have fewer people admitted to prison, even if (as argued in Chapters 4 through 7) those still sentenced would probably get longer terms? Do you prefer to have parole boards empty prisons as quickly (or slowly) as they can? Your choice of numerator(s) will depend on your priorities for control: *who* to include (e.g., men or women), *what* to include (e.g., felonies or misdemeanors), *where* to include (e.g., prisons, jails, mental institutions), and *when* to include (e.g., population on one day or all those entering prison during a year).

Still other kinds of numerators will be chosen if your primary interest is in controlling recidivism. The problems of measuring and controlling recidivism are considered in Chapter 10.

MEASURING INCARCERATION RATE DENOMINATORS

Conventionally, as with offenses known to the police, incarceration rate denominators are expressed in hundreds of thousands of inhabitants of the jurisdictions in question. This is the denominator used in national statistics in the United States (e.g., N.C.J.I.S.S., 1971; 1975; 1976a; 1976b) and in international comparisons (e.g., Waller and Chan, 1974). But all inhabitants are not "at risk"; many of them could not be sent to prison regardless of what they did. Although exceptions can be made, in the United States, children under the age of seven will seldom, if ever, be sent to juvenile institutions, and children between fourteen and eighteen (depending on the jurisdiction) usually cannot be sent to prison or jail. Arguably, only those old enough to be incarcerated should be included in rate denominators.

Rates of responsiveness to criminality can be developed, comparable to those of responsiveness to crime. Published rates of responsiveness by incarceration are usually classified as "disposition of defendants." U.S. national figures have been compiled only for the federal courts (Administrative Office of the United States Courts, annual), not for their state counterparts. There one finds (in the 1975 *Annual Report*, pp. xi–107), for instance, that 45.5 percent of the 76.1 percent of those charged and convicted in U.S. federal courts in 1975 were sent to prison. In other words, less than half of those convicted were incarcerated, compared to about a third of those who were charged.

As with numerators, there are special issues of incarceration rate denominators with measures of recidivism. These issues are discussed in Chapter 10.

CURRENT TRENDS

The state of knowledge of incarceration rate trends can be summed up in a word: unclear.

U.S. jail censuses are so rare as to be useless in projecting trends. Most recently, there were two national censuses, conducted by the N.C.J.I.S.S. (1971; 1975). This is insufficient to predict trends, since one has no basis for gauging a margin for error. One guess is as good as another.

Prior to 1971, rates of felons held in state and federal prisons had remained fairly stable for half a century (Blumstein and Cohen, 1973). As mentioned above, these data cannot be compared to those from 1971 on (N.C.J.I.S.S., 1976b: iii–iv). The trends from 1971 through 1974 indicate that the number of prisoners in state and federal institutions, whose sentences were at least a year and a day per 100,000 inhabitants, dropped 1.0 percent from 1971 to 1972 and then rose during the next two years to 103.6 per hundred thousand—6.9 percent above the 1971 level (N.C.J.I.S.S., 1976b: 1).

U.S. imprisonment rates once appeared to be near the upper

limit (H. Pepinsky, 1977). However, these N.C.J.I.S.S. figures show otherwise. As mentioned in Chapter 4, by 1976, the U.S. adult prison population was reported to have climbed to an all-time high (R. Wilson, 1977). The 1971–1974 national figures not only change, but change roughly parallel to national police "offenses known" figures for the same period (F.B.I., 1975: 55). The F.B.I. figures are dominated by property offenses plus robbery. (Although robbery is classified by the F.B.I. as "violent crime" because it entails at least an implicit threat of force against a person, the threat of force is used to obtain property, making robbery a property offense, too.) While other offenses against the person climbed steadily through the early 1970's, property offenses and robbery declined from 1971 to 1972, increased somewhat from 1972 to 1973, and increased several times over from 1973 to 1974. Is it true that incarceration rates, like arrest and conviction rates, follow police "offenses known" trends? Figures for one kind of incarceration rate for four years are a scant basis for generalizations, but it will be worth following the trends to see whether the parallel continues.

As yet, there is no reason to believe that jail rates would parallel imprisonment rates. This remains to be seen (Waller and Chan, 1974: 48). Unfortunately, U.S. jail censuses are too infrequent to extrapolate trends.

Waller and Chan's (1974: 60–63) survey of trends in various Western countries indicates many fluctuations in rates of those held in prisons, jails, and juvenile institutions per 100,000 population in this century. Unfortunately, the figures are too confused to interpret. The only clear generalization that emerges is that rates can change dramatically during depressions and wars.

EVALUATING CHANCES OF CONTROLLING INCARCERATION RATES

Although little can be inferred from trend data within countries, patterns of incarceration rates across nations are highly suggestive. Waller and Chan (1974) have done a masterful analysis of these patterns. The following discussion is based on their work.

First, the pattern: The United States leads Waller and Chan's

(1974: 58) list of fifteen countries, with a rate of 200.0 persons incarcerated per 100,000 population. Poland follows with 189.7. Then comes Australia, with 128.2, followed in order by Finland, New Zealand, Canada, England and Wales, Denmark, Sweden, France, Italy, Japan, Spain, Norway, and finally, by the Netherlands at 22.4.

Waller and Chan (1974: 64–65) note that this ranking for incarceration rates is similar to the ranking for homicide rates. It was argued in Chapter 7 that, in the long run, crime rates should rise or fall together, also in places with less crime, violence would be rarer but usually more serious when it did occur. Furthermore, homicide contributes little to U.S. incarceration. Building on Waller and Chan's finding, higher incarceration rates appear to reflect not only more widespread violence but probably the other features of a society in which tolerance of strangers (Chapters 6, 7) is the norm.

Waller and Chan (1974: 65) cite the status of alcohol and drugs in different societies as a possible factor in incarceration rates. Consider, for example, the many Americans in jail for offenses like public drunkenness and, in countries with low incarceration rates, the relatively high percentage of people jailed for driving while intoxicated. Note the contrast: the United States, with the highest incarceration rate in Waller and Chan's study, jails drunks who are causing a nuisance in one area, while countries with low incarceration jail them for causing trouble by moving around too freely. Does this reflect a tendency for countries with low incarceration rates to restrict mobility, while countries with high rates stimulate mobility? Perhaps so.

Waller and Chan (1974: 65) cite public responses that favor reporting offenses and giving stiff sentences to help boost incarceration rates. That is, the same society that generates high crime rates will increase incarceration. This, too, is consistent with the idea that tolerance of strangers implies incarceration. Waller and Chan also mention levels of urbanization, literacy, and advanced education as possible factors in public attitudes toward incarceration. However, they do not elaborate on this proposition, and these factors do not differ greatly across the countries studied.

Waller and Chan (1974: 65) suggest that alternatives to imprisonment might affect incarceration rates, including probation, preventive detention, and use of mental institutions. Ironically, as noted in Chapter 4, as such alternatives are developed, they soon come to supplement rather than supplant imprisonment. The United States has pioneered an amazing array of alternatives; they are increasingly used as incarceration rates remain high. The more a society resorts to incarceration, the more it tends to develop and use other forms of official supervision and confinement.

Finally, Waller and Chan (1974: 65–66) propose that war and amnesty affect incarceration rates. If the country is invaded, as was Japan in World War II, incarceration rates go up. If, instead, the country simply sends its men to war (relatively few women being incarcerated in any society Waller and Chan examine), like the United States in World War II, its rates of incarceration decline. Waller and Chan also cite Italy, France, and Finland as examples of places where dramatic declines in prison populations have been brought about by amnesty. Amnesties have also been granted in the United States. This happened in the State of Georgia several years ago when Governor Maddox freed large numbers of prisoners in order to reduce crowding. Amnesty has never been used continuously, and probably never will be, to control incarceration rates permanently, but it can be used as a temporary expedient.

According to Waller and Chan, the requirements for control of incarceration rates are the same as those for the control of crime rates—convictions, arrests, offenses known, and victimizations by population. The United States can reduce its high rate of incarceration by war or momentarily by amnesty. But if Americans hope to keep the rate low in peacetime, they must learn to deal differently with each other. They must try not to treat their families, neighbors, and co-workers like strangers; they must reduce their level of violence by moving less often; and they must depend less on criminal justice and other official confinement services.

Thus, incarceration rates seem to behave like other rates of *crime*, apart from the characteristics of offenders. But that is strange, since incarceration rates are supposed to represent rates of *criminality*. What happened? After all, incarceration has long been treated as a problem of individual traits. We have assumed that there is something peculiar about people who are in jail and especially about those in prison. Let us backtrack and see whether incarceration rates can be controlled like rates of criminality. May I spoil the surprise? When incarceration is treated as criminality, incarceration becomes virtually uncontrollable. As discussed below (see the section on ethical issues), if we use this strategy, we have chosen *not* to control (and, by extension, not to change current rate trends in) incarceration. The ethical imperative for explanation is then considered more important than control. This author chooses to pursue control. The following section will help to show why treating incarceration as criminality seems doomed.

INCARCERATION AS CRIMINALITY

What if the nineteenth-century Italian surgeon, Lombroso (1968, originally published in Italian in 1898), is right? What if much of a nation's crime is caused by genetic defects, in persons Lombroso called "atavisms" (genetic throwbacks)? How does this knowledge help us design a crime control strategy? Does it not limit us to three choices? One choice is fatalism: to resign ourselves to live among confirmed criminals, and simply try to compensate the victims. Another choice is eugenics: to confine or kill the atavisms or, at least, to sterilize them or otherwise discourage their fertility so that they will disappear from succeeding generations. The third *potential* choice is psychosurgery or other biological transformation of each atavism at first diagnosis, to block the body chemistry of violence or aggression. The knowledge that genetic defects cause crime implies no further options for success in crime control. This limited use of knowledge is the basic shortcoming in all explanations of criminality.

A fourth alternative—giving criminals what they need to make up their deficiencies and be normal—is a logical impossibility. Just as two wrongs don't make a right, so further tampering with someone who already has a history of deviance cannot make the person normal. Garfinkel's (1967) case study of Agnes is illustrative. At one point, Agnes has male reproductive organs and yet identifies herself as a woman. She then has surgery. Now she may be treated as a transsexual, or as a woman with a peculiar problem of sterility and an unusual past. Although she maintains that she has always been a woman, can she or others ever take her sexuality for granted? The only way she can maintain her identity as a normal woman is by keeping her personal history a secret, which in itself is abnormal. She has not been made normal, but more distinctive, more deviant from the norm.

Kitsuse (1962) reveals another facet of the problem. Once it is suggested that a person is deviant (gay in Kitsuse's study), other aspects of the person's appearance and behavior—once assumed normal—now become redefined as further evidence of deviance. What then happens if the suggestion of deviance is refuted? The person remains in a special class of normality: one who gave the appearance of being deviant. Why is it suggested that officials should resign for even the appearance of impropriety? Because the appearance of deviance alone is a powerful test of the person's trustworthiness. Once considered deviant, it is hard to be treated as normal. As Goffman (1963) makes clear in his study of how people cope with being different, deviants may hide their stigma from others, but in so doing will guide their own behavior by the personal realization that they are different or abnormal. Even if the experience of being treated for deviance does not create a deviant self-identity (Lemert, 1972), the person becomes vulnerable to being charged with another form of deviance: amnesia, stupidity, denial, repression, or undue secretiveness.

Researchers have recently tried to refute the logic of stigmatization by pointing to deviants who were deviant before being so labeled (Gove, 1975). Such evidence is off the point. The issue is not whether deviance is independent of the label, but whether special treatment for deviance can make people normal. If we wish to prove that deviants cannot be made normal, we would have to find signs of deviance in the past behavior of people who seem normal in the present. Aye, there's the rub. The deed cannot be imagined, let alone be done. Deviance can be compounded or at best forgotten, but not undone. The only conceivable approximation of this is to turn the deviance into some form of nonconformity defined as "productive," which entails, among other things, powerful sponsorship (P. Pepinsky, 1961). Once someone's criminality is confirmed, only three courses of treatment remain open: (1) refusing to tolerate the deviant, (2) becoming more tolerant and expanding the deviant's role in society, or (3) concealing the criminality. Acts of intolerance of deviance cannot conceivably be belied, not only in the realm of genetics, but in other realms of explanation as well.

No one has yet taken a person who behaves deviantly because of "genetic defect" and made the person normal. In the foreseeable future, no one will.

The problem is not limited to genetic explanations of criminality. Not only is it now inconceivable to make a deviant normal, but no one, I submit, really *believes* it conceivable. If it were, it should be reflected somewhere in social science research. For all the studies of why people become deviant, I know of no empirical study (i.e., as opposed to speculation) of why deviants become normal. The American Friends Service Committee (1971)— Quakers—who helped to establish the Philadelphia prison system as a humane alternative to capital and corporal punishment (Rothman, 1971)—has led the way in sponsoring recent statements that enforced rehabilitation of criminals is an unattainable goal. The Goodell Committee on Incarceration has reaffirmed this position (Von Hirsch, 1976). This may go a little too far. In Chapter 10, we shall consider whether enforced rehabilitation of offenders is possible. Many things might be done to make the life of offenders in communities more tolerable for themselves and for others. The point here is that knowing why some people rather than others commit crimes in a criminogenic environment contributes nothing to their rehabilitation. This is J. Wilson's (1977: 47–70) argument.

Some further examples:

Remember the various theories of criminality reviewed in Chapter 1? There is a common theme underlying most of them. The causes of criminality arise in one's youth (if not before birth), and these causes either include poverty or are associated with it (H. Pepinsky, 1976: 106–115). Suppose poverty does cause people to become criminals. If, then, we give a poor juvenile delinquent (for example) a lot of money, will this cure the delinquency? Not according to conventional wisdom, which holds that paying criminals and delinquents to behave well only rewards and encourages wrongdoing. Knowing that poverty has caused the delinquency indicates no cure; it shows no way to undo the damage that poverty has done, except by changing the entire social structure to eliminate poverty for all. This is the problem with a thesis like Bonger's (1969): that poverty breeds egoism (or selfishness), which, in turn, breeds crime. We are left with the implication that crime is inevitable in a given social order.

So it is with the longstanding (Duesterberg, 1979; Rothman, 1971) thesis that crime or delinquency is caused by family breakdown, which is a product of poverty (e.g., Miller, 1958). What do you do with a child who is delinquent because of a broken family? Return the child to babyhood and provide a set of warm, loving parents who are good role models? This is not provided by state institutions or even by foster homes. In fact, by the time the problem is revealed, it is too late to return to those crucial early years.

Today, with compulsory universal education, a new theory has emerged: Trouble in school leads to delinquency (Cohen, 1955; Hirschi and Hindelang, 1977). The problem is either that failure in school breeds resentment, which leads to delinquency (Cohen), or the stupidity that produces failure in school also produces delinquency (Hirschi and Hindelang). But as Illich (1971) observes, failure is an inevitable part of Western education. Schooling is used to cull the talented from the untalented, the socially deserving from the undeserving. Certification—grading—is fundamental to the system. And as the recent turmoil in U.S. higher education over "grade inflation" indicates, those who support the Western model of formal education believe it works only if it discriminates good students from bad. As I can attest from personal experience (I once lost a job in large part because over a couple of terms I had given all students in large undergraduate classes A's), no grading system in which all students do well is considered fair. If teachers are doing their job, some students must be worse than others. Some students must fail, and as with other societal rewards and punishments, most of the failure will probably occur among the poor and dispossessed. In the United States, it would be practically un-American for poor students to do as well as rich ones.

What does this say about trouble in school as a cause of delinquency? Again, it suggests that the poor and dispossessed are bound to produce more than their share of delinquents. Again, instead of pointing out a way of reducing delinquency or criminality, this explanation is simply a rationalization of why delinquency and criminality have to be expected from some people, especially the poor.

In reaction to this bias against the poor, some criminologists, like Quinney (1974), have argued that instead of seeing poverty as a cause of criminality, we should realize that criminality causes poverty. Being rich and successful, showing some control over the economy, these—not poverty—are to Quinney indicators of criminality. This is but a mirror image of the traditional explanations of criminality. One side of the social order breeds virtue, the other criminality, and the mirror just reverses the sides. This explanation of criminality—this isolation of characteristics of one group of individuals as the source of crime—like the traditional explanations, implies that criminality is inevitable. Rich crooks can be killed or confined, but not redeemed. And no reason is given to believe that poor folks who overthrow their rulers, and then become rich and powerful themselves, will not become criminals, too.

There is a gray area between the treatment of incarceration as a sign of crime versus criminality. Those who end up in institutions can be seen as socially retarded because of a lack of tolerance and support. If normal maturity is regarded as an end that most people reach early in life, then criminals can almost be redeemed by being raised to that level of maturity a few years later. Warren (1969) makes the best convincing case. She has developed a scale with five levels of "interpersonal maturity." Warren believes that delinquency stems from the frustration of those with only a limited chance of interpersonal growth. These people cannot relate to teachers and other authority figures on the interpersonal level at which these people operate. Her remedy is to match problem youths with counselors who communicate well on their level. When the youths have received support and affection in terms they can understand and appreciate at their own level, they will be prepared—again with appropriate support—to move to a higher level. The fourth level of maturity is, according to Warren, as high as most people reach. At this level, they know how to conform to adult expectations. At the fifth level, the person is able to empathize with other points of view. If problem youths can be brought up to the fourth level, they will function normally in society.

Warren's research has shown that her course of treatment reduces the risk of problem youths returning to institutions. (We shall return to her research in Chapter 10.) Her results have been criticized as indicating not that the youths were changed by the treatment, but that officials were more lenient toward Warren's treatment group than toward a comparison group (Lerman, 1968). For this reason, Warren's explanation of incarceration falls in a gray area. It is not clear whether her theory concerns the problems of delinquents or the problems of responding to delinquency. Much of Warren's success probably comes from the love and support she gives to others. She may succeed because she focuses on the method of treatment rather than as a problem with the youths themselves. She succeeds by giving youths in trouble the social acceptance and political sponsorship they have not had before. For Warren, incarceration reflects a problem of crime produced by how other people interact with certain youths. Warren succeeds in controlling crime (or delinquency) by treating incarceration as a sign of crime—a problem shared by offenders and non-offenders—rather than criminality.

Warren has almost succeeded in developing a theory of how deviants become normal, but not quite. Instead, she treats incarcerated youths as responding normally to the level of social support they receive. For Warren, delinquent youths' needs are like others; the problem is not in their character. Warren's youths are not really deviant to begin with.

Thus, the problem remains: Treat incarceration as a normal behavioral issue and incarceration rates may be controllable. Treat incarceration as evidence of criminality and no control strategy is indicated except killing, confining, or incapacitating the deviants.

Ethical issues involved in these three strategies are considered later in this chapter. For now, I argue that this approach will fail to reduce incarceration rates, let alone the crime rates considered in Chapters 4 through 7. Incapacitation will probably—in the long run—increase rather than decrease crime rates (see Chapter 6). In brief, as a society comes to punish more of its members more severely, this greater willingness to hurt others is unlikely to stop with a certain group of criminals. It can be expected to generate more crime and more need for official protection.

There is another practical issue to be considered—and here, geneticists like Dobzhansky (1973) and Hirsch (1975) are especially helpful. According to their research, there are so many genetic combinations that, identical twins aside, every human being who has *ever* lived has been genetically unique—substantially different from any other human being. Given this incredible variety, it is unlikely that any substantial group of people in one society at one time will be genetically similar that they will behave alike regardless of environment.

Furthermore, the role of the environment must be considered. If some persons are "genetically predisposed" to shoot when shot at, for instance, their genes "make" them shoot people only when the environment provides guns and a victim who shoots first. Genes and environment *interact* to produce behavior. In theory, then, behavior can be changed by changing either genes or the environment. There is no logical basis to believe otherwise. Even if a person has shown repeated violent behavior under one set of circumstances, this does not imply that the behavior will hold under all circumstances. Without considering the ethical issue of whether everyone is worth redeeming, everyone—including those incarcerated—is in theory redeemable if others are tolerant, supportive, and imaginative enough to change the environment sufficiently to get the behavior they want.

Some suggest that offenders can be treated successfully for criminality just as a patient can successfully be treated for a physical disease such as malaria. The medical analogy is worthwhile; the conclusion that offenders can successfully be treated as criminal "patients" is not. Who does the doctor treat for malaria? The one who complains of symptoms of the disease. In the realm of crime, who bears the symptoms of the "disease" of burglary? The burglar? No, the burglar complains only of the treatment. It is the complainant or the victim who bears the symptoms. In the case of a social as opposed to a physical disease, usually someone other than the offender asks for treatment. If the victim of crime is cured, someone other than the offender must be made well. Treatment of the offender alone cannot cure the "patient."

By analogy to malaria, the victim of burglary is most like the patient and the offender like the anopheles mosquito, the carrier of the disease. We could not very well control malaria if control strategies had focused on making the anopheles mosquito safe to live among people. Instead, the greatest successes have come in treating *potential* victims (as by giving them quinine) or in controlling the mosquito's breeding grounds (as by draining the swamps where it breeds). If success in crime control is to come from copying the success of medical science, then we should concentrate on *both* making people invulnerable to crime *and* altering the social environment that breeds crime. Rehabilitating the carrier of the disease of crime, like making the anopheles mosquito safe for society, is a waste of crime control resources (Pepinsky, 1978b).

And so, using scientific logic, the issue of whether crime is caused by criminals or by society is nonsense. In that mythical state of perfect knowledge, we would understand that any criminal behavior was caused by the biology of the criminal, the personal history of the criminal, and the social setting—all working together. Change *any* of these elements and the behavior may be changed. Again using scientific logic, in an imperfect state of knowledge, the criminologist can choose to analyze incarceration *as though* it is caused by biology, personal history, *or* social context. The choice rests not on what really causes crime, but on the practical, political, and ethical gains and losses from generating one kind of knowledge rather than another. If I argue that incarceration ought to be explained by social context, it is not because social context alone causes crime. It is because knowledge about social context is more useful for controlling crime in general and incarceration rates in particular than is knowledge about biology and personal history. It is conceivable that incarceration rates by population could be reduced, and the incarceration rates increased, using knowledge about the relationship between social contexts and incarceration rates. This kind of control could scarcely be accomplished by using knowledge of the biology and personal history of those incarcerated. For this reason, explanations of incarceration based on criminality should be laid to rest.

SIDE EFFECTS OF CONTROLLING INCARCERATION RATES

To begin with, if incarceration rates were reduced and rates of response to crime increased, these changes would rest on the same foundation as control of rates of conviction, arrest, offenses known and victimization by population. Therefore, the same side effects should occur. In addition, if officials and citizens became more selective about sending people to jail and prison, they would have less regard for the remaining inmates. Thus, one would expect that prison and jail conditions would deteriorate. This might not be as bad as it seems. Inmates who "enjoy" life varying from rat-infested jails to modern correctional facilities seem to be equally unhappy under all circumstances. A library could be filled with literature on inmate life in various kinds of institutions. Goffman (1961) especially provides a vivid, quite generalizable account of what it is like to be confined. Without denigrating the richness and variety of life in institutions, my impression is that the overwhelming reality of life in any institution is the sense of being caged. For most inmates, conditions of incarceration are rotten and oppressive in the best institutions—and decline from there. How much worse can prison conditions get?

There are many arguments that prison conditions can and should be improved in many ways, whether as a matter of legal right (Rubin, 1973) or of correctional philosophy (Murton and Hyams, 1970). Control of incarceration rates would probably undercut these attempts to improve inmates' conditions.

POLITICAL CONSIDERATIONS

In 1971–1972, the Massachusetts Commissioner of Youth Services closed several of the state's training schools in favor of using community homes and facilities (Ohlin et al., 1975). But he could not close them entirely (Ohlin et al., 1976: 13–14). As of the most recent date, after reporting that no training schools or training school wards were officially open for 1973 and 1974 (N.C.J.I.S.S., 1977a: 26–31), Massachusetts opened two training schools housing forty-six wards as of 1975 (N.C.J.I.S.S., 1977b: 20–21). The Commissioner has changed jobs several times. A brilliant job of reducing incarceration is being undone.

For one thing, the experiment was bound to fail because the change was superficial. It did not rest on basic changes in the way the people of Massachusetts responded to personal conflict, and old habits soon resurrected old incarceration practices. Unless the public participates in major social change, the change cannot be expected to endure. Also, as with policing, the livelihoods of many people rest on continued criminal justice activity. In fact, whole communities often grow up around institutions of confinement, from which guards (or warders or staff or counselors) are drawn generation after generation. After all, it is safer to have inmates in geographically isolated institutions than in major cities. Hence, not merely individual jobs but the lives of entire communities may depend on inmate populations. Correctional workers, too, work against the attempt to reduce incarceration rates, unless they themselves are offered job security. Meanwhile, as Villaume (1978) reports, the U.S. correctional bureaucracy is feeding on its insecurity and expanding more (while perhaps doing less). Control of incarceration rates will occur only when correctional workers cooperate. And this will not happen unless they are shown that they will benefit from the change (Pepinsky, 1978a).

ETHICAL ISSUES

First, there are ethical issues of choice between treating incarceration rates as measures of crime or of criminality. Here, I will make a blatant political statement: The explanation of criminality is morally indefensible unless the research findings are *never* applied to treating criminals. At this point, you are welcome to disagree with me. In fact, I hope you will, as an exercise in independence from the "expert" criminologist. And if you disagree, you will have a lot of company.

In part, the moral beliefs that cause me to take a political position here also lead me to reject any explanation of incarceration as criminality. Recently in social science, there has been an emphasis on the need for researchers to remain "value neutral" about what their findings mean (a position commonly taken in books on research methods, like Lin, 1976). The idea that scientists ought to remain neutral about moral implications is ascribed (falsely, I think) to Weber (as by Gouldner, 1968). In his classic lecture on "science as a vocation," Weber (1946, originally lectured in 1918, first published in 1919) argues that scientists cannot derive political positions merely by applying the logic of scientific inquiry. Speaking of the scientist as teacher, he said, " 'To let the facts speak for themselves' is the most unfair way of putting over a political position to the student" (p. 146). The introduction to the idea of ethical issues in Chapter 3 of this book is essentially a restatement of Weber's argument. Weber stressed that the scientist is in a position to know which of several means is most useful in reaching a desired goal. But beyond this, the scientist cannot prove which of several goals is preferable. At the same time, the scientist must recognize that his or her definition of a research problem inevitably rests on political preferences, which Weber calls "presuppositions."

My view of incarceration as a measure of crime is a presupposition. To another researcher, incarceration may be a measure of criminality. Science cannot prove which preference is correct. But while I state that my approach is political, those who try to explain criminality (such as Hirschi and Selvin, 1967) stress that their preference is value neutral. Why the difference? Perhaps those who choose to explain criminality are as concerned over the use of their knowledge as I am. Possibly, if their knowledge indicated a positive approach, rather than killing, confinement, or incapacitation, they would be willing to acknowledge political meaning. Value neutrality is a shelter for those whose research findings can have no positive uses.

If killing, confinement, or incapacitation of criminals even produced a longtime reduction of crime in a society, applied knowledge of criminality might be justified. As it is, explanations of criminality, cloaked in value neutrality, can only reinforce the idea that crime is out of control, and worse, is uncontrollable. Explanations of criminality are fatalistic. However, human beings in various societies have demonstrated that crime control *is* possible. Admittedly, in a country like the contemporary United States, crime control would entail a lengthy, fundamental reordering of society, but even here, crime control is conceivable. If, on balance, people want to maintain a social order with uncontrolled crime, so be it. But let that choice be an affirmative one. Let those who decide accept moral responsibility for not trying to control crime, not because it appears that crime *cannot* be controlled but because they believe that it *should* not be controlled. This, at least, would be a more honest rationale for the explanation of criminality than value neutrality.

To a limited extent, explaining criminality can be defended

as a heuristic aid to crime control. If the strategies surveyed in Chapters 4 through 7 work to control crime, they must keep people from becoming criminals. Even if explanations of criminality offer no hope of redeeming criminals, perhaps they can help us learn how to keep people from becoming criminals in the first place. Will crime control measures make people in one society behave like people in another society? To answer this, we must try to guess what people in the old order want. If a crime control measure works as planned, it will be in part because former criminals can now get what they want in legitimate ways. But even in a society with incarceration rates as high as that of the United States, known criminals are such a small portion of the population that a crime control measure is bound to affect far more people than the "criminal element" alone. Our instruments of social engineering are too crude to focus on criminals alone. That is why incapacitation strategies probably generate more crime than they prevent. If explanations of criminality are to be useful in designing crime control strategies, the explanations must describe features of criminal behavior common to most people. If a planner can discover what features of life criminals share with the rest of us, and what we are all struggling for together, then the planner may be able to devise a way for people to get what they want with less crime. For instance, if one supposes that all Americans want recognition for being special people, and if a common way of doing so—for criminals and noncriminals alike—is to get wealthy faster than other people by "private enterprise"—legitimate or illegitimate—then opening noncompetitive channels to achieve recognition may reduce criminal behavior (H. Pepinsky, 1976). But again, it is explanations stressing the similarities between criminals and noncriminals that can aid in planning crime control strategies. There is no justification for trying to explain why criminals become different from the rest of us, unless we simply wish to put other people down.

If incarceration rates are taken to represent crime rather than criminality, the central ethical issue remains: should we become strangers to our own kind and kinder to strangers? The more Americans become so—and in consequence, the more they put each other in jail and prison—the kinder they become toward inmates. At least, more attention is given to inmate rights, safety, and comfort. Is a lower crime rate worth a lessening of social concern for inmate welfare? Each person alone must decide.

CONCLUSION

It appears that the only good use for incarceration measures is the same as those for convictions, arrests, offenses known, and victimizations. Progress toward crime control can be assessed in terms of reduced rates of incarceration by population and increased rates of incarceration by conviction. Progress in crime control cannot, it seems, be measured by changes in characteristics of those incarcerated.

This is not to say that all measures of criminality rates have been shown to be useless. Certain refinements have been made on the use of incarceration to tell us about criminality. One refinement—self-reporting—extends information about criminality to include more people than are counted in incarceration measures. The other refinement—measures of recidivism—extend information about a more limited sample than all those incarcerated. In the next few chapters, we will see whether either of these refinements is more useful than simple incarceration rates.

REFERENCES

Administrative Office of the United States Courts. Annual. *Annual Report of the Director*. Washington, D.C. United States Government Printing Office.

American Friends Service Committee. 1971. *Struggle for Justice*. New York: Hill and Wang.

Blumstein, Albert D., and Jacqueline Cohen. 1973. "A theory of the stability of punishment." *Journal of Criminal Law and Criminology* 64 (June): 198–207.

Bonger, Willem (Austin W. Turk, ed. and trans.). 1969. *Criminality and Economic Conditions*. Bloomington: Indiana University Press.

Bureau of the Census. 1974. *Statistical Abstract of the United States—1974*. Washington, D.C.: United States Government Printing Office.

Cohen, Albert K. 1955. *Delinquent Boys: The Culture of the Gang*. New York: Free Press.

Dobzhansky, Theodosius. 1973. "Differences are not deficits." *Psychology Today* 7 (December): 97–101.

Duesterberg, Thomas J. 1979. *The Social Origins of Criminology in Nineteenth-Century France*. Bloomington, Ind.: Indiana University (dissertation).

Federal Bureau of Investigation. 1975. *Crime in the United States: Uniform Crime Reports—1974*. Washington, D.C.: United States Government Printing Office.

Garfinkel, Harold. 1967. *Studies in Ethnomethodology*. Englewood Cliffs, N.J.: Prentice-Hall.

Goffman, Erving. 1961. *Asylums*. Garden City, N.J.: Doubleday.

———. 1963. *Stigma*. Englewood Cliffs, N.J.: Prentice-Hall.

Gouldner, Alvin N. 1968. "Anti-minotaur: the myth of a value-free sociology." *The American Sociologist* 3 (May): 103–116.

Gove, Walter R. (ed.). 1975. *The Labeling of Deviance: Evaluating a Perspective*. New York: Wiley.

Hindelang, Michael J., Michael R. Gottfredson, Christopher S. Dunn, and Nicolette Parisi. 1977. *Sourcebook of Criminal Justice Statistics—1976*. Washington, D.C.: United States Government Printing Office.

Hirsch, Jerry. 1975. "Behavior genetic analysis and its biosocial consequences." Pp. 348–367, in Clarence J. Karier (ed.), *Shaping the American Educational State: 1900 to the Present*. New York: Free Press.

Hirshi, Travis, and Michael J. Hindelang. 1977. "Intelligence and delinquency: a revisionist review." *American Sociological Review* 42 (August): 571–587.

Hirschi, Travis, and Hans C. Selvin. 1967. *Delinquency Research*. New York: Free Press of Glencoe.

Illich, Ivan. 1971. *Deschooling Society*. New York: Harper and Row.

Kitsuse, John I. 1962. "Societal reaction to deviant behavior." *Social Problems* 9 (Winter): 247–256.

Kittrie, Nicholas N. 1971. *The Right to Be Different*. Baltimore: Johns Hopkins Press.

Lemert, Edwin M. 1972. *Human Deviance, Social Problems, and Social Control*. Englewood Cliffs, N.J.: Prentice-Hall (second edition).

Lerman, Paul. 1968. "Evaluative studies of institutions for delinquents: implications for research and social policy." *Social Work* 13 (July): 55–64.

Lin, Nan. 1976. *Foundations of Social Research*. New York: McGraw-Hill.

Lombroso, Cesare (Henry P. Horton, trans.). 1968. *Crime: Its Causes and Remedies*. South Hackensack, N.J.: Patterson Smith (reprint of 1911 edition).

Miller, Walter B. 1958. "Lower class culture as a generating milieu of gang delinquency." *Journal of Social Issues* 14 (November): 5–19.

Murton, Thomas O., and Joe Hyams. 1970. *Accomplices to the Crime*. New York: Grove Press.

National Criminal Justice Information and Statistics Service. 1971. *1970 National Jail Census*. Washington, D.C.: United States Government Printing Office.

———. 1975. *The Nation's Jails—1972*. Washington, D.C.: United States Government Printing Office.

———. 1976a. *Prisoners in State and Federal Institutions on December 31, 1974*. Washington, D.C.: United States Government Printing Office.

———. 1976b. *Survey of Inmates of State Correctional Facilities—1974: Advance Report*. Washington, D.C.: United States Government Printing Office.

———. 1977a. *Children in Custody: Advance Report on the Juvenile Detention and Correctional Facility Census of 1974*. Washington, D.C.: United States Government Printing Office.

———. 1977b. *Children in Custody: Advance Report on the Juvenile Detention and Correctional Facility Census of 1975*. Washington, D.C.: United States Government Printing Office.

Ohlin, Lloyd E., Robert B. Coates and Alden D. Miller. 1975. "Radical correctional reform: a case study of the Massachusetts youth correctional system." Pp. 280–317 in Robert M. Carter, Richard A. McGee and E. Kim Nelson (eds.), *Corrections in America*. Philadelphia: Lippincott.

Ohlin, Lloyd E., Alden D. Miller, and Robert B. Coates. 1976. *Juvenile Correctional Reform in Massachusetts*. Washington, D.C.: United States Government Printing Office.

Pepinsky, Harold E. 1976. *Crime and Conflict: A Study of Law and Society*. New York: Academic Press.

———. 1977. "Stereotyping as a force for increasing crime rates." *Law and Human Behavior* 1 (September): 299–308.

———. 1978a. "Communist Anarchism as an alternative to the rule of criminal law." *Contemporary Crises* 2 (July): 315–327.

———. 1978b. "Social historians: write your criminologists!" Paper presented at Social Science History Association Meeting, Columbus, Ohio (November 5).

Pepinsky, Pauline Nichols. 1961. "The social dialectic of productive nonconformity." *Merrill-Palmer Quarterly of Behavior and Development* 7 (April): 127–137.

Pollak, Otto. 1950. *The Criminality of Women*. Philadelphia: University of Pennsylvania Press.

Quinney, Richard. 1974. *Critique of Legal Order: Crime Control in Capitalist Society*. Boston: Little, Brown.

Rothman, David J. 1971. *The Discovery of the Asylum: Social Order and Disorder in the New Republic*. Boston: Little, Brown.

———. 1975. "Behavior modification in total institutions." *Hastings Center Report* 5 (February): 1–12.

Rubin, Sol. 1973. *The Law of Criminal Correction*. St. Paul, Minn.: West (2nd ed.).

Villaume, Alfred C. 1978. "Parkinson's law and the United States Bureau of Prisons." *Contemporary Crises* 2 (April): 209–218.

Von Hirsch, Andrew. 1976. *Doing Justice: The Choice of Punishment.* New York: Hill and Wang.

Waller, Irvin, and Janet Chan. 1974. "Prison use: a Canadian and international comparison." *Criminal Law Quarterly* 17 (December): 47–71.

Warren, Marguerite Q. 1969. "The case for differential treatment of delinquents." *Annals of the American Academy of Political and Social Sciences* 381 (January): 47–59.

Weber, Max. 1946. "Science as a vocation." Pp. 129–156, in H. H. Gerth and C. Wright Mills (eds. and trans.), *From Max Weber: Essays in Sociology.* New York: Oxford.

Wilson, James Q. 1977. *Thinking About Crime.* New York: Vintage Books.

Wilson, Rob. 1977. "U.S. prison population again hits new high." *Corrections Magazine* 3 (March): 3–22.

FOOD FOR THOUGHT

1. Which incarceration rate numerator is the best indicator of a society's tendency to confine people for wrongdoing? Which denominator should be used in this measure?

2. There is a lot of speculation as to why so fewer women than men are incarcerated in all societies. What do you think accounts for the difference, and how could you test your explanation?

3. If you could set your own standards, how would you decide whether a convicted person should be incarcerated?

4. What is the strongest argument for *not* abandoning attempts to explain what makes criminals different from noncriminals?

5. Would reduced incarceration rates by population be worth a worsening of prison conditions?

6. Should an author of a criminology text refrain from taking political or ethical positions? Should criminologists in general be value neutral?

CHAPTER NINE

Should
Self-Reporting Rates
Be Controlled?

This chapter differs in format from earlier chapters on crime and criminality. There are no separate sections on the measurement of rate numerators and denominators or on current trends in self-reporting rates. Instead, much of the chapter consists of a historical review of self-report research.

There are several reasons for this. For one, the researchers are less concerned with the amount of self-reported crime and delinquency than with explaining why people commit offenses. There has been so little measurement of self-reported crime rates that only one researcher, Gold (see Gold and Reimer, 1975), has even begun to analyze how these rates change over time. Therefore, to examine only measurements of rates and trends would distort the progress of self-report research.

In Chapter 8, I noted that it seems futile to try to use knowledge of incarceration rates to explain what makes criminals different from the rest of us. Self-report data, in contrast, may prove more useful. Researchers who have generated self-report data have done the most sophisticated work on this question to date. Self-report research largely succeeds in transcending official biases regarding who is labeled criminal and who is not. For the last twenty years, self-report researchers have mainly studied young people—adolescents—in many instances trying to figure out what triggers repeated delinquency. One major self-report study is entitled *Causes of Delinquency* (Hirschi, 1969). If there is anything to be gained from trying to figure out what makes some people criminals, it should be found in self-report data. Although I believe that there is no point in trying to explain criminality, self-report literature may prove useful. To be frank, I doubt it. Self-report literature is reviewed here in the hope that explanations of criminality will finally be dissipated.

There are relatively few major self-report studies to review. Thus, a chronological survey of this literature can be done here, in contrast to other areas in which the research literature is too vast to be covered. This survey of the literature offers two benefits to readers. For the person new to criminology, the survey presents the type of literature review that occurs elsewhere in the field. After dealing with the material in this chapter, you should be able to handle standard criminology journals and monographs with confidence. (After reading this chapter, you might want to look up one of the studies reviewed and see how easy it is to read.) For those of you with a special interest in self-report research, this extended review of the literature will be helpful.

ORIGINS OF SELF-REPORT RESEARCH

The Great Depression taught Americans compassion for the underdog. In the 1930s, jobs were so hard to get that people could hardly be blamed for being unemployed. Under President Franklin D. Roosevelt's "New Deal," the government took the role of providing for the welfare of citizens who could no longer fend for themselves. The name of the law that provided income to retired and disabled Americans—the Social Security Act—captured the spirit of the times.

Criminologists were caught up in this spirit. Perhaps, they thought, criminals should not be blamed for their status. According to Robison (1936), children labeled delinquent were unfairly discriminated against. She argued that officials charged children "from the wrong side of the tracks" with offenses they overlooked in middle-class children. Hence, she argued, most delinquents acted no worse than many middle-class children who were never charged or adjudicated guilty of wrongdoing.

Sellin (1938) argued that much crime was caused by what

he termed "culture conflict." Culture conflict took two forms. For one, Sellin believed it likely that the many immigrants from other countries would be found guilty of crime for doing what was normal in their native societies, such as conducting family vendettas. For another, given the mixture of backgrounds and experiences of people in U.S. cities, Sellin thought it highly probable that each individual learned unique standards of behavior. Thus, it could easily happen that city residents, doing what they thought entirely proper, would violate the law. Sellin's message: Let us consider the possibility that criminals are as normal as any of us, and simply get trapped in the demands of foreign cultural standards.

The year that Sellin's book appeared, Tannenbaum (1938) published another explanation of why people become criminal. Tannenbaum argued that any one of us can commit an unlawful act. By chance, some of us get caught. When we are caught, we are called "criminals" or "deviants." We normal people, who happened to commit a wrongful act, are now treated as abnormal people who are characteristically criminal. If we are denied the opportunity to play the role of normal people, we become the deviants we have been declared to be and embark on criminal careers. Why, according to Tannenbaum, are criminals criminal? Because they have been caught and labeled as such. It is the people who respond to crime—notably, officials—rather than habitual criminals themselves who launch criminal careers.

The following year, 1939, Sutherland (1940), a noted criminologist, delivered a controversial Presidential Address to the American Sociological Association. In the speech, Sutherland coined the term "white-collar crime." He argued that the stereotype of crimes being committed predominantly by poor people was false. Rich folks, particularly business and professional persons, committed just as much crime as poor folks. The difference between the rich and the poor was that the rich had the power to get the law written and enforced in their favor. Hence, crime was something common even to pillars of the community. There was nothing necessarily deviant or unusual about committing crimes.

For all these suggestions that "nice" people were no less crooked than those convicted of crimes, only isolated cases of white-collar crime were found. The climate was right for attempts to find out how much crime was committed among supposedly law-abiding citizens. The findings of three such studies were published in the 1940s. The idea of the studies was to find out from people how much hidden crime they had committed. While victim surveys were designed to find hidden *crime*, self-report surveys (so called because persons were asked to report their own criminality) were designed to find hidden *criminality*. Early surveys were little more than exposés. Porterfield (1946) gave questionnaires to a group of students entering Texas Christian University in Fort Worth, who admitted having committed practically every offense for which other youths had been brought before the local juvenile court. To Porterfield, the striking features of these reports was that these students had almost never been caught. Porterfield (1943) also reported little difference in what those who had and had not been caught had done, except that those put in training schools could be expected to be channeled into further trouble with the law, while college kids would probably turn out to be respectable community members whose white-collar crime went unpunished.

The second exposé was a survey of adult men and women by Wallerstein and Wyle (1947). It remains one of the few published U.S. self-report surveys of adults. Questionnaires were mailed to persons holding various types of jobs. A total of 1,698 were returned—mostly from the New York City area, and some from upstate New York, Pennsylvania, Ohio, and California. People from high-status occupations were *over*represented in the returns. Modeled on the Porterfield questionnaire, this one asked respondents whether they had committed any of 49 offenses for which, under New York State law, they could, under some circumstances, have been sentenced to more than a year in prison. They were asked to distinguish offenses committed before the age of sixteen (at which time they would have been treated as adults under New York State law) from those committed thereafter. On the average, men reported having committed 18 of the 49 offenses as adults and 3.2 offenses as juveniles. The average for women as adults was 11, plus 1.6 as juveniles. While minor offenses—malicious mischief and disorderly conduct—were the most commonly reported, more than 25 percent of the men and 8 percent of the women reported stealing cars; 17 percent of the men and 4 percent of the women committing burglary; and 11 percent of the men and 1 percent of the women committing robbery. Wallerstein and Wyle (p. 111) even report: "A self-styled criminologist over sixty gave up after reading the questionnaire and returned it with the sweeping comment, 'Too much trouble, I've done them all.' "

The third of these early surveys was the most sophisticated. Murphy et al. (1946) obtained data from the Cambridge-Somerville Youth Study outside Boston. In this project, caseworkers maintained close contact with many youths from low-income families throughout their adolescent years; detailed records were compiled. Murphy et al. found records for 114 boys aged eleven to sixteen. Included in these records was "a great deal of information concerning misdeeds that had never become a matter of official court complaint." Murphy and the caseworkers jointly reviewed each boy's record and conservatively tabulated, in separate categories, violations of city ordinances, arbitrarily classified minor offenses, and serious offenses. Of the 114 boys, 13 had no violations as far as the caseworkers knew, 61 who had violations had never had court complaints filed against them, and the remaining 40 had official records of alleged wrongdoing. On the average, each of the 40 "official delinquents" had committed more offenses in each of the three categories than had the 61 "unofficial delinquents." But each unofficial delinquent had still committed about 3 serious offenses, 12 ordinance violations, and 30 minor offenses.

These early studies, then, showed that most people who never got into trouble with the law repeatedly committed offenses. Even serious offenses were not uncommon among ostensibly law-abiding people.

DELINQUENCY AMONG THE LAW-ABIDING MIDDLE CLASS

This was the end of U.S. self-report research for a decade. Then, as computer technology began to facilitate more sophisticated statistical analyses of large data sets, researchers once again tried to figure out how—if at all—official delinquents differed from other youths. Now, they began surveying large samples, comparing official delinquents to those without records, including apparently respected middle-class youths. The first of this group of studies was by Short and Nye (1958). More than 500 high school boys and 500 high school girls (aged sixteen and seventeen) from several Midwestern and Western communities, and 125 boys and 48 girls in Western training schools, were given a questionnaire asking whether they had committed each of 23 offenses at all, or "more than once or twice." Training school boys and girls were generally more likely to have committed at least one offense, and more than once or twice, than the others. The exceptions: homosexual relations among boys, driving without a license for girls, and game violations among both boys and girls. Still, high proportions of other boys and girls had committed most of the offenses commonly committed by the training school youths.

It is a worldwide, almost universal pattern—both in official statistics and in self-reporting—that girls and women commit fewer offenses of most kinds, and less often, than boys and men (Jensen and Eve, 1976). Short and Nye's data fit this pattern.

The researchers also tried to discern differences in self-reported delinquent behavior at different socioeconomic levels, in sex and age groups, and training schools versus high school youths. As in most U.S. self-report research (exceptions: Reiss and Rhodes, 1961, and Gold, 1966, discussed below), socioeconomic level made little difference in the kind of delinquency involved. Greater delinquency of certain types in the lowest socioeconomic groups was equaled by greater delinquency of other types in the highest socioeconomic groups. Thus, this and most other U.S. self-report studies do *not* show that poor children are likely to be more delinquent than rich ones. In fact, Akers (1964), using Nye and Short's items in a study of 836 junior high school students in a Northwestern Ohio city of 275,000, also found no relationship between socioeconomic level and delinquency.

Midwestern and Western children reported much the same behavior, except that Western boys and girls were far less likely to report drinking and deliberate property damage. (Short and Nye see a pattern of "somewhat more widespread" delinquency in the Midwestern high school samples; however, I cannot see this pattern.)

There is little difference in the patterns of self-reported offenses between sixteen and seventeen year olds. Small wonder. Since these are adjoining ages, members of one age group have a good chance of being closer in birthdate to someone in the other age group than to someone in the same age group (e.g., on January 1, someone born December 31 is farther from someone born on Christmas Day of the same year (although the same age) than someone born January 4 of the next year (although a year younger). The seventeen year olds are being asked to confess to the offenses of a sixteen year old, plus any others in the preceding year (or earlier, in the case of training school youths). In other words, the reporting period for a seventeen year old is generally the same as that of the sixteen year old. Among high school students, this problem might have been overcome by asking them to report only those offenses they had committed during the preceding year. However, that would have made the high schoolers incomparable to the training school youths who had been confined for at least part of the period.

Thus far, self-report research had established the following: Practically every American who had reached adolescence had committed a variety of offenses, boys and men more so than girls and women, and those who had been caught more so than those who had not. Short and Nye made a lot of the fact that the self-reported offenses scaled well. This meant that—separately by sex for high schoolers and for training school youths—there were seven to fifteen offenses that fell into a hierarchy: anyone who had committed a higher offense in the scale had probably committed all the lesser ones as well. Thus, the higher the offense confessed, the greater the variety of offenses probably committed. Getting scales as nearly perfect as Short and Nye's is a major achievement. It is an aesthetic triumph to be able to summarize the pattern of confessions about so many offenses in a short scale. But Short and Nye were unable to discover from the scales what made people more or less likely to commit or report offenses of any kind. All that Short and Nye reported new about the characteristics of delinquents was that males confess to having done more than females (which Wallerstein and Wyle, 1947, had already discovered) and that those who are caught confess to more offenses than those who have not (which Murphy et al., 1946, had already discovered).

Nye (1958) elaborated on the data in a book of his own. He emphasized the finding that officially biased differences between delinquents and nondelinquents were far greater than self-reported differences. For instance, while 19.7 percent of all boys in the sample came from broken homes, and a slightly higher percentage of "most delinquent" boys in the high school sample came from broken homes (23.6 percent), fully 48.1 percent of the training school boys came from broken homes. Nye inferred that this was an artifact of juvenile justice politics.

Nye found a small but consistent difference between the attachment to parents of self-reported delinquents and nondelinquents. He speculated that one of the reasons girls were less delinquent than boys was the greater attachment of girls to their parents. But the differences associated with attachment to parents were smaller than those found by Hirschi (1969), which—as we shall see later in this chapter—are still too small to inform policy.

A study by Reiss and Rhodes (1961) concluded that there is a strong relationship between socioeconomic level and delinquency. Most of the study is an analysis of juvenile court data—not self-report data—for Davidson County, Tennessee. As is common in U.S. studies of criminal and juvenile court data, lower-class persons get into more trouble, and more serious trouble, than other socioeconomic groups. In the self-report portion of their study, Reiss and Rhodes interviewed 158 white boys, ages ten to sixteen, plus the 2 others each boy named as his closest friends. Through a complex set of inferences—such as the usual type of offense committed by each boy and his associates, and the delinquency pattern—Reiss and Rhodes classified some boys as "career oriented delinquents" and some as "peer oriented delinquents." The researchers found 2 of the 158 boys to be career delinquents. Both of them had fathers with blue-collar rather than white-collar jobs. There were 9 peer oriented delinquents, 7 of them with blue-collar fathers and 2 with white-collar fathers. This does not exactly show a close relationship between socioeconomic level and delinquency, but it did seem to impress Reiss and Rhodes.

Even so, it was a bit absurd for other self-report researchers at the time to claim that there was *no* relationship of class to delinquency. After all, researchers who had compared official delinquents to hidden delinquents consistently reported that official delinquents committed more serious offenses, and more often, than those who merely self-reported delinquency. U.S. criminological research has always shown that official delinquents are disproportionately lower class. This was corroborated in self-report findings of the early 1960s. When self-report researchers had found delinquency *unrelated* to class, they had (a) looked for a relationship separately within groups composed exclusively of official delinquents or peer delinquents (like Short and Nye, 1958), and/or (b) had classified all those who had committed offenses two or three or more times as serious delinquents, overlooking the possibility that class might begin to make a difference only with youths with hundreds of offenses.

Nonetheless, there is good reason to believe that patterns of self-report data can differ substantially from official delinquency data patterns. Chambliss and Nagasawa (1969) showed this by comparing the proportions of different racial groups of high school boys who scored high on self-reporting (whites, 53 percent; blacks, 52 percent; Japanese, 36 percent) to the proportions of the sample who had been arrested (whites, 11 percent; blacks, 36 percent; Japanese, 2 percent) or who had been referred by teachers for discipline. If self-report data are given more credence as measures of criminality or delinquency, then findings based on official data are highly suspect.

We return to the relationship between status and delinquency in considering Gold's (1966) study, below.

EARLY EXPLANATIONS OF DELINQUENCY

Dentler and Monroe (1961), like Reiss and Rhodes, tried to discover what predisposes children to delinquency. They gave questionnaires to about 1,000 junior high school students in three Kansas communities (a middle-class suburb, a rural farm town, and a rural nonfarm town), asking them whether they had committed any of fourteen offenses. Of these offenses, five—theft offenses— scaled well. Girls and boys were combined in the same scale. Then, Dentler and Monroe analyzed which factors might discriminate those who had committed (a) none of the five offenses from (b) those who had committed either of the lower two offenses on the five-item scale from (c) those who had committed any of the three higher offenses. This was their way of asking: What makes boys and girls more or less likely to steal? As one would expect, boys were more likely to have stolen than girls, and the chances increased somewhat as children got older. Consistent with Short and Nye's findings, the father's occupation and education (i.e., socioeconomic level) made little difference. Nor did the community in which the child lived, or whether the child came from an intact or a broken family. It also made little difference whether the child had a working mother.

But at last, some intriguing relationships between other variables and self-reporting began to appear. For one, eldest children were less prone to report theft than others.

Caution is in order as we begin to find variables related to self-reported crime. Recall the discussion of false positives (type I error) and false negatives (type II error) from Chapter 3. The relationship between birth order and theft is substantial. According to Dentler and Monroe's figures, the probability of an eldest child's being a thief is .40, while the probability for other children is substantially larger—.53. However, if all but the eldest children were isolated or treated so as to keep them from stealing—that is, if 58 percent of the children in Dentler and Monroe's sample were isolated for special treatment—35 percent of the thieves would remain untreated (false negatives) and 47 percent of the children isolated or treated would not have been thieves if left alone (false positives).

Does knowing in which ways eldest children differ from others improve the choice of children for treatment? If, instead of isolating or treating all but the eldest children, a *random* selection of 58 percent of all the children had been removed, on the average, 42 percent of the thieves would have remained in the community, while 52 percent of those removed would not have been thieves anyway. There is not much to gain by being selective about who is treated as delinquent, is there?

As you go through this chapter, you can repeat this comparison of a random sample to a selective sample. In random selection, the average percentage of false positives (isolating or treating people unnecessarily) equals the percentage of nondelinquents in the whole community. The average percentage of false negatives in random selection (leaving delinquents at large and untreated) is equal to the total percentage of all persons left alone in the community. Thus, if a 10 percent random sample were removed from Dentler and Monroe's communities, the average level of false negatives would have been 90 percent of the thieves remaining at large, while the average level of false positives would still have been 52 percent removed unnecessarily. It is rare that any systematic selection of persons predicted to be due for special treatment will be much of an improvement on random selection. This shows how bad is our ability to predict individual behavior.

This particular predictor (and others evaluated in this chapter) is a single variable, in this case birth order. One might suppose that if a combination of variables were used as a predictor, predictions would become more precise. In most studies, including self-report studies, the data are not presented in a way that permits this hypothesis to be tested. The only study that I know of in which the hypothesis has been tested is Wenk and Emrich's (1972), whose results are analyzed in detail in Chapter 10. As we will see there (and as argued briefly in Chapter 3), the prediction of violent recidivism becomes *worse* as more variables are added to the prediction equation. Prediction error becomes compounded rather than being reduced. I infer that as a rule single variable predictions will be stronger than multiple variable predictions—that if the single variable predictions discussed in this chapter are weak, adding more variables would make them weaker still.

In Dentler and Monroe's data, the variables most strongly related to self-reported theft were children's ratings of their families and of how they got along there: whether the children thought they were treated equitably (weakly related); whether the children saw their own families as being poor, average, or superior; how obedient the children reported themselves to be in the family; and the children's reported confiding in their parents.

Obedience in the family was the variable most strongly related to self-reported theft. If the very disobedient children (8 percent of the sample) had been taken out of the communities as potential delinquents, 86 percent of the thieves would have been left (false negatives), while 42 percent of the children removed would not have been thieves if left in the community anyway (false positives). If we only wished to pick out the high-theft types—those scoring three through five on Dentler and Monroe's five-item scale —removing the 8 percent of children who were disobedient at home would have rid the community of only 73 percent of the *major* thieves (27 percent false negatives), but 74 percent of those removed would not have been major thieves (false positives).

The level of false negatives could have been reduced by removing all those not confiding in their fathers. Only 49 percent of the major thieves would have remained. However, 86 percent of the nonconfiding group would not have been major thieves if they had been left alone. Also, removing all those not confiding in their fathers would have affected 34 percent of all children in the community.

You can begin to see the hazards of using measures of criminality to pick out potential delinquents or criminals for isolation or treatment. The more potential thieves selected, the more people are selected unnecessarily. In predicting individual wrongdoing—except in cases of gross recidivism, to be considered in Chapter 10—mistakes are bound to overshadow successes.

SELF-REPORTING AS A MEASURE OF CRIME

Dentler and Monroe's self-report study revealed few differences in delinquency. Clark and Wenninger (1962), in contrast, found a pervasive difference through a range of offenses among youths of four Illinois communities. In each community, a sample of about 300 children in sixth through twelfth grades was given a questionnaire asking whether they had ever committed each of thirty-six offenses once, twice, three times, or four or more times. Although both boys and girls were polled, Clark and Wenninger do not mention the proportions of each sex in the samples, nor are their data analyzed by sex. Youths throughout an industrial city did not differ much from those in a specifically lower-class urban area, nor did those in an upper-class urban area differ from rural youths. But consistently higher percentages of the youths in the former two areas reported having committed offenses at all, once or twice, or three or more times than youths in the latter two communities. The only exceptions were looking at dirty pictures or books, being out at night when supposed to be home, tampering with someone's car, tractor, or bicycle, hanging around pool halls or bars or around trains or train stations. Less than 10 percent of youths in any community admitted to beating up innocent children ever, vandalizing property in a church or public building, and arson. Otherwise, it was not that the differences were dramatic; they were simply consistent. Socioeconomic status differences were insignificant within each community but significant across communities.

Clark and Wenninger's findings begin to suggest that the community itself can make more of a difference in the possibility of delinquency than can differences among youths within each community. Is it possible that Short and Nye (1958) and Dentler and Monroe (1961) failed to get much differences among communities simply because the communities they studied were so similar?

Self-report studies done in Scandinavia allow us to explore this possibility. In 1961, Christie et al. (1965) gave questionnaires to more than 3,500 young men (aged seventeen to twenty) in three Norwegian communities, asking whether they had ever committed each of twenty-five offenses. Elmhorn (1965) gave questionnaires the same year to 950 boys and girls, aged nine to fourteen, in Stockholm, asking whether they had ever committed each of twenty-one offenses. The Scandinavian offense descriptions differ markedly from the U.S. descriptions—which also differ strongly among themselves. Still, some rough comparisons are possible. The most striking difference between Scandinavian and U.S. respondents is for vandalism. Short and Nye's (1958) figures for ever committing vandalism are: Midwestern boys, 60.7 percent; Western boys, 44.8 percent; training school boys, 84.3 percent; Midwestern girls, 21.6 percent; Western girls, 13.6 percent; and training school girls, 65.4 percent. Among the older men in Christie et al.'s Norwegian sample, only 17.2 percent report ever having committed vandalism.

Then there is robbery. Again, Short and Nye have the U.S. data except for Western youths, whom they were not allowed to poll on this question. The figures for robbery are: Midwestern boys, 6.3 percent; Midwestern girls, 1.3 percent; training school boys, 67.7 percent; and training school girls, 36.7 percent. Just 1.8 percent of the older Norwegian men admitted to having robbed anyone, compared to 3 percent of the younger Swedish boys and girls.

Clark and Wenninger's (1962) figures for breaking and entering range from a low of 16 percent of lower-class urban youths to 42 percent of rural youths. In their questionnaire, the offense was worded as follows: "Gone into another person's house, a shed, or other building without their permission." It is possible that the lower-class urban youths interpreted this to include houses but not apartments. Otherwise, it is hard to imagine how only 16 percent of them reported breaking and entering, compared to 31 percent of industrial city youths. At any rate, only 11.9 percent of the older Norwegian men reported ever having broken and entered, while 6 percent of the younger Swedish boys and girls reported having broken into someone's slot machine, bookstall, shop, apartment, or house *and* taken something.

Scandinavians did report an amount of petty theft and pilfering comparable to American youths, but the figures suggest that Scandinavian youths are less inclined to vandalize private property, to steal, or to enter other people's premises without their permission. Just as, in preceding chapters, we have seen that the social climate people live in may strongly influence how much they report other people's crimes, Clark and Wenninger and a comparison of Scandinavian and U.S. findings suggest that environment can make a substantial difference in youthful self-reporting. It is intriguing to note that Christie et al. actually find self-reported crime, weighted by seriousness, more likely among those with *more* formal education and with *higher*-status parents. In Norwegian culture, Christie et al. surmise, questionnaires may be biased *against* the socially privileged. Differences in questions asked and in ages sample make such a conclusion a little tenuous at this point. However, the comparisons we can make suggest that self-report data can be used to measure crime rather than criminality—to pick out cultures that generate more crime or delinquency than others, rather than to pinpoint certain individuals.

A different kind of evidence on the role of social climate in delinquency is presented by Voss (1963). Using sixteen of Short and Nye's (1958) items, Voss gave a questionnaire to seventh graders in Honolulu—a total of 273 boys and 366 girls. Like Short and Nye, he scaled the responses on a six-item scale. Those reporting the fourth or a higher offense he labeled "most delinquent"; those reporting only the third, a lesser, or no offense on the scale he called "least delinquent." He then compared the percentages of those most delinquent within each of six ethnic groups, separating boys and girls into the categories: Caucasian, Hawaiian, Chinese, Japanese, Filipino, and "others." The ranking for boys was others, 63.2 percent most delinquent; Chinese, 45.8 percent; Caucasian, 44.1 percent; Hawaiian, 38.0 percent; Filipino, 27.8 percent; and Japanese, 26.6 percent. Among girls, Hawaiian, 57.6 percent were most delinquent; Caucasian, 50.0 percent; Filipino, 44.4 percent; Chinese, 29.8 percent; Japanese, 26.4 percent; and others, 23.1 percent. Note that Voss's data indicate wrongdoing to be about equally likely among girls and boys, a rare finding in delinquency research. (In Illinois, Berger and Simon [1974] also found fourteen- to eighteen-year-old girls more likely than boys to self-report a couple of categories of offenses. Black girls from intact homes reported three or more thefts more often than others, and black girls from broken homes were more likely than others to report drug use.) For Voss, the proportions of each ethnic group in official records ranked differently. For instance, Chinese boys were least likely to have gotten into trouble with the police, suggesting a distinction between a personal knowledge of wrongdoing and what becomes visible to the police. The Chinese might have recognized wrongdoing among themselves, but settled their own problems more than other cultural groups. At any rate, Voss's findings, too, suggest that one's culture can make a difference in how much wrongdoing one reports.

Another issue arose in self-report research. Questionnaires had seemed preferable to caseworkers' records in Murphy et al.'s (1946) study: (a) anonymous questionnaires might make people communicate more freely than someone who could identify them; (b) data on larger samples could be gathered more quickly and less expensively than in the Cambridge-Somerville Youth Study; and (c) youths could be surveyed by questionnaire who would never see a caseworker, especially middle-class and rural youths. But what if children could not read, or else misread, the questionnaire, or took advantage of their anonymity to lie or give silly responses, or made ambiguous responses that no one could detect? What if the respondents answered before searching their memories carefully? If the errors were randomly distributed, the relationships among variables found by researchers would not be affected. On the other hand, in Dentler and Monroe's study, it is plausible to suppose that those children who reported that they obeyed and confided in their parents felt a special need for adult approval, and hence were more likely to fail to report offenses they had actually committed. Also, the children who reported disobedience and distance from their parents might have been inclined to play a joke on the researchers and make up offenses they had not in fact committed.

THE HEYDAY OF INTERVIEWING

After Reiss and Rhodes (1961), criminologists began to feel that interviews would be a better means of collecting data than questionnaires. Interviewers might be able to establish rapport with respondents, clear up ambiguities in responses, pick out inconsistencies in responses and press respondents for honesty, and work with respondents to probe their memories. Accordingly, Erickson and Empey (1963) limited themselves to a small random sample with in-depth interviewing regarding twenty-two offenses. The sample consisted of 50 high school boys (aged fifteen to seventeen) who had never been to court, 30 who had been to court once, 50 offenders on probation, and 50 incarcerated offenders.

In their eagerness, the interviewers may have induced respondents to "confess" to far more than they actually had done. Let us remember that according to U.S. crime measurement specialists, self-reports are generally honest—*over*reporting is negligible—while *under*reporting is substantial. In any case, Erickson and Empey got record high reporting from the boys they interviewed. Murphy et al. (1946) had 323 violations reported for one boy in a Boston area slum. Erickson and Empey do not give their highest figure, but they do have a category for boys reporting 501 or more violations. It is true that their sample could have been as much as a year older than the boys in Murphy et al.'s, with more time to accumulate offenses. However, Erickson and Empey's sample was drawn from a staid, Mormon environment in Utah. This makes Erickson and Empey's high figures rather remarkable. In Short and Nye's (1958) study, 62.7 percent of Midwestern high school boys and 60.6 percent of Western high school boys reported ever having stolen things worth less than $2. Only 42 percent of Dentler and Monroe's (1961) Kansas boys reported this much or more theft. In Erickson and Empey's sample of boys who had never been to court, 92 percent reported having stolen things worth less than $2. It appears that interviewing is capable of bringing out the worst in children, although a restrained interviewer might get rates comparable to those from questionnaires and although it has been argued (as by Krohn et al., 1975) that relationships among variables may not change from one method to the other.

Erickson and Empey reiterated the finding that official delinquents self-reported having committed more offenses more often than those who had seldom, if ever, gotten into trouble with the law. Among persistent offenders who had been to court, 65 percent had been in trouble for the most serious offense they self-reported. In general, though, court records better reflected the most serious self-reported offense than patterns of self-reported offenses.

Self-reported truancy distinguished official nonoffenders and one-timers in court from those with longer official records, although 66 percent of the former reported having skipped school. Using truancy to predict delinquency might entail a great deal of type I and type II error. Interestingly, the strongest discriminant of official from unofficial delinquents was habitual smoking. In this case, habitual smoking may have resulted from the official label of delinquent rather than act as a cause or predictor of delinquency. Smoking is taboo among Mormons, and habitual smoking would mark a Utah resident as an outsider. Habitual smoking was most prevalent among youths in training schools, where many might have learned to smoke and where cigarettes were probably used as a kind of money. Utah children would probably not start smoking habitually until they knew that they were outsiders and had nothing to lose by defying Mormon doctrine. Note that in a survey like Erickson and Empey's, in which all the data are gathered at once, there is no way of telling which events preceded others. The data themselves give no indication of whether smoking or delinquency comes first.

Reiss and Rhodes (1964) published another study—again of white boys in Davidson, County, Tennessee, aged twelve through sixteen. The data were collected in 1957 in interviews of 299 boys and their two closest friends. Each boy was asked whether he had ever committed auto theft, theft of under $2, theft of more than $50, theft of from $2 to $50, assault, or vandalism. The idea was to see whether the likelihood of such delinquency depended on the actions of one's friends. Reiss and Rhodes classified each of the 299 boys as blue-collar or white-collar; career oriented delinquent or peer oriented delinquent; conforming nonachiever, nonconforming isolate, conforming achiever, conforming isolate, or hyperconformer.

Using Sutherland's (1924) theory of "differential association," which suggests that crime and conformity are learned from contact with others, Reiss and Rhodes supposed that delinquent boys especially should have delinquent friends and conforming boys especially have nondelinquent friends. Reiss and Rhodes failed to find support for this hypothesis in their data. They did find that blue-collar boys were more likely to report auto theft, theft over $50, and assault, and all boys theft of $2 to $50—one or more times—if their best friends reported having done the same. They also found that all boys were more likely to report vandalism or theft of less than $2 more than once if their best friends reported having done the same. Does this mean that delinquent boys attract one another as friends, or that one boy's delinquency encourages another's? This line of research has not been pursued. Again, type I and type II error might result in trying to apply Reiss and Rhodes's findings to treatment.

Following Reiss and Rhodes (1964), there has been much controversy over whether delinquency involves mainly a group or an individual. Vaz's (1965) findings for middle-class boys supported Reiss and Rhodes. Later self-report studies (by Lerman, 1967, 1968; Erickson, 1971; and Hindelang, 1971, 1976) have shown that group support is less critical for individual acts than had once been supposed, especially in studies relying on official data. These studies do not explain what *does* cause delinquency, but they suggest that we may know *less* than we thought about why youths do or do not commit offenses. At this point, no new ideas of what makes delinquents different from the rest of us, or about relative rates or trends in delinquency, have emerged.

After a certain kind of research has gotten well underway, researchers usually begin to measure its reliability and validity.

Clark and Tifft's (1966) study of "polygraph and interview validation of self-reported deviant behavior" was a sign that self-reporting research had come of age. These researchers gave 45 male University of Illinois students a questionnaire asking them whether they had committed each of thirty-five offenses since entering high school. The students were then invited back—for "interviews," they were told—in a few weeks. Of the group, 40 returned. They were then told that inaccuracies were likely on questionnaires administered in groups. They were asked to fill out the questionnaire again, this time to be followed by a polygraph (lie detector) test on the responses. Without their knowledge, the polygraph examiner had a record of their responses on the first questionnaire to compare to the second. When the examiner thought a student might be lying on the second questionnaire, he invited the student to change his response; almost invariably, the response was changed. The second questionnaire was then compared by Clark and Tifft to the first. When differences appeared, Clark and Tifft assumed that the second answers were correct. The researchers then calculated the rates at which the items had been under- and overreported on the first questionnaire. They concluded that three of the items had been responded to initially with complete accuracy: running away from home (admitted to by 5 students), attempted homicide (admitted to by no one), and attempted suicide (admitted to by 1 student). The least accurately reported item was one familiar to you from earlier research: whether the students had stolen something worth less than $2. In the end, 35 of the 40 students admitted to such petty theft (87.5 percent). Of the remaining 5 students, 2 had originally overreported the offense, and 25 of the 35 who finally reported it had not done so originally. Here is a hint of how Empey and Erickson (1963) might have gotten a greater percentage of reporting of this offense by interviewing than had Short and Nye (1958) or Dentler and Monroe (1961) by using questionnaires alone. Interviewers who cajole respondents can draw out a lot of otherwise unstated reports. The method of data collection can make the biggest difference in self-reporting rates.

The students also responded to the items on the "lie scale" of the Minnesota Multiphasic Personality Inventory (MMPI). This personality profile, which asks such questions as "Do you ever get angry at anyone?" is designed to see whether respondents will give socially desirable even if obviously untrue responses. For example, everyone gets angry at some people sometimes. However, a person concerned with giving socially desirable responses might deny this. None of the 40 students scored unusually high on the lie scale.

Nonetheless, within the range of normal behavior, self-report respondents might feel compelled to report offenses and respond accordingly even when they were not sure they had committed the offenses in question. Hardt and Bodine (1965) had suggested that bids for social approval could lead respondents to lie to researchers. And as Reiss (1977) has pointed out, human memory for specific events rapidly becomes unreliable. Reiss suggests interviewing persons to find out which offenses they have committed in the prior *week*, arguing that respondents' memory should be trusted no longer. Error in self-reporting need not simply be a matter of honesty, but of perception (was it theft when I took my little brother's toy and broke it?) and memory. As self-report respondents move from questionnaires to interviews, if they feel that researchers want them to report offenses, they may subconsciously reconstruct their pasts to include imagined offenses. They may feel a lessening of anxiety when they conjure up an offense to report. If this action makes a self-report respondent more relaxed in an interview, if conjuring up an offense breaks the tension, a polygraph examiner may believe that the respondent is finally telling the truth. This, as much as the fear of confessing to crime, could account for the large percentage of students who confessed in Clark and Tifft's final interviews.

It is possible that when interviewing yields more offenses than questionnaires, it is because interviewed respondents make up fictitious offenses. However, without independent, firsthand knowledge of day-to-day lives of respondents prior to their self-reports, there is no way of confirming this.

GOLD'S RESEARCH

Gold (1966) has made the most painstaking effort to overcome the problem of fabricating offenses. Gold began a career of self-report research with his Ph.D. dissertation, which showed that wealthy boys got into less trouble with the police than poor boys who committed the same offenses (Gold, 1963). The same data are reanalyzed in a later book (Gold, 1970), but the results were clear by 1966.

Gold's 1966 study describes the most sensitive, carefully conceived and executed self-report interview procedure thus far used by anyone. First, in 1960 (once data are collected, it can take a long time for a study to get into print), he drew a random sample of practically all boys and girls, aged thirteen through sixteen, in the Flint, Michigan, school district. Of the 600 youths initially selected, 36 refused to be interviewed and 42 had moved out of town; 522 were then interviewed.

Local college students were trained as interviewers. Each youth was interviewed by a college student of the same sex and race.

A letter was sent to the parents of those selected announcing a study of what teenagers do in their spare time. The interviewer then called and arranged to drive the youth to some public building, such as a community center or a firehouse, for the interview. Interviews were conducted outside the home so that confessions would remain confidential. Gold surmises that most of the refusals of interviews were by parents loath to have their children carted off by strangers.

At the interview, youths were told that the study was about hidden delinquent behavior; assured of anonymity and confidentiality; told that truthfulness was especially important; informed that this was a random sample; and then given a chance to withdraw from the study. One youth did so.

As a compromise between the threat of having to confess offenses in person and the obscurity of responses checked off on a questionnaire, each youth was handed a deck of fifty-one cards containing "a statement describing something a fellow or girl might have done, like the first one . . . ," which the interviewer read aloud. Most of the cards described delinquent acts (which would be crimes if committed by adults) or status offenses (for which only children could be locked up, like truancy), but some of the cards described approved activities, like getting on the school honor roll or helping charity drives. Youths were asked to set aside the cards describing things they had done in the last three years. If they admitted having done the act more than once, the interviewer asked only about the two most recent occurrences. At the end of the interview, each respondent was asked standard demographic questions about such things as parents' occupations. On the average, each interview took an hour and a half, with a range of from thirty-five minutes to two hours.

The researchers were especially sensitive to the possibility that the respondents would exaggerate. Gold acknowledges the difficulty of knowing when overreporting occurred. He argues only that it would have been difficult for youths to make up offenses and carry off the lie throughout detailed questioning by the interviewers. Incidents which the researchers believed too trivial or dubious for police action were not included. These included carrying a Boy Scout knife (a concealed weapon?), being in a minor fight on the playground (an assault?), or driving the family car around the block without permission (unauthorized use of a motor vehicle or auto theft?).

The researchers took additional steps to try to find out how much their respondents might be concealing. From teachers, youth workers, "other interested adults," and youths who had already served as informants, the researchers got the names of youths who might report on people they knew. From information gained from 40 of these informants, the researchers found 125 other youths who had been identified as wrongdoers. Each of them was assigned to a regular interviewer, who was not told that the youth was any different from those in the regular sample. The researchers scored these special youths as "truth tellers" if they either (a) recounted the incidents told by informants, (b) confessed to more recent offenses of the same kind, or (c) confessed to more serious offenses (in terms of a scale developed by Sellin and Wolfgang, 1964). The youths were classified as "questionables" if they confessed to similar, but not identical, offenses to those described by informants. The rest of the youths were classified as "concealers." Concealment did not vary appreciably by race, sex, or socioeconomic level. Of the 125 youths in the special sample, 72 percent (90) were classified as truth tellers, 11 percent (14) as questionables, and 17 percent (21) as concealers. Breaking and entering, property destruction, and carrying concealed weapons were found to be the offenses most often concealed by the 9 concealer boys, while the 12 concealer girls failed to confess to breaking and entering, property destruction, unauthorized use of a motor vehicle, gang fighting, miscellaneous theft, and fornication.

Gold acknowledged that this procedure tells nothing about concealment by youths who alone commit offenses in secret. The procedure has some other problems Gold did not mention. As stated earlier, the chief problem is the validity of the criterion. Who is to say whether the informants were exaggerating or concealing or misremembering offenses? Is it not possible that the informants, after being interviewed, informed on the researchers, too, so that the youths in the validation sample already knew what informants had said and kidded the researchers by corroborating this information?

Leslie T. Wilkins, of the State University of New York at Albany, has used a pertinent illustration of the problems of criterion validation in his research design class. The illustration is based on a study in which he participated some years ago. In a plant that sorts and crates eggs by size, the eggs pass down a conveyor belt one by one. Each egg passes over a scale. Each egg that weighs more than a certain amount (say, six ounces) is automatically moved to one side as a jumbo egg. The process is repeated further along the conveyor until only small eggs are left, and the sorting is completed. Someone in the plant has a bright idea. It is possible that there is error in the weighing and sorting. Some jumbo eggs might be getting by the first scale undiverted. The solution: to introduce a second scale just further on to catch the jumbo eggs that have gone by the first scale. Here is a neat system of criterion validation. The second scale checks the validity of the first.

Or does it?

When Wilkins and others checked the eggs sorted through this process, they found a small percentage of error in *both* scales. Fewer jumbo eggs slipped through, to be sure, but more of the smaller eggs were mistakenly diverted into the jumbo pile as well. In fact, introducing the second scale had made more of the smaller eggs end up in the jumbo pile than jumbos ending up elsewhere. The effect of the second scale was to cheat the consumer. Herein lies the fallacy of using a second measure to check the accuracy of the first. The second measure itself is susceptible to error. If the second measure is subject to biasing forces similar to the first, its error is apt to *compound* the error of the first measure. In Gold's study, there may be more error among his truth tellers than there is concealment and exaggeration among the respondents in the regular sample. His informants have made it harder, not easier, for him to gauge whether his respondents are telling the truth. Here is an instance in which a researcher has been *too* careful about collecting and interpreting data.

Gold paid no attention to what percentage of the respondents had committed each kind of offense. He did add up the overall frequency of offenses reported by each respondent, and also added up a seriousness score (the Sellin-Wolfgang, 1964, seriousness score for each offense, added to the seriousness scores for other offenses) for each respondent. He then considered whether status differences were related to the frequency or seriousness of self-reported offenses. Gold found that the lower the status of the boys (measured in terms of fathers' occupations), the more often and more seriously they reported offenses. He found no status differences in self-reporting among girls. (Again, boys reported more than girls. Gold had only lower-middle and low-status black youths in his sample. These two groups turned out practically the same as the white youths of the same sex, and Gold concentrated his analysis on status differences of white boys alone.)

In general, the relationship of seriousness scores to other variables was the same as that of frequency scores. Let us take a close look at Gold's frequency figures for the different status groups of white boys. In the high-status group of 28 boys (whose fathers were professionals, managers, etc.): 35 percent reported 0–1 offense; 29 percent 2–4 offenses; 25 percent 5–7 offenses; and 11 percent 8 or more offenses (average frequency—3.4). In the upper-middle-status group of 100 boys (whose fathers were skilled workers, foremen, white-collar workers, etc.): 20 percent reported 0–1 offense; 39 percent 2–4 offenses; 25 percent 5–7 offenses; and 16 percent 8 or more offenses (average frequency—4.3). In the lower-middle-status groups of 42 boys (whose fathers were semiskilled workers, etc.): 26 percent reported 0–1 offense; 36 percent 2–4 offenses; 19 percent 5–7 offenses; and another 19 percent 8 or more offenses (average frequency—4.4). In the low-status group of 25 boys (whose fathers were unskilled laborers, unemployed, etc.): 8

percent reported 0–1 offense; 16 percent 2–4 offenses; 40 percent 5–7 offenses; and 36 percent 8 offenses or more (average frequency—7.6).

Since only the two most recent offenses of each kind were reported for each boy, these figures favored boys who committed many of just one, two or three kinds of offenses over boys who committed occasional offenses of many kinds. For example, a boy who had reported 2 days of truancy, 2 thefts, 1 act of vandalism, 3 fights, and 1 illegal entry into a home would rate high in frequency—would have been classified as having committed 8 or more offenses—while a boy who had been prepared to admit 20 major thefts, but only that offense, would have been counted as having reported just 2 offenses. However, those who committed many offenses of one kind may also have committed many kinds of offenses. Also, unless there were reason to believe that only low-status boys committed many kinds of offenses but relatively few offenses of each kind, the distinction would probably make no difference in Gold's figures.

Note that the big difference in frequency of self-reporting is between low-status boys and the other three groups. Even lower-middle-status boys are not so different from high-status boys.

Since the sample was random, the proportions of boys in each status group were probably roughly the same as the proportions for all boys in Flint, aged thirteen to sixteen, at the time the survey was taken. Based on this assumption, we can estimate the type I and type II errors that would have resulted from successful treatment of low-status white boys (13 percent of the white boys) from Flint before 1961 as potential delinquents. For type I error, 8 percent of the low-status boys would have reported none or 1 offense if they had been left alone, 24 percent 4 or fewer offenses, and 64 percent less than 8 offenses. For type II error, treating the low-status boys would have left out 85 percent of the boys who reported more than 1 offense; 78 percent more than 4 offenses, and 75 percent more than 7 offenses. Would it have been worthwhile to treat 13 percent of the boys in order to lower the number of those committing 8 or more offenses by 25 percent (75 percent false negatives), even if only 36 percent of the low-status boys would have turned out to be 8-or-more-offenses types themselves if left alone (64 percent false positives)? Status does not discriminate the good boys from the bad too well, does it? (For those who are familiar with the measure of correlation called "Kendall's tau," the correlation coefficient of status to frequency of offenses is a mere $-.12$.)

Altogether, self-report findings suggest caution in associating criminality with socioeconomic level. Higher-status youths do a lot of bad things, too, and it is by no means certain that lower-status youths are more delinquent than middle-class or upper-class youths. On the other hand, Gold's data indicate that someone who has committed a lot of delinquent acts, will probably turn out to be lower class.

The relationship between delinquency and socioeconomic level, as reflected in self-report research, is like the relationship between illness and age. If you look at the ages of those who get sick most often and who fail to recover and die, they are most likely to be very young or very old. But people get sick often at all ages. In most cases, even the very young and the very old recover. Some middle-aged people who get sick die, too. Knowing that seriousness and rate of illness are related to age is not a very sound basis for planning how to prevent illness or how to treat illness once it occurs. If self-report findings are to be taken at face value, seriousness and rate of delinquency are related to socioeconomic level, but socioeconomic level is not a very sound basis for planning how to prevent or treat delinquency.

As to information that official offenders—and, to a lesser extent, self-report offenders—come disproportionately from low-status groups, even if the information had practical value, it would still have been a waste of considerable time, expense, and effort to gather a lot of data on the point. Once we realize that the definition of crime and criminality is essentially political (see Chapter 7, on reassessing what a measure of crime measures), we understand that such definitions in any society favor those with political and economic power. The more powerful can draw the legal line between what is and what is not considered crime. They are able to conceal incriminating information about themselves. They can marshal more resources to combat accusations of criminality. The more powerful can (and do) argue, even if convicted of crimes, that because they start from a higher social position, they have more to lose and are thus punished more than the poor by any particular sanction. Therefore, they deserve to be convicted of lesser offenses than the poor and to get lighter sentences in order to receive equal punishment. The more powerful can (and do) argue that the community cannot afford to lose their services by punishing them for crime as much as the poor are punished. The more powerful can (and do) argue that because they have more elaborate, stable, "respectable" community ties, they require less monitoring, supervision, rehabilitation, and less deterrence than do the poor. Who has a better chance of winning the political game of defining and controlling crime and criminality? Those with greater political power, of course. What confers political power? Wealth and status, of course. Therefore, is it not inevitable that crime and criminality would be associated with low socioeconomic status? Why need criminologists belabor the obvious? And since there is more room for political maneuvering in the official world of criminal justice than there is in private self-report questionnaires and interviews, why not take it for granted that the socioeconomic differences in self-reported criminality will be narrower and more confused than officially measured differences?

It may not be morally palatable that the poor suffer more than the rich by being labeled criminal or delinquent, but it is a practical inevitability. In a political revolution, the powerful may change places with the powerless, so that as in contemporary China, the new criminals come disproportionately from the formerly wealthy class (Pepinsky, 1978). This is a variant of the rule that current socioeconomic level is negatively related to criminality. Crime controllers may wish to reduce the ascription of criminality among all social groups, but not to obliterate the distinction between rich and poor unless and until everyone has equal wealth and social standing. And in this case, there could be no such thing as criminality anyway.

In subsequent research, Gold (in Gold and Reimer, 1975) is also the only self-report researcher (a) to have drawn a national sample to estimate self-reporting rates per year, and (b) to have sampled at different points in time to check for self-reporting trends. Gold and Reimer compare figures from two national surveys—one in 1967 and the other in 1972—for black and white boys and girls aged thirteen to sixteen. The data collection procedure was the same as in Gold's study in Flint, except that respondents were asked about only seventeen offenses and about the three, rather than two, most recent times they had committed each offense during the preceding three years. Gold and Reimer's general finding was that drug and alcohol offenses were up for both boys and girls in 1972, and that a number of other offenses, including theft and breaking and entering, were down for both sexes.

The study is disappointing. No doubt, selection of the sample, data collection, and data analysis were meticulous, time-consuming, and expensive, but the number of respondents was so small as to make 1967–1972 comparisons tenuous at best. The largest group in both samples consisted of white boys. There were 408 white boys in the 1967 sample and 270 in the 1972 sample. Gold and Reimer concluded that the difference in reporting alcohol fraud was highly significant. The average frequency of the offense per white boy in 1967 was just .05, while the 1972 average was .12. This meant that the offense was reported throughout the samples about 20 times in 1967 and 32 times in 1972. If there had been 13 more reports in 1967 and 11 fewer in 1972, the averages for the two years would have been equal. It is true that the difference in alcohol fraud found by Gold and Reimer is statistically highly significant. The .05/.12 difference was great enough to indicate that if 100 additional random samples of 408 white boys had been drawn from the same population as the original sample in 1967, 100 samples of 270 white boys drawn for 1972, and each 1967 sample paired with one of the 1972 samples, the odds were less than even that the average frequency in *any* of the 1972 samples would have been less than in its 1967 mate (i.e., in statistical jargon, the difference was significant at the .01 level). The problem was that the 1967 and 1972 samples were drawn from different populations. Although the sex, race, and age distributions in each sample were roughly the same as for the country as a whole, there was a lot of room for error in having a sample of 408, let alone a sample of 270, represent all white boys aged thirteen to sixteen in the United States. Since the 1967 and 1972 samples were drawn from different populations, similar differences in reporting alcohol fraud might have existed in the different areas in either 1967 or 1972. If the samples had been drawn from the same populations, they would still probably be unrepresentative of the country as a whole. Gold and Reimer's data cannot tell us whether alcohol fraud was more or less likely among American white boys aged thirteen to sixteen in 1972 than in 1967. The result may look plausible. It substantiates rumors that teenage drinking has increased in recent years. Nevertheless, Gold and Reimer's findings are not very strong evidence for this conclusion.

The differences in reported marijuana smoking are extreme— far more so than for any other offense. Among white boys, .04 episode (16 reports) of marijuana smoking *per capita* were reported in 1967, .42 (113 reports) in 1972. Black girls were the only group not to report much marijuana smoking in 1972—.09 *per capita* or just 3 reports among the 34 respondents. The differences for boys and for white girls are striking enough to tell us that marijuana smoking was probably more prevalent in 1972 than in 1967. Otherwise, like the differences in alcohol fraud, these differences are too small to generalize from with any confidence.

Recall, too, the problems of inferring trends from measures of less than three points in time. Even if one takes at face value the finding that, for example, thefts were lower in 1972 than in 1967, it could be that thefts had gone down before 1972 and were on the way up again. To be confident that a trend is moving in a certain direction, the trend line has to have a chance to move in both directions; this requires measures of at least three points in time.

Since Gold and Reimer's are the only self-report data for more than one point in time—and inadequate as these data are for inferring a trend—self-reporting trends are still unknown. One might hope to infer trends by comparing rates in different studies, but given differences in data collection and classification methods, such inferences would be tenuous. As with victim surveys, the expense of collecting self-report data probably means that good self-reporting trend data will not soon appear.

HIRSCHI'S STUDY

Hirschi (1969) has done a major book-length self-report study of the *Causes of Delinquency*. His sample was huge. In 1964, over 5,500 students in junior and senior high schools in Western Contra Costa County (outside San Francisco) were given an extensive three-part questionnaire, including self-report items. After the questionnaire had been readministered to 2,100 students who had answered it unsatisfactorily the first time, 4,077 completed questionnaires were obtained for analysis. However, Hirschi did not try to analyze the questionnaires from girls, and he decided that the questionnaires from black boys were too unreliable to use. Hence, most of his analysis was limited to data on 1,300 white boys in his sample.

The first section of the questionnaire asked about the student's attitudes toward school work, teachers, participation in school activities, school attendance, and discipline in school. Finally, item 67 began asking the student about having committed each of six offenses (a) never, (b) more than a year ago, (c) during the last year, or (d) during the last year and more than a year ago. (For much of the analysis, responses [b] and [c] were coded as *one delinquent act*, [d] as two or more acts.) The six offenses were: (1) theft of things worth less than $2, (2) theft of things worth from $2 to $50, (3) theft of things worth more than $50, (4) unauthorized use of a car, (5) vandalism, and (6) assaults on anyone other than brothers and sisters. Then came questions about trouble with the law, attitudes toward and beliefs about best friends, leisure activities, and a few questions about general attitudes. The section contained 144 questions in all. Students marked answers for this and other sections on IBM sheets marked with their names (although assurances of anonymity were given).

The second section of the questionnaire asked demographic questions about the student's family, such as parents' occupations, the student's religion, and where the student had grown up. Then came questions about the student's neighborhood, the student's employment history, and attitudes toward and aspirations for work and education. Again, there were a few concluding questions on general attitudes, with 144 questions in all.

The third section of the questionnaire asked about the student's home life, followed by items on the student's racial attitudes. There were 144 questions in this section, too.

School teachers administered the first round of the questionnaire. In at least one school, the questionnaire was given in three consecutive school periods; in most schools, on three consecutive days. The research staff administered the second round of the questionnaire to those who had not given satisfactory responses the first time.

Hirschi obtained two additional sets of data. Sheriff's and police records for the county were reviewed to find official records on boys in the sample. These records were used to show (a) that most boys who had been in trouble with the law reported similar offenses in the self-report questionnaire, and (b) that lower-status boys were discriminated against by the law more than was warranted by the self-reporting of boys from different status groups. Otherwise, comparisons of official and self-reported data were largely absent from the study; only self-reports were analyzed.

The other set of data was drawn from school records. It consisted of standardized test scores and grade point averages in selected subjects.

The results of the data analysis were fairly straightforward. The only significant variables in whether white boys reported none, one, or two more offenses were (a) school performance and (b) self-reported communication with parents. Now, if you were doing well in school, and your teacher gave you a questionnaire—with your name on the answer sheet—asking you how much you had broken the law, might you not figure that you had a lot to lose and should be especially discreet? If you were doing poorly in school, would you not be inclined to say to yourself, "What the heck, I'll show them," and report all you could (especially if your teacher were making you answer 432 questions and giving you nothing for it)? So much for bad school performance leading to delinquency.

Traditionally in the United States, schoolchildren have two sets of authority figures: parents and teachers. The same psychology that accounts for the inverse relationship Hirschi found between school performance and self-reported delinquency should also account for the inverse relationship he found between students in self-reporting of delinquency and their reporting of how well they got along with their parents. Those who have an investment in proclaiming good relationships were probably those who stood to lose by self-reporting delinquency; those who had nothing to lose by damning their parents probably had nothing to lose by exaggerating their delinquency. So much for poor communication with parents leading to delinquency.

Otherwise, the idea of answering such a long questionnaire is so irritating that frivolous responses and no meaningful results are likely. This Hirschi discovered.

Hirschi's analysis was meticulous for all the good it did, given the original data. This can happen when concern for gathering data outweighs concern for knowing the respondents.

Consider type I and type II error. The inverse relationship between communication with the father and self-reported delinquency was the strongest relationship in Hirschi's study. If the 9 percent of the white boys who reported no communication with fathers had been treated as potential delinquents, Hirschi's data show that 39 percent of them would have been unnecessarily treated, report having committing no offenses if left alone, and that 57 percent would have reported less than 2 offenses if left alone. Meanwhile, treatment of the noncommunicating white boys would have left 88 percent of those who reported one offense, and 79 percent of those who reported two or more offenses, to continue committing offenses without treatment.

Isolation of more boys—of the three lower (of five) categories of boys by intimacy of communication with fathers—would have been far more successful in treating those who would otherwise have been delinquent. The type II error (false negatives) would have been reduced so that less than 30 percent of those reporting at least one offense and less than 25 percent of those reporting two or more offenses would have remained untreated. This success in preventive treatment of "dangerous" white boys would have come at some cost. Only 22 percent of the white boys would have been left alone. As to type I error (false positives), of those treated, 53 percent would not have self-reported even one offense if left alone, and 79 percent would have reported fewer than two offenses.

The error tradeoff would have been worse if white boys had been diagnosed as potential delinquents and isolated because of poor performance rather than because of failure of intimacy with fathers. Lerman's (1968) figures for valuing stable grades are stronger than Hirschi's figures for school performance. According to Lerman's figures from interviews of 151 New York boys aged ten to thirteen, treating those who did not value stable grades— half the population—would have taken care of 64 percent of the delinquents, with 57 percent of those treated being false positives.

For the number of boys reporting 2 or more offenses among the 125 boys aged fourteen to nineteen in Lerman's sample, removing those who did not value stable grades—69 percent of the population—would have failed to cover 80 percent of those reporting 2 or more offenses, with type I error down to 40 percent.

Many of the problems with Hirschi's study are not peculiar to Hirschi; they are inherent in trying to figure out what makes delinquents and criminals "different." In any researcher's attempt to discriminate between good persons and bad, uncontrollable biases are bound to affect the data. Hirschi might have avoided the problem of students telling teachers what they were supposed to hear, only to replace it with some other problem, like that of official bias toward youths. And if any data on criminality are to be used, they will probably be so imprecise that using these data to select some individuals for especially good or bad treatment is morally questionable. Even the best explanations of why some persons become delinquent or criminal while others do not are of little demonstrable value.

Readers who are nevertheless interested in pursuing Hirschi's line of research should see Hindelang's (1973) replication of Hirschi's study using a rural sample from upstate New York. Hindelang's findings are about the same as Hirschi's, except that among rural respondents attitudes toward peers were unrelated to attitudes toward parents and favorable attitudes toward peers were positively correlated with self-reported delinquency.

ELLIOTT AND VOSS'S STUDY

Elliott and Voss's (1974) study is far more elaborate than Hirschi's. In 1963, these researchers studied over 2,000 students entering ninth grade in eight California schools and continued to collect data on them, year by year, for the next three years. The primary objective of the study was to determine the relationship between dropping out of school and delinquency.

In each of the four years, the students in the original sample were given questionnaires. Those who changed schools were given the questionnaire in the new school. Those who had dropped out of school were contacted by a trained interviewer, who administered a modified questionnaire. Students were allowed to refuse to answer the questionnaire. Five refused. Of the 2,658 students who completed the first questionnaire, 235 (9 percent) were missing by the fourth year. The lengthy questionnaire contained items gauging success or failure in career plans and school activities, asking whether students felt accepted at school and at home, asking students to confess wrongful acts (described below), asking about closeness to parents and about feelings toward school, gauging attachment to school activities and the community, checking on exposure to those who had committed delinquent acts or dropped out of school, checking on parent support, and asking about commitment to peers and to parents. Teachers were asked eight questions about each student. In the first year of the study, parents or guardians of 2,617 of the respondents were interviewed by interviewers matched to the respondents by sex and by ethnicity (Spanish-speaking, if applicable). School, police, court, and probation office records were obtained for respondents as well.

There were thirteen questions about wrongful acts. One of these, about drug use, was asked only in the fourth year. Ten of the remaining twelve items—about offenses ranging from stealing less than $2 to using force to get money from others—were used in constructing a scale. The items were classified as to whether they were misdemeanors or felonies under California law. Then, each student was given a "delinquency status" scale score of from 0 to 5; 0: no self-reported or official recorded delinquent act; 1: one or more nonserious self-reported acts (misdemeanors under California law); 2: one or more serious self-reported acts (felonies under California law); 3: one or more police contacts for alleged misdemeanors; 4: one or more police contacts for alleged felonies; 5: adjudicated delinquent in court.

Elliott and Voss attempted to determine what was related to delinquency status in two ways: (a) delinquency status as of ninth grade, and (b) delinquency status as it changed from year to year.

The surprises in Elliott and Voss's findings are especially notable. Dropping out of school was *negatively* related to both measures of delinquency. The relationship between success in school and either measure of delinquency was negligible. So was success at home for boys, and whether one felt lost or oriented at home.

So was exposure to delinquency. So was socioeconomic level. The most significant relationships: most strongly, as commitment to peers (*regardless* of whether they were delinquent) and as feelings of not knowing what was right or wrong in school increased, so did delinquent status; then, as commitment to parents declined, delinquent status increased. These findings applied equally to boys and girls, except that for girls, too, as feelings of success at home declined, delinquent status increased.

Elliott and Voss claim that commitment to peers, normlessness in school, and commitment to parents are predictive of delinquency. I doubt it. There is no way of computing type I and type II error from Elliott Voss's data as presented. They depict relationships among the variables by what are known as "correlation coefficients." A correlation coefficient of zero indicates no relationship between variables. A coefficient of 1.0 or −1.0 indicates that the value of one variable can be perfectly predicted from the other. The coefficient of 1.0 indicates that one variable increases by a fixed amount whenever the other does, while −1.0 indicates that one variable decreases by a fixed amount while the other increases by a fixed amount. Elliott and Voss's three "strongest predictors" correlate with delinquency status and its growth at levels of around .30 (or −.30 in the case of commitment to parents). Correlation coefficients this high are hard to get in studies of individual differences, but they are so low as to imply a *large* margin for type I and type II error in prediction. The Farrington (1973) study, discussed below, reports a correlation of .38 between self-reported delinquency at age fourteen to fifteen and boys' delinquency in the next three years. Farrington's correlation statistic is different, but his coefficient is roughly analogous to those reported by Elliott and Voss. Farrington's data do permit calculation of levels of type I and type II error, and as we shall see, the predictive value of his data is unimpressive.

Elliott and Voss do report one extremely high correlation each for boys and girls: that between delinquency status in the ninth grade and year-to-year gains in delinquency status thereafter. For boys, the coefficient is .94; for girls, .92. This supports a thesis of the chapter on recidivism—that by far the best predictor of future wrongful behavior is past wrongful behavior. This will be discussed further in Chapter 10.

THE CAMBRIDGE STUDY IN DELINQUENT DEVELOPMENT

This was a ten-year study of 411 boys who lived in a lower-class district of London. Farrington (1973), among others, reports on it. The boys were eight to nine years old when the data collection began in 1961. Of particular interest to us, at the ages of fourteen to fifteen, 405 of the boys were interviewed. As in Gold's (1966) study, they were asked to sort out cards according to how often they had committed each offense. There were 38 cards in all. For purposes of data analysis, the boys were given the number of the offenses to which they confessed ever having committed, from 0 to 38, as a delinquency score. The scores actually ranged as high as 31. Records were obtained of boys who were official delinquents by the time they were interviewed. These 47 boys were eliminated from a follow-up check on which of 358 of the boys were adjudicated delinquent in the next three years (51).

The first set of official records enabled the researchers to run a criterion check of how honest the self-reporting had been. Farrington's figures raise no new issues about whether criterion checks establish that self-reporting is honest and true, except that Blackmore (1974) rechecked the records and argued that the concordance between official records and the Cambridge study's self-reporting was not as high as the Cambridge researchers (Gibson et al., 1970) had claimed. (Remember the eggs!)

It was mentioned above that Farrington's (biserial) correlation between the self-reported delinquency score and official delinquency in the subsequent three years was .38. This indicated to Farrington that self-reported delinquency was predictive of boys' getting into trouble with the law. But to illustrate the tradeoff in type I and type II error: Farrington's data suggest that even if all boys reporting 10 or more of the 38 offenses (110—30.7 percent—of the 358 boys in the follow-up sample) had received successful preventive treatment, 74.5 percent of the adjudications of delinquency would have taken place among the boys left alone (false negatives), while 45.1 percent of the boys treated would never have been adjudicated delinquent if left untreated (false positives).

Farrington also reported some characteristics that distinguished the 25 percent of the 405 boys with higher delinquency scores (those admitting at least 13 of the 38 acts) from the rest. He reported that four characteristics distinguished these exceptionally delinquent boys from the others at a high level of statistical significance. One characteristic was whether the boy's parents had been separated. However, two-thirds of the boys with separated parents had delinquency scores below 13 (type I prediction error), and more than two-thirds of those with scores at 13 or above had both parents living together (type II prediction error). Another distinguishing feature of high-level self-reported delinquents was that they had criminal parents. However, just over two-thirds of boys with criminal parents scored below 13 on the delinquency scale, and just over two-thirds of the high-level delinquents had no criminal parents. Poorly supervised children were especially likely to score 13 or above, but just over two-thirds of these children scored less than 13 and 73.3 percent of those who scored 13 or higher were well supervised. Boys with I.Q. scores of 90 or below were "characteristically" delinquent at a level of 13 or above. However, 68.9 percent of the low I.Q. boys scored below 13 on the delinquency scale, and among high-level delinquents, 66.0 percent had I.Q.'s above 90.

Again, the point is not that Farrington's research is bad. Rather, his findings reflect problems of research that tries to figure out what makes some people in a community more prone than others to crime or delinquency. In Chapter 11, I will argue that these problems are unsurmountable.

TITTLE'S RESEARCH

In 1972, Tittle (1977; Tittle and Villemez, 1977) collected 1,993 self-report hour-long interviews from 57 percent of a randomly drawn sample of members of households, aged 15 and above, in Iowa, New Jersey, and Oregon. It is interesting to compare their data to Wallerstein and Wyle's (1947), the only other interstate data for a range of offenses committed by adults. Tittle's respondents were asked whether, during the past five years, they had stolen something worth at least $5.00 or more than $50.00, had smoked marijuana, had gambled illegally, had hurt anyone on purpose, had lied to a sweetheart had cheated on their income tax, or had failed to stand during the playing of the national anthem. Forty-seven percent admitted to having lied to a sweetheart, 32 percent to having gambled illegally, 21 percent to having stolen something worth about $5, and only 7 percent to having stolen something worth about $50.

In one analysis of his data, Tittle (1977) finds little indication that the socioeconomic level of respondents is related to their criminality—another entry into this longstanding controversy. Tittle also finds a slightly greater tendency for those who have risen above their parents' socioeconomic level to self-report offenses than for those whose level remains the same, with somewhat less self-reporting still for those whose level has declined between generations. As Tittle acknowledges, the difference that this "intergenerational mobility" makes is not very great.

In the same survey, Tittle collected data on respondents' estimates of the likelihood that they would commit the same "tomorrow if they had an extremely strong desire or need to do so." In his second analysis (Tittle and Villemez, 1977), he found that some types of fear of sanction—fear of loss of respect more than of legal sanctions—as well as ratings of how desirable the acts would be to commit, plus ratings of how morally offensive respondents considered the acts to be, were related to whether respondents reported any likelihood that they would commit the acts in the future. Tittle is to be commended for being one of the few researchers who has tried to use measures of *future* criminality to test predictions. (Farrington, 1973, above, who collected data from respondents over time, is another.) But it is tenuous to assume that respondents will in fact do what they say they will do. Leslie T. Wilkins tells of having done a study in England in which an attempt was made to predict who would donate blood during the coming year. The strongest predictor was indeed announced intention to donate blood, but the prediction was negative (a correlation of −.60 between intention and donation). That is, those who made the biggest display of their willingness to give blood were those least likely to give blood, while those who in fact gave blood apparently felt no need to announce their intention to do so. And so, from Tittle's data, it is hard to tell anything about who in fact would commit offenses in the future.

HARDT AND PETERSON-HARDT

A study has recently appeared which gives a fitting climax to this review of self-report research. Its title is, "On determining the quality of the delinquency self-report method" (Hardt and Peterson-Hardt, 1977). Ironically, after the increased popularity of interviewing, and after arguments that the choice between interviews and questionnaires is trivial, Hardt and Peterson-Hardt argue that questionnaires are preferable. They give respondents a greater sense of anonymity and promote greater candor than interviews. If Hardt and Peterson-Hardt's premise is that respondents would report more offenses in questionnaires than in interviews, what of the relatively high rates of reporting sometimes obtained in interviews? Whatever the relative merits of questionnaires and interviews the history of this controversy illustrates a fact of scientific life: a truth that is rejected as obsolete may later supersede its successor. The growth of scientific wisdom is not a simple evolution from inferior to superior knowledge. Today's old-fashioned stupidity may well emerge as tomorrow's highest wisdom. Whatever ideas a criminologist or any scientist rejects may well return. And so, the criminologist should keep an open mind to the possibility that whatever is claimed to be right or true today will seem wrong or false tomorrow.

Hardt and Peterson-Hardt gave questionnaires to 914 boys in seventh through ninth grades in nine sections of a Mid-Atlantic U.S. city of 250,000. (Some researchers prefer to keep the names of their locations secret, figuring that this gives needed protection to respondents.) They asked the boys whether they had committed any of 25 offenses during the preceding week, preceding year, ever, or never. It would have been interesting to see figures for the preceding week, but apparently the numbers were so low that the researchers failed to report them.

As the title of their study indicates, Hardt and Peterson-Hardt were more concerned with issues of method than of substance. Accordingly, their findings add nothing significant to our substantive knowledge. As expected, status is slightly related to self-reported delinquency, self-reported delinquency is related to official delinquency, and number of self-reported delinquent friends is related to official delinquency. The findings do say a lot more about the accuracy of self-report data from questionnaires than about self-reported delinquency itself.

Respondents were asked whether they had been warned or ticketed by the police. Their responses were checked against data in the county juvenile offender registry. Of the 190 boys who reported having been ticketed, 56 (29 percent) had no official record. Of the 672 boys who reported never having been ticketed, 39 had a record (6 percent). By this criterion, overreporting official delinquency exceeded underreporting. This datum makes this study unique.

Of course, this attempt at criterion validation of self-reports, like Gold's (1966) use of informants, has the problems of compounding error inherent in using an extra scale. For instance, many official records might have gotten lost before the researchers looked for them.

Hardt and Peterson-Hardt used a set of five social desirability, or lie scale, items as Clark and Tifft (1966) had done. By this criterion, there was little indication of misreporting.

One interesting indication of some accuracy in the boys' recall was their reporting of theft from parking meters. Just over a year before the questionnaires were administered, the city had installed theft-proof parking meters. The number of those reporting theft from parking meters during the preceding year was just 28 percent of the number reporting parking meter theft more than a year previously. By contrast, the number reporting theft from other coin machines during the preceding year was 67 percent as much as those reporting having committed the same offense more than a year before. This is an interesting example of construct validation (see Chapter 3).

The researchers concluded that self-report data obtained from questionnaires are highly valid indicators of who has committed how many offenses. On the other hand, in a review of issues of validity in self-report research, Van Alstyne and Laub (1977) end on a note of skepticism. By now, you are in a position to arrive at your own judgment.

EVALUATING CHANCES OF CONTROLLING
SELF-REPORTING RATES

The conclusions reached by Scandinavian self-report researchers are thought provoking. Christie et al. (1965: 115) conclude that, for the sake of social equality, perhaps lower-status persons should be less subject to official control and more subject to informal response to wrongdoing. Elmhorn (1965: 146) says:

Measures aimed at reducing the number of offenses and the damage thereby caused to the public should, for example, not be limited to the most serious category of juvenile delinquents; to a certain extent they should also be adapted to the average of your people. At the same time isolated offenses and individual offenders should be judged and dealt with by authorities and private persons in the context of what is normal, i.e. of what is average for the age group in question, not on the empirically false premise that crime is an abnormal rarity among children. Despite certain difficulties in placing the results of the inquiry in wider contexts, one may perhaps say that they have nevertheless made it possible to regard the delinquency of young people in a more realistic way than before, which should be an advantage both from the point of view of effectiveness and from that of justice.

Is this not the lesson of self-report research for crime control planners and criminologists? Self-report findings have made it harder, not easier, to maintain that criminals and delinquents differ from the rest of us. U.S. self-report data come closer to establishing that *all* Americans are crooked than to distinguishing certain characteristics about some people who often commit serious offenses. If we try to use self-report data to infer criminality, and then apply these data to predicting who the crooks in our society will be, we end up making embarrassing errors. The strangest feature of U.S. self-report research is that so many of the researchers devote much of their effort to isolating who the criminals and delinquents are and what makes them special—when, above all, the data indicate that Americans who are looking for criminals and delinquents might as well look at themselves.

How could self-reporting rates be changed? Not by trying to pick out individual criminals and delinquents for special treatment. Self-report data suggest two approaches to controlling self-reporting rates. One approach is to change the social context in which self-reporting occurs. The other approach is to change the method of data collection.

Self-report data do not strengthen the prospect of controlling self-reporting rates by changing the respondent's culture. The differences among communities in Clark and Wenninger's (1962) and Voss's (1963) studies are not great, nor are differences between U.S. and Scandinavian self-reporting rates. One could surmise that U.S. self-reporting rates would drop if crime rates were reduced by using the strategies discussed in Chapters 4 through 7. But it is also possible that persons across cultures with different levels of crime are still equally likely to self-report crime. If that were the case, we would have to get used to unchanged self-reporting rates regardless of the social order.

On the other hand, there is strong reason to believe that self-reporting rates could be changed by changing the data collection methods. For instance, Empey and Erickson's (1963) rates could probably have been lowered substantially by switching from interviews to questionnaires. The ultimate way to reduce self-reported crime, of course, is to refrain from collecting self-report data by *any* means. The idea is outrageous only if self-report data have more worthwhile applications than no data. To date, self-report data indicate little such usefulness.

SIDE EFFECTS OF CONTROLLING SELF-REPORTING RATES

Although some professional criminologists might be put out of work, the effects of controlling self-reporting rates would otherwise be like those of controlling incarceration and other crime rates. In the U.S., reduced self-reporting rates would represent a lessening preoccupation with criminality. Americans would be able to take it for granted that persons convicted of crimes were despicable without having to explain what made them that way. As crime rates dropped, and fewer people were charged with more serious crimes, Americans would lose interest in criminality and self-reporting rates would fall away.

POLITICAL CONSIDERATIONS

There are three ways for those at the top of the social hierarchy to rationalize their position. One is the authority of tradition (Weber, 1947, written just before Weber's death in 1920, published in successive chapters over several years thereafter), which Americans lack. Another is the threat of extinction by an outside enemy (including nature), which is unconvincing to most Americans. The third is the scientific premise that some people are better, more deserving of wealth and power, than others. In the U.S., the desire of powerful people to extend the criminal justice system to lesser folk rests on this premise. If the premise is to be legitimated, it must be supported by those who have the authority to speak on behalf of science. In the field of U.S. criminology, as long as high social status is to be defended, criminologists need to be paid to figure out what makes criminals and delinquents deserve lower status and less wealth. This research objective, as we have seen, precludes control of self-reporting rates.

If U.S. self-reporting rates are brought under control, Americans will believe either that nature or another outside enemy is on the verge of destroying them, that being at high socioeconomic level has become indefensible, or that high social economic level is a traditional birthright. Given the political options, most Americans may remain content with uncontrolled self-reporting rates.

ETHICAL ISSUES

Let us consider one issue here: Is it better to risk error in discriminating among individuals in a society? Or to risk error in changing a society for everyone?

Americans prefer discrimination among individuals to social change that might affect all Americans, for better or worse. This practice is so strongly ingrained that even Rawls's (1971) revolutionary work on philosophy of justice focuses on individual members of a society rather than the society itself.

Consider the crime control stategies discussed in Chapter 7. If those strategies succeeded in controlling U.S. crime rates, all

Americans would be equally susceptible (a) to having their chances of mobility reduced, (b) to having chances of being victimized by crime reduced, (c) to acting more bigoted and being more discriminated against, and (d) to having less official protection. Strategies for controlling rates of *crime* fail to apply knowledge of individual differences in criminality. If such a strategy goes awry, everyone is equally threatened. This means that there is more risk in implementing a strategy to control crime rates than to control rates of criminality. If the former strategy fails, everyone may suffer. If the latter strategy fails, those treated as criminals may suffer most, while the risk of change to others is minimized.

This chapter has stressed the risk of type I and type II error in trying to give special treatment to those thought to have criminal characteristics. One alternative is to ignore the control of crime and criminality so that the risks of change are minimized. The other is to subject every member of the society equally to the risks of social change. If everyone is equally at risk, then at least the bad effects of the change will not work injustices among individuals any more than a lightening bolt strikes some people rather than others unjustly.

On the other hand, there is something to be gained from limiting the risks of social change. If, despite the great type I error necessary to control type II error in isolating potential criminals, we continue to believe that special treatment for potential criminals is preferable to extending risks of crime control to the whole society, then we will have a moral preference for basing crime control strategies on identifying the criminals among us. As is clear by now, I reject this alternative. But the moral choice of whether to try to find, explain, and control criminality remains a personal one.

CONCLUSION

Thus far, we have dwelled upon issues of criminality so that the people involved might be specially controlled. One possibility for controlling criminality remains: Trying to keep official criminals out of legal trouble in the future. This issue—of the possibilities of controlling recidivism—is the subject of the next chapter.

REFERENCES

Akers, Ronald L. 1964. "Socio-economic status and delinquent behavior: a retest." *Journal of Research in Crime and Delinquency* 1 (January): 38–46.

Berger, Alan S., and William Simon. 1974. "Black families and the Moynihan Report: a research evaluation." *Social Problems* 22 (December): 145–161.

Blackmore, John. 1974. "The relationship between self-reported delinquency and official convictions amongst adolescent boys." *British Journal of Criminology* 14 (January): 38–46.

Chambliss, William, and Richard D. Nagasawa. 1969. "On the validity of official statistics: a comparison of white, black, and Japanese high school boys." *Journal of Research in Crime and Delinquency* 6 (January): 71–77.

Christie, Nils, Johannes Andenaes, and Sigurd Skirbekk. 1965. "A study of self-reported crime." Vol. 1, pp. 86–116, in Karl O. Christiansen (ed.), *Scandinavian Studies in Criminology*. South Hackensack, N.J.: Fred B. Rothman.

Clark, John P., and Larry L. Tifft. 1966. "Polygraph and interview validation of self-reported deviant behavior." *American Sociological Review* 37 (August): 516–523.

Clark, John P., and Eugene P. Wenninger. 1962. "Socio-economic class and area as correlates of illegal behavior among juveniles." *American Sociological Review* 27 (December): 826–834.

Dentler, Robert A., and Lawrence J. Monroe. 1961. "Social correlates of early adolescent theft." *American Sociological Review* 26 (October): 733–743.

Elliott, Delbert S., and Harwin L. Voss. 1974. *Delinquency and Dropout.* Lexington, Mass.: Lexington Books.

Elmhorn, Kerstin. 1965. "Study in self-reported delinquency among schoolchildren in Stockholm." Vol. 1, pp. 117–146, in Karl O. Christiansen (ed.), *Scandinavian Studies in Criminology*. South Hackensack, N.J.: Fred B. Rothman.

Erickson, Maynard L. 1971. "The group context of delinquent behavior." *Social Problems* 19 (Summer): 114–129.

Erickson, Maynard L., and Lamar T. Empey. 1963. "Court records, undetected delinquency and decision-making." *Journal of Criminal Law, Criminology, and Police Science* 54 (December): 456–469.

Farrington, David P. 1973. "Self-reports of deviant behavior: Predictive or stable?" *Journal of Criminal Law and Criminology* 64 (March): 99–110.

Gibson, H. B., Sylvia Morrison, and Donald J. West. 1970. "The confession of known offenses in response to a self-reported delinquency schedule." *British Journal of Criminology* 10 (November): 277–280.

Gold, Martin. 1963. *Status Forces in Delinquent Boys.* Ann Arbor, Mich.: University of Michigan, Institute for Social Research.

———. 1966. "Undetected delinquent behavior." *Journal of Research in Crime and Delinquency* 3 (January): 27–46.

———. 1970. *Delinquent Behavior in an American City.* Belmont, Calif.: Brooks/Cole.

———, and David J. Reimer. 1975. "Changing patterns of delinquent behavior among Americans 13 through 16 years old: 1967–1972." *Crime and Delinquency Literature* (December): 483–517.

Hardt, Robert H., and George E. Bodine. 1965. *Development of Self-Report Instruments in Delinquency Research: A Conference Report.* Syracuse, N.Y.: Syracuse University Youth Development Center.

Hardt, Robert H., and Sandra Peterson-Hardt. 1977. "On determining the quality of the delinquency self-report method." *Journal of Research in Crime and Delinquency* 14 (July): 247–261.

Hindelang, Michael J. 1971. "The social versus solitary nature of delinquent involvements." *British Journal of Criminology* 11 (April): 167–175.

———. 1973. "Causes of delinquency: a partial replication and extension." *Social Problems* 20 (Spring): 471–487.

———. 1976. "With a little help from their friends: group participation in reported delinquent behavior." *British Journal of Criminology* 16 (April): 109–125.

Hirschi, Travis. 1969. *Causes of Delinquency.* Berkeley, Calif.: University of California Press.

Jensen, Gary J., and Raymond Eve. 1976. "Sex differences in delinquency: an examination of popular social explanations." *Criminology* 13 (February): 427–448.

Krohn, Marvin, Gordon P. Waldo, and Theodore G. Chiricos. 1975. "Self-reported delinquency: a comparison of structured interviews and self-administered checklists." *Journal of Criminal Law and Criminology* 65 (December): 545–553.

Lerman, Paul. 1967. "Gangs, networks, and subcultural delinquency." *American Journal of Sociology* 73 (July): 63–83.

———. 1968. "Individual values, peer values, and subcultural delinquency." *American Sociological Review* 33 (April): 219–235.

Murphy, Fred J., Mary M. Shirley, and Helen L. Witmer. 1946. "The incidence of hidden delinquency." *American Journal of Orthopsychiatry* 16 (October): 686–696.

Nye, F. Ivan. 1958. *Family Relationships and Delinquent Behavior.* New York: Wiley.

Pepinsky, Harold E. 1978. "On the correct handling of contradictions." *Juris Doctor* 8 (April): 16–23.

Porterfield, Austin L. 1943. "Delinquency and its outcome in court and college." *American Journal of Sociology* 49 (November): 199–208.

————. 1946. *Youth in Trouble*. Fort Worth, Tex.: Leo Potisham Foundation.

Rawls, John. 1971. *A Theory of Justice*. Cambridge, Mass.: Harvard University Press.

Reiss, Albert J. Jr. 1964. "An empirical test of differential association theory." *Journal of Research in Crime and Delinquency* 1 (January): 5–18.

————. 1977. Comments on papers presented in session on "The Validation of Self-Report Measures of Illegal Behavior," American Society of Criminology Meeting, Atlanta (November 19).

————, and Albert Lewis Rhodes. 1961. "The distribution of juvenile delinquency in the social class structure." *American Sociological Review* 26 (October): 720–732.

Robison, Sophia M. 1936. *Can Delinquency Be Measured?* New York: Columbia University Press.

Sellin, Thorsten. 1938. *Culture Conflict and Crime*. New York: Russell Sage.

————, and Marvin E. Wolfgang. 1964. *The Measurement of Delinquency*. New York: Wiley.

Short, James F. Jr., and F. Ivan Nye. 1958. "Extent of unrecorded juvenile delinquency: tentative conclusions." *Journal of Criminal Law, Criminology, and Police Science* 49 (December): 296–302.

Sutherland, Edwin H. 1924. *Criminology*. Philadelphia: Lippincott.

————. 1940. "Is 'white-collar crime' crime?" *American Sociological Review* 5 (February): 1–12.

Tannenbaum, Frank. 1938. *Crime and the Community*. Boston: Ginn.

Tittle, Charles R. 1977. "Sanction fear and the maintenance of social order." *Social Forces* 55 (March): 579–596.

————, and Wayne J. Villemez. 1977. "Social class and criminality." *Social Forces* 56 (December): 474–502.

Van Alstyne, David H., and John H. Laub. 1977. "The validity of self-reported delinquency: a review." Paper presented at Session on "The Validation of Self-Report Measures of Illegal Behavior," American Society of Criminology Meeting, Atlanta (November 19).

Vaz, Edmund W. 1965. "Middle-class adolescents: self-reported delinquency and youth culture activities." *Canadian Review of Sociology and Anthropology* 2 (February): 52–70.

Voss, Harwin L. 1963. "Ethnic differentials in delinquency in Honolulu." *Journal of Criminal Law, Criminology, and Police Science* 54 (September): 322–327.

Wallerstein, James S., and Clement, J. Wyle. 1947. "Our law-abiding lawbreakers." *Probation* (March-April): 107–112, 118.

Weber, Max (Talcott Parsons, ed. and trans.). 1947. *The Theory of Social and Economic Organization*. New York: Free Press.

Wenk, Ernst A., and Robert L. Emrich. 1972. "Assaultive youth: an exploratory study of the assaultive experience and assaultive potential of California Youth Authority wards." *Journal of Research in Crime and Delinquency* 9 (July): 171–196.

FOOD FOR THOUGHT

1. How would you measure how many offenses a person has committed?

2. By what criterion should a person be called a delinquent? A criminal?

3. Should persons ever be specially treated for delinquent or criminal tendencies on any basis other than offenses they have been found guilty of committing? If no, why not? If yes, upon what basis?

4. Using self-reporting measures, why might rich people be more criminal than the poor in Norway and less criminal than the poor in the United States?

5. What do you think makes males more likely than females to report—and be reported for—committing offenses?

6. For the sake of crime control, is it more moral to use strategies that distinguish delinquents/criminals from others, or to use strategies that are equally likely to affect all members of the society?

CHAPTER TEN

Should Recidivism Rates Be Controlled?

We come now to one last approach in attempting to control criminality—that of trying to keep delinquents and criminals from getting into trouble with the law again.

Unlike the literature on self-reporting, that on diagnosing, predicting, and treating recidivism is extensive. But the history of recidivism is one of frustration. As recent writers like Wilkins (1969), the American Friends Service Committee's (1971) research group, Gottfredson (1975), and Von Hirsch (1976) have recognized: to this day, (a) little is known about what makes people more or less likely to recidivate, and (b) the range of alternatives for dealing with recidivism remains limited. Since recidivism literature has been reviewed many times, as by the above authors, and since the study of recidivism has yielded so little, the recidivism literature will not be reviewed here. The details can readily be found in other sources. Here, instead, I will concentrate on summarizing the limitations on attempts to control recidivism.

MEASURING RECIDIVISM RATE NUMERATORS

Recidivism rate numerators are official measures of personal failure—of ways that offenders have gotten into more trouble with the law. Issues raised by measuring these failures concern who, what, when, and where to measure.

One of the categories of recidivism numerators is that of re-arrest. Whose rearrest should be measured? The sex of those meas-ured has not been at issue. Apparently, recidivism rates are the one measure of criminality in which the sex of the offender does not affect the results. But the *age* of those measured *can* be impor-tant. As Wilkins (1969: 56) has reported, recidivism studies con-cur in the finding that those who get into trouble with the law early in their lives are somewhat more likely to recidivate than older persons. While some studies of rearrest include data for ju-veniles (see Wolfgang et al., 1972), others omit them (see Califor-nia Bureau of Criminal Statistics, 1969: 111–113). One could well argue for developing separate rearrest numerators for different age groups, as permitted by Wolfgang et al.'s (1972) data.

The issue of which offenses to include in rearrest numerators is trickier. As discussed in Chapter 4, there are many ways to clas-sify offenses by seriousness, and researchers may only be inter-ested in more serious recidivism. This was the case in Waller's (1974) Canadian study of rearrest for indictable offenses only. On the other hand, if, like Belkin et al. (1973), one is interested in modeling trends in complete sets of arrest figures like those pub-lished by the F.B.I. (annual), rearrest numerators will include mi-nor offenses, too.

How many prior offenses should recidivists have before one begins to count their rearrests? As Wilkins (1969: 41) has re-ported, some people believe that recidivism should not begin to count as such before the second or third or even subsequent offense has occurred.

Recidivism rates consist of so-called "time series data." That is, at least two measures are taken in each case in the rate figure, one following the other. For each case in rearrest rate figures, re-arrest in the numerator will correspond to an earlier arrest in the denominator. Among cases of arrest included in the denominator, how long a subsequent period should be searched for rearrests? Obviously, the longer the period allowed, the higher the rearrest rate will be. Among recidivism rate numerators, though, there does not appear to be a long spread of rearrests in most cases (at least, not in the United States), since the average rearrest rate is so high. Belkin et al. (1973) estimated that for U.S. rearrests of all ages for all offenses, 86.5 percent of those arrested would be rearrested within half a year and 88.5 percent rearrested within a year and a half.

The spread of reconvictions appears to be far longer than that of rearrests. Among all those convicted of offenses in the London Metropolitan Police District in March-April 1957, about 25 percent were reconvicted within a year, 35 percent within two years, 40 percent within three years, almost 50 percent within four years, and just over 50 percent within five years (British Home Office Statistical Research Unit, 1964: 43). The lower probability of reconviction and the greater probability of incarceration seemingly account for the greater time lag in reconviction.

On the other hand, how long should one wait *before* starting to count rearrests? The situation is ambiguous. Suppose two persons are rearrested twelve months after an initial arrest. One has been in jail during six of these months, and the other on the streets and on probation for nine months. Who has recidivated earlier: the offender rearrested three months after treatment ended or the offender who recidivated six months after returning to the streets?

The longer people stay out of trouble with the law while at liberty, the less likely they are to get back into trouble regardless of treatment. For instance, among those on probation, chances of being rearrested are high at first and then decline rapidly as time passes. If, therefore, a person is on probation for three years, chances of recidivism are minimal, just as the chances are minimal for someone who has been at liberty for three years without ever having been on probation. If the effectiveness of probation in preventing recidivism is being evaluated, the recidivism figures can be made to look good by imposing long probation terms and including only those who "finish their full term of treatment" in the numerator. Wilkins (1975) has argued that this is a dishonest way of evaluating treatment, and that recidivism should begin to be counted as soon as offenders have the opportunity to commit new offenses.

Especially in a society as mobile as the United States, offenders may move around quite a bit. They may be rearrested in different jurisdictions from those in which their initial arrests are recorded. If these rearrests are undetected or otherwise uncounted, one can argue that recidivism rates are understated.

It is the usual practice for students of recidivism to use one of several numerators other than rearrest: convictions, adjudicated violations of probation or parole, or return to institutions like prisons. In general, measurement of these numerators poses the same problems as does measurement of rearrest.

Some additional issues arise in the use of these latter measures. Note that the several categories are not mutually exclusive. Therefore, different kinds of recidivism rate numerators cannot simply be averaged together to make them more complete. Instead of being prosecuted and possibly convicted of a subsequent offense, the person may be sent to an institution following a probation or parole violation hearing. This practice is common in the United States, since the standards for hearing and adjudicating probation and parole violation are not as rigorous or demanding as those of trying and convicting someone of a new offense. Of course, a person's parole or probation may be revoked for having done something that is not a crime, such as failing to keep appointments with a probation or parole officer, getting married, or leaving the jurisdiction without the probation or parole officer's permission, going to a bar, staying out after curfew or "consorting with known felons." On the other hand, an offender who is thought guilty both of technical violations and of a serious offense may be prosecuted and convicted to stress the seriousness of an offense and perhaps to extend commitment for a longer period than mere revocation would allow (the maximum term for probation violation being whatever sentence would have been allowed or had already been set and suspended for the earlier offense, and for parole violation, the amount of the prison sentence remaining when the offender was released on parole). It is possible for a person both to suffer revocation and to be reconvicted, especially if acts are committed in more than one jurisdiction. Finally, a person may be continued on probation or parole even though a violation has occurred, or may be reconvicted without being incarcerated.

It is also possible for someone to abscond from probation or parole without being caught and qualifying for inclusion in any of the above recidivism rate numerators.

Comparison of figures for adult Americans placed on parole between 1968 and 1974, and followed up for one to three years, indicates that the lowest numerators are for absconding and for return to prison following reconviction for a major offense. Each of these figures is only about 30 to 60 percent as large as the figures for return to prison for technical parole violations. And a one-year follow-up of those released from prison in New York State indicates that figures for rearrest are higher than those for technical parole violation and absconding (Moseley, 1977). These data give a limited idea of the relative size of various numerators. They indicate that relatively high recidivism numerators could be obtained by counting rearrests over a period of several years, while relatively low rates could be obtained by counting those reconvicted of major offenses within a short period after completing extended treatment in the community.

Given the common use of recidivism rates to compare effectiveness of various treatment programs, it is important to note that such comparisons should be based on use of equivalent numerators (Wilkins, 1975).

MEASURING RECIDIVISM RATE DENOMINATORS

All the issues of measuring recidivism rate numerators arise in measuring the denominators—in selecting populations of those defined as initially having gotten into trouble with the law. In addition:

Wilkins (1969: 95–98) has analyzed a problem peculiar to recidivism rate denominators. As he has pointed out, denominators may easily confound kinds of persons being treated with kinds of treatments being given. Most frequently, recidivism studies address two questions: (a) What kinds of offenders are most likely to recidivate? (b) What kinds of treatment lead to least recidivism? That is, is the offender or the treatment to be held responsible for recidivism?

Those who measure recidivism rate denominators must distinguish the two possibilities. If recidivism rates of different kinds of offenders are to be compared, the treatment they receive should be held constant or equal in the denominators. If recidivism rates resulting from different programs of treatment are to be compared, types of offenders should be held constant or equal. To cite a simple example, suppose it is found that those released from prison are more likely to be reconvicted than those placed on probation. Does this indicate that those sent to prison are more likely to recidivate in the first place, or that probation prevents recidivism more effectively than imprisonment? This problem of confounding is extremely difficult to overcome. Many ways of trying to avoid confounding treatments and persons are evaluated below, in the section "Evaluating Chances of Controlling Recidivism."

There is another problem of comparability in recidivism rate denominators. If trends are to be evaluated, it can also be difficult to figure out whether changes in rates over time are attributable to the changing character of offenders or to changes in effects of treatment. Let us look at recidivism rate trends.

CURRENT TRENDS

Comparable recidivism figures are scarce. As Moseley (1977: 194–195) has pointed out, the F.B.I.'s (annual) figures for recidivism among those paroled in the United States are so vague and apparently sloppy as to be meaningless. The F.B.I. reports on small samples of parolees without saying how the samples are selected, is ambiguous about its follow-up period, and uses arrests in its numerators while acknowledging that most of the arrests fail to lead to conviction (and perhaps even to parole violations). The only carefully documented trends are from the Uniform Parole Reports Project (Neithercutt et al., 1975), following up return to prison after parole across the United States for one and two years after paroles granted between 1968 and 1972. These figures show that rates of return to prison declined somewhat during these years because returns for technical parole violations declined (a) from 15 percent to 9 percent over one-year periods and (b) from 20 percent to 15 percent over two-year periods. Of the 27,259 reported paroled in 1972, 20,173 (74 percent) were still succeeding on parole after two years (Moseley, 1977: 194–195). Rates of absconding and of return to prison following conviction of major new offenses scarcely changed.

The decline in technical violation rates remains to be explained.

Wilkins (1969: 14), while suggesting that recidivism has

risen, notes that at various places and times, the chances of reconviction for those on probation are about one in five, and for those released from prison, about one in two (substantially different from the percentage of those returned to prison following convictions for major new offenses within two years of parole in 1972: 6 percent). As you can see, our knowledge of recidivism rate trends is skimpy indeed.

EVALUATING CHANCES OF CONTROLLING RECIDIVISM RATES

Among the many studies of what causes or prevents recidivism, there is agreement on only two points: recidivism is more likely among those who get into trouble with the law (1) earlier and (2) more often (Wilkins, 1969: 56). In sum, of all that is known about recidivism, the only reliable predictor of recidivism is the prior official record of criminality.

The pitfalls of predicting recidivism are well illustrated by a study of 4,146 youths admitted to the Reception and Diagnostic Center of the California Youth Authority in 1964–1965 (Wenk and Emrich, 1972). To see how well they could predict parole violations for violent offense, Wenk and Emrich performed the following experiment.

Each youth in the group was followed up for fifteen months after release on parole. Of the 4,146 youths, 104 became violent parole violators.

The 4,146 youths were randomly divided into two groups of 2,073, each containing half the 104 violent recidivists. Each youth in one-half of the sample was given a score on each of eighteen variables, ranging from prior history of violence to number of months incarcerated. Then, beginning with history of violence, each variable was added to an equation with recidivism. As variables were added, each one was given a weight indicating how strongly it should be scored in calculating a total "recidivism score." The higher the total score, the stronger the prediction that an individual would recidivate.

Then the researchers applied the equation to the *other* random half of the 4,146 youths. The 260 or so youths in this group with the highest recidivism scores were classified as "violent prone." First, the 260 youths with the most serious prior history of violence were so classified. The researchers checked to see how accurate their predictions were. Then they used the equation with two variables—history of violence and race—weighted in relation to one another, and approximately the same number of youths were again classified as violence prone. Again, the accuracy of the prediction was checked. Then the equation using three variables (history of violence, race, and association of alcohol use with delinquency) was applied, and so forth.

In the prediction using history of violence alone, of the 260 predicted violent, 232 turned out not to be violent recidivists (false positives or type I error of 89.2 percent), while 24 of the 52 violent recidivists were classified as nonviolent (false negatives of type II error of 46.2 percent). As Wilkins (1974) put it, this finding suggests that we could lock away half of the young violent recidivists if we were prepared to lock up nine of every ten offenders unnecessarily.

The strangest feature of the experiment was that the prediction became *worse* as the number of variables in the equation was increased. When race was added to history of violence, of 260 predicted violent, 239 turned out to be peaceful (type I error of 91.9 percent), and 31 of the 52 recidivists were classified as nonviolent (type II error of 60.0 percent). This trend generally increased as prediction equations with more and more variables were used.

Why did the predictions with more variables do progressively worse than the one using history violence alone?

The answer: The error in each predictor was more than likely to compound the error in the next. This happened because the kinds of variables were interrelated rather than independent of one another. For instance, in Wenk and Emrich's equation, a history of alcohol associated with delinquency use was added to a history of violence. Alcohol use predicts violence because people often commit violent acts while drunk. Therefore, alcohol use does not tell much more about a person's likelihood of future violence than can be told from the history of violence alone.

On the other hand, someone with a high alcohol use score would be predicted to be violent in the future even with a low score for history of violence. But the main reason alcohol use predicts violence is that it accompanies a history of violence. The possibility of scoring high for alcohol use and low for history of violence thus increases the chances that nonrecidivists would mistakenly be classified as likely recidivists—type I error. The addition of predictors to Wenk and Emrich's equation increased the number of ways youths could mistakenly score high enough to be classified as likely recidivists.

Sure enough, of the 260 youths Wenk and Emrich classified as the most likely recidivists based on history of violence alone, 28 (11 percent) turned out to be recidivists. By the time 16 more variables had been added to the equation, of 248 classified as the most likely recidivists, only 11 (4 percent) recidivated. In consequence, more of the actual recidivists were not included in the violence-prone category, and type II error increased as well.

In conclusion, for the most accurate prediction, only the official record of prior offenses should be considered.

Moreover, if recidivism is unlikely in the population being studied, the best prediction is that no one will recidivate. This can be seen by adding the number of false positives and false negatives in Wenk and Emrich's prediction. In their best prediction, using history of violence alone, there were 204 false positives and 24 false negatives, for a total of 256 prediction errors in the sample of 2,073. And only 52 of the 2,073 actually recidivated. If Wenk and Emrich had predicted that *no one* would be a violent recidivist, they would have made only 52 prediction errors. Wenk and Emrich also reported having tried to predict recidivism from the second half-sample back to the first, but these predictions fared much worse than the first set.

Because their study was careful and honest, Wenk and Emrich's findings nicely illustrate the pitfalls of predicting recidivism. The limitations of prediction were so clear that Leslie T. Wilkins, in a foreword to the study, concluded:

Something different must be attempted if we are to seek to control the behaviors we find repulsive. . . . Perhaps this study should be "the last word" for some time in the attempt to "predict" violence potential for individuals.

This is a remarkable statement, coming as it did from a man who had gained international renown for a pioneering delinquency recidivism prediction study he had co-authored two decades earlier (with Herman Mannheim, 1955). In a recent conversation with me, Wilkins confirmed that he has seen nothing since Wenk and Emrich's study to make him waver in his rejection of the very kind of research upon which his own criminological reputation was founded. It is extremely rare that an eminent scholar like Wilkins is moved to publicly reject a prior line of research. Wilkins' change of heart is a strong indication of how extraordinary the problems of predicting recidivism are.

Prediction research has not failed for lack of inventiveness. In correspondence, Wilkins has reported to me on his attempts to use "nonlinear" statistical models to predict recidivism. Wenk and Emrich's prediction formula was "linear"; that is, in their equations, chances of recidivism increased in a steady line as the values of the variables increased. But what, for example, of the possibility that greater alcohol use breeds violence only if accompanied by a prior history of violence? To account for such possibilities, Grygier (1966) has tried using nonlinear prediction methods as has Wilkins. Wilkins reports that this introduces more "noise," more error, into the prediction than simple use of linear models. Like caroming the billiard ball, or adding an extra scale to weigh the eggs, combining values of variables compounds rather than reduces error. Some with prior alcoholism but no prior violence then commit violence, and many with past violence but no alcoholism do so, too. The simpler the predictor, the better.

Admittedly, if one is trying to predict property offense recidivism as well as violent recidivism, prior record alone can become a strong predictor—reducing false positives to a minimum, especially for young offenders. A British Home Office Statistical Research Unit (1964) study of all those (more than 4,000) convicted in the London Metropolitan Police District during March and April 1957 is the strongest available evidence of such predictability. Records of prior convictions were obtained for each convict, and then a check was made for reconvictions during the next five years.

The results were: (a) of those aged eight to eleven at the time of conviction, 53 percent of those with no prior conviction recidivated, compared to 68 percent of those with one prior conviction and all of those with two or more prior convictions; (b) of those aged twelve to thirteen, recidivists included 51 percent of those with no prior convictions, 71 percent of those with two prior convictions, and 100 percent of those with four or more prior convictions; (c) of those aged fourteen to sixteen, recidivists included 43 percent of those with no prior convictions, 72 percent of those with two prior convictions, and 100 percent of those with five or more prior convictions; (d) of those aged seventeen to twenty, recidivists included 42 percent of those with no prior convictions, 68 percent of those with two prior convictions, and 100 percent of those with ten or more convictions; (e) of those aged twenty-one to twenty-nine, 30 percent of those with no prior convictions recidivated, as opposed to 62 percent of those with two prior convictions and 100 percent of those with more than fifteen prior convictions; (f) of those aged thirty to thirty-nine, 15 percent of those convicted for the first time recidivated, as opposed to 42 percent of those convicted for the third time and 85 percent of those with more than fifteen prior convictions; and (g) of those older than 39, 9 percent of those convicted for the first time recidividated, compared to 41 percent of those convicted for the third time and 79 percent of those with more than fifteen prior convictions. For those of all ages, the major steps in increasing probability of reconviction were: 36.2 percent of those convicted for the first time, 57.5 percent of those with one prior conviction, 77.2 percent of those with four prior convictions, and 83.1 percent of those with more than fifteen prior convictions. By the time those in any single age group had four prior convictions, their odds of reconviction were better than even, while they were better than even for those with just one prior conviction for each age group as high as those aged twenty-one to twenty-nine.

If these figures are representative of other times and places (and there is no reason to believe they are not), reconviction seems likely for those with prior records. Also, the younger the convict, the better the chances of recidivism.

(This is *not* to say that any convict will have a prior record. False negatives remain high. Of those convicted in March-April 1957 in the British Home office sample, 46 percent had no prior convictions. As the Van Dine et al. [1977] study indicates and as discussed in Chapter 6, even if all recidivists were eliminated, that would still leave a lot of new people continuously getting into trouble with the law. To repeat: even if there were no recidivists, crime rates would probably remain high in England and the United States. Crime rates could not be well controlled by controlling recidivism.)

The remaining problem is that there is no known way to reduce a person's chances of recidivism. As far as anyone knows, the probability remains just as high after a prison term as it was before (Von Hirsch, 1976). If, because of youth and a prior record, a person is considered dangerous enough to be locked up, recidivism research gives no reason to believe a person will be less dangerous after release.

Based on criminological research to date, we are capable of picking out likely recidivists and killing, isolating, or otherwise incapacitating them. However, we have found no way of making recidivists less dangerous, and research so far indicates that nothing we do to recidivists will help us control crime rates much or for long.

There have been a number of claims to success in treating recidivism. These claims, too, have been thoroughly reviewed. The reader is again referred to Wilkins (1969), the study sponsored by the American Friends Service Committee (1971), and Von Hirsch (1976) for more detailed reviews of the treatment literature. In general, no individual studies will be singled out for criticism here. There are so many studies evaluating treatment in prisons alone that it would be misleading and unfair to find fault with just a few of them. Wilkins (1969: 75) has reported that several hundred studies of outcomes of prison treatment were published in English between 1940 and 1960 alone. Here, we will review the general problems with claims to success.

The most common problem here is that no comparisons are made between those who were treated and like persons who were not. Often, those selected for treatment have no long prior records; thus, the prognosis for success would be good even if they were left alone. Also, among those with long prior records are a few who do not recidivate. Therefore, if treated persons do not get into further trouble with the law, one cannot say that the treatment made them behave unless the recidivism rate is substantially higher among an equally select group of untreated offenders. As Bailey (1966) found in his review of 100 evaluation studies, the more rigorous the comparison between those receiving treatment and others, the lower the chance of finding that the treatment reduces recidivism.

Where comparisons are made, the method used often loads the results in favor of the treatment group. The fairest method of comparing treatments is to assign persons to the treatment and nontreatment groups randomly, so that there can be no systematic difference between them. However, as a political and ethical matter, random assignment is seldom possible. Imagine the problems of setting up an experiment in which some offenders are randomly sent to prison while others are set free. Nonetheless, in several major research projects, subjects have been randomly assigned to special treatment. In one such project, the Provo Experiment in Utah, there was virtually no difference between those receiving standard versus special treatment (Empey et al., 1964). In another, the Community Treatment Project in California, the specially treated group recidivated less than did those receiving standard treatment (Palmer, 1974). However, as Hood and Sparks (1970: 207) note, this result could apparently be obtained only when officials were sympathetic to the special treatment group and therefore overlooked parole violations deemed unacceptable for the standard group.

A similar result was obtained in another random assignment study (Berntsen and Christiansen, 1965) and in one of different parole treatments (Havel and Sulka, 1962). In these studies, the only special groups to do better were "medium risk" groups. The high risk and low risk groups showed no treatment difference. This suggests that the better results from treatment were obtained with those whose recidivism was most subject to discretionary interpretation by officials, while in clearer cases of recidivism, or the lack thereof, officials were harder put to make discretionary interpretations in favor of the special treatment group. Only if officials who reported recidivism did not know who had received the special treatment could this best have been avoided. These results suggest one promising path to "success" in reducing rates of recidivism. If officials can be made to believe enough in the treatment to disregard offenses among those they treat, recidivism rates (obviously) will decline. As argued in Chapter 7, the only way to reduce rates of criminality is to treat them as rates of crime, as by making officials less inclined to treat some individuals (e.g., recidivists) as abnormal people.

The problem with relying on a special treatment technique, like that in the California Treatment Project, to reduce recidivism is that officials' romance with the special treatment is bound to wane after a few years. Once the special treatment becomes routine, official evaluation of violations of the offenders can be expected to become routine, too. Hence, recidivism rates can soon be expected to rise to their old levels.

To sustain reductions in recidivism rates, the tendency of officials to find and report crime must be changed by grander crime control strategies, like those reviewed in Chapter 7.

Otherwise, random assignment of subjects to different treatments has not shown that one treatment controls recidivism better than another. By extension, these studies give no reason to believe that one treatment works better than none at all.

Since random assignment to treatments is so hard to arrange, most evaluations of treatment have relied on other ways of matching subjects of different treatments for comparison.

One of these methods has been to compare the subjects of the different treatments on a number of bases, such as age, race, seriousness of current offense, and length of prior record. Generally, one treatment works better than another in a few comparisons among many attempted. This result would be expected even if the treatments had had no effects on recidivism. Consider an analogy. If you pick out two pennies, flip each four times, get four heads with one coin and four tails with the other, chances are better than 99 out of 100 that the weight of the coins is distributed differently. Now, suppose you take 100 pairs of pennies, and in flipping one of the 100 pairs you happen to get the four heads and four tails. This result is not so extraordinary, is it? In fact, the odds are better than 3 in 4 that the result will occur among like coins. Neither is it so extraordinary to compare treatments in many different ways and get large differences in recidivism in a few comparisons.

Another approach to making comparisons is to develop equations, like Wenk and Emrich's (1972) prediction equation, from the special treatment group. The next step is to see whether there are more successes in the special group separately among those predicted to do well and poorly. This, as Wilkins (1969: 89) wrote, "Under almost any imaginable conditions . . . would load the dice in favor of the experimental group."

If one relies on officials, such as judges, to select the group for special treatment, the experimental group will probably consist of low recidivism risks.

Finally, as mentioned above, if the special treatment group is living in the community and their recidivism is measured only after the treatment is completed, the early recidivism will not be counted (or be counted as failure to complete the treatment) and low recidivism rates are to be expected regardless of treatment (Wilkins, 1975).

Otherwise, there are no research findings indicating that treatment reduces the risk of recidivism. As Greenberg (1977: 141) concludes, consistent with the earlier survey by Lipton and Wilks (1975): "The blanket assertion that 'nothing works' is an exaggeration, but not by very much."

The fact that no effective treatment for recidivism has been found does not rule out the future. But such a finding is unlikely. As discussed in Chapters 8 and 9, explanations of what makes criminals or delinquents different from the rest of us are of little use in figuring out how to make them like us. While there may be little type I error in predicting that those with serious prior records will recidivate, this record is established and cannot be changed by treatment. Knowing a prior record does not tell us what could reduce chances of recidivism. If the prior record is the only distinguishing feature of the likely recidivist, then nothing is known about what to treat in that person. Knowing someone is a likely recidivist is like knowing that a car is a "lemon." After different parts of the car have broken down continually for a long time, it is a safe bet that something will soon go wrong again. But if you only know that things keep going wrong and have been unable to isolate any troublesome system in the car, you have no way of preventing future breakdowns as long as the car remains in use.

Sources of trouble in known recidivists are bound to be hard to isolate. Generally, most recidivists are like the rest of us. Most of their behavior is similar to ours. In many respects, especially among property offenders, even most of the illegal activity itself is usually carried out just as the rest of us would conduct our day-to-day affairs. Thus, any cause of illegal activity must be consistent with a recidivist's overwhelmingly normal behavior. Conversely, anything that succeeds in changing only the criminal behavior for the better without worsening the recidivist's normal behavior must be extremely refined and selective. Figuring out how to use imprisonment to make a recidivist a normal, law-abiding citizen is somewhat like determining how to use napalm bombs to kill only the guerrilla soldiers in a group of several hundred peaceful villagers. With the crude tools we now have, such refinement is impossible. Just as the only potentially successful way to ferret out the guerrillas is to get close to the villagers, the only persons who can control recidivism are those close at hand when a potential danger arises—those who live and work where the recidivist lives, works, and preys. This is what leads Monahan (1978) to speculate that predictions that someone will be violent in a few minutes or hours in a community setting, as a basis for a short-term emergency mental health commitment, should be far more accurate than long-term predictions of violence for institutionalized offenders. It is practically inconceivable that a recidivist who has been released to the community could be controlled from prison, let alone by officials in probation and parole offices, in squad cars, or even on foot patrol. This, again, takes us back to the crime control strategies reviewed in Chapter 7.

Nor—as some, like Schwitzgebel (1972), have suggested—is electronic monitoring or stimulation—as by brain implant—a promising means to control recidivism. Even if the implant in the brain could be made more selective than the napalm on the village, countertechnology might well confound the implant—jamming, removing, or in some other way disabling it or neutralizing its effects. The shortsightedness of using control hardware is that those who oppose it cannot—in the final analysis—be prevented from escalating the war by countertechnology (as in the nuclear arms race), unless of course, the control technology is itself so disabling as to make its subjects into almost totally nonfunctioning zombies. Simply killing recidivists would be cheaper, simpler, and in the long run, arguably just as humane.

There is some chance that trying too hard to control recidivism worsens the problem. Lemert (1972) has theorized that the more people do to confirm that those committing deviant acts are deviant persons, the more committed the actors will become to deviant behavior. Mannheim and Wilkins (1955), in England, in a procedure replicated in California (Havel, 1963), worked out a prediction equation for calculating the "base expectancy" that anyone sentenced in a jurisdiction would recidivate regardless of treatment. Different treatment methods could then be compared to see how violation rates following treatment compared to the base expectancy rates of those being treated. By this criterion, Mannheim and Wilkins (1955) found that boys on probation did *slightly* better in relation to expectations than did those placed in institutions, and Havel (1963) found that adults did at least as well in less supervised as in more closely supervised parole. But since there is so much room for error in treating recidivism, and since supervision and punishment in theory might just as well discourage as encourage recidivism, harsher or more tightly monitored treatment procedures and lighter measures are probably about equally ineffective. This is not to say that harsh measures like imprisonment do no harm to people, but that the harm is probably too diffuse and varied in effect to lead to increased recidivism.

As figures like those of the F.B.I. (annual) consistently indicate, career criminals eventually stop recidivating in most categories of offenses. Consider again an analogue with flipping pennies. Suppose 100 of us are given a penny to flip until we get seven heads in a row. The game is to see how long it takes all of us to get the seven heads.

If you wanted to bet on whether any one of us would get seven heads in the next seven flips and stop, *no matter how many flips were already done*, the odds would be better than 99 out of 100 that the flipper would fail. This is like predicting whether someone repeatedly convicted of property offenses will be reconvicted if released. The odds are excellent that the offender will fail once again to stop recidivating.

On the other hand, it is a safe bet that all the 100 flippers would eventually get seven heads and that all the coin flipping would be over—sometime.

Given a group of eighteen-year-olds each with a long burglary record, most of them will be at large but no longer recidivating fifteen years later. But release any of them just after conviction, and the odds of recidivism are high. And even if you wait for fifteen years, and find one of the group who has kept on recidivating and has once again just been reconvicted, the odds of that person's recidivism are still as high as or higher than ever. The recidivism will probably stop sometime, but it is a poor bet that it will *this* time.

We are still left with some options. We can decide that some crimes are serious enough to be intolerable and, after someone has been convicted of (or arrested for?) the crime often enough, lock the person up for a longer than normal period, perhaps for life. This kind of "habitual offender" law is on the books of many states in the United States, and as "preventive detention" in England. The person can commit no crimes in the outside world while in prison.

If the person is dangerous enough to lock away, and time spent in prison does not reduce the risk of recidivism, what rational reason can there be to let the person go? If the purpose of imprisonment is to reduce the likelihood of committing crimes, then one might argue that prison sentences should never be for less than life (with no chance for early release). Everyone incarcerated (with the possible exception of those detained pending trial) would die in prison.

If this policy were implemented, unless incarceration were limited to very rare cases like second convictions of murder, incarceration rates would soon swell far beyond what they are in the United States. Conservatively, the average U.S. prison term would be fifty years, compared to an average of less than three years today. Again conservatively, to control U.S. incarceration rates, only about 5 percent as many persons could be sent to prison each year for life as are now imprisoned yearly. And local jails would not be used to control recidivism at all.

In theory, older recidivists might be easier to catch and defeat than younger ones. If prison space were limited, prisoners over a certain age (fifty or sixty?) might be released to make room for younger recidivists. If this policy were followed, the decreased danger presented by older recidivists would be offset by the greater cost of providing food, shelter, and other social services to the older offenders who had lost community ties and the capacity to fend for themselves outside after years of imprisonment.

Incapacitating recidivists to keep them from doing harm in the outside world requires nothing more than secure confinement. If imprisonment is to be used for retribution in order to keep retribution impartial and out of private hands (see Chapter 6), the punishment of imprisonment need not necessarily last a lifetime. If the expense were not prohibitive, recidivism might be controlled by allowing prisoners to import their families and set up communities as they saw fit. Since no treatment has been shown to reduce the risk of recidivism, no treatment facilities in prison would be needed or warranted. If there were isolated, open places in the world to be settled, these might be used to establish penal colonies in which the need for supervision to prevent escape was minimal (as Australia was originally used by the English for a penal colony, and as the Soviets have used parts of Siberia), although historically such attempts at "transportation" have been brutal. (For an excellent account of the history of punishment, including transportation, see Fairwether, 1975.) Under these circumstances, the expense of life imprisonment would be minimized.

SIDE EFFECTS OF CONTROLLING RECIDIVISM RATES

The biggest risk of using prisons to control recidivism is that prison populations grow unmanageably. This is the dilemma that confronts Americans. On the one hand, Americans freely use prisons to isolate people predicted dangerous to outside communities. On the other hand, prison facilities become so crowded that continued increases in prison populations become untenable. Under these circumstances, pressure is strong to release prisoners regardless of their prior records. The only available rationalization for release of someone initially deemed too dangerous to be left at large is that the prisoner has been cured of criminality. In this climate, Americans have shown themselves willing to keep trying the new treatments "experts" offer, just as incurably ill patients, in desperation, sometimes invest fortunes in obscure treatments of doubtful value. The dilemma of U.S. attempts to cage dangerous criminals supports the proliferation of treatment programs—(a) in prison, (b) in the community in an attempt to make imprisonment unnecessary (witness the transitory fad for "community corrections," reflected by the President's Commission on Law Enforcement and Administration of Justice, 1967), and (c) in the community to control the dangerousness of released prisoners (e.g., O'Leary's, 1972, plea for parole). As the number of those employed in vain to treat and cure recidivism grows, the employees themselves become a powerful lobby for expanding attempts to rehabilitate offenders.

Unless a society limits itself to imprisoning only as many persons as the society can afford to keep in prison for life (or perhaps at least until old and infirm enough to be readily controllable in the community), a growing rehabilitation bureaucracy and the frustration of repeated failure are bound to result. Ineffectual rehabilitation is liable to become an albatross around the neck of those who use imprisonment freely to incapacitate dangerous recidivists.

POLITICAL CONSIDERATIONS

If Americans were to give up on the idea of curing dangerous offenders, what would they do with all they have invested in rehabilitation programs?

We can recognize and support the good intentions of those who aim to help offenders without confusing helping offenders with controlling recidivism.

Various kinds of assistance and counseling can be given to offenders without forcing the offenders to accept the help. Currently, U.S. offenders are often induced to accept help by the prospect of "getting off light": avoiding prosecution or incarceration, or gaining early release from prison on parole. This tradeoff is justified by the belief that if help is received and reduces the chances of recidivism, formal sanctions will be unnecessary. But since there is no reason to believe that help or treatment in any form influences recidivism rates, what is the point of trying to force offenders to accept the help? Led by the sponsorship of the American Friends Service Committee (1971), many criminologists have concluded that there is no point in the practice, and that offenders should be left free to reject help without penalty. The Indiana Penal Code (1977) no longer allows the parole board to release persons early, so that help in prisons might be chosen freely without special inducement.

Even if help is no longer made compulsory, offers of help may still be suspect to offenders. Americans deem it vital that for clients to trust their clinicians, clergy, doctors, and lawyers, whatever the helper learns will remain confidential and not be used to hurt the client. By contrast, in U.S. prisons, those who help offenders are responsible for keeping their clients in line. Offenders who confess wrongdoing to a prison counselor may have the information used against them. Under these circumstances, the offenders are more likely to try to con the helper than to trust the helper with their problems. We have seen that there is little the helper can do to curtail recidivism under any circumstances. If we are going to bother with the trouble and expense of employing helpers for offenders, what is to be lost by obligating the helpers to keep information about their clients in confidence? Doesn't a criminal trial lawyer have the same obligation? We should recognize that all the helpers we employ cannot supervise their wards effectively as long as offenders do not trust them.

In other words, there is no reason to take jobs away from those currently employed to treat recidivism as long as we free these people to gain the trust and confidence of their clients.

Meanwhile, as long as likely recidivists were kept in prison to prevent their recidivism, some people would have to be employed just to keep the prisoners in custody. This is bound to be a thankless job. It can at least be made less frustrating by not expecting the custodians to help rehabilitate the prisoners, too.

In general, the greatest political obstacle to giving up the pretense of treating recidivism would be the job threat to those employed to give treatment. By guaranteeing job security, and by making the expectations of the employees more realistic than that of preventing recidivism, the change should be welcomed.

ETHICAL ISSUES

If attempts to treat recidivism are abandoned, will criminal justice sanctions lose their humanity? When Americans began to build prisons in the early nineteenth century, the prison movement was led by humanitarians—notably the Quakers—who argued that an attempt to rehabilitate offenders was morally superior to capital and corporal punishment (Rothman, 1971). It is ironic indeed that some American Quakers (American Friends Service Committee, 1971) have now sponsored the leading argument that giving up the pretense of rehabilitation by imprisonment—and avowedly using prison only as punishment for wrongdoing—is a morally superior position.

It does seem cold-hearted, does it not, to decide that the person who is dangerous enough to lock away is irredeemable. Which is worse: after more than a century of failure to continue to hold out hope that offenders can be rehabilitated, or to give up on offenders we find too great a threat to keep in our communities?

Some might argue that it is more humane to execute offenders than to imprison them for life. Perhaps capital punishment should be substituted for imprisonment. Or if humanity toward recidivists is at issue, perhaps they should be given a choice between suicide and imprisonment.

There is a more fundamental moral issue: How much should the control of recidivism be guided by the interests of offenders? One might argue that incapacitation of recidivists is more expensive than it is worth, and that those who cannot be tolerated in society should simply be killed to save expense and to channel moral outrage at persistent criminals.

Does youth deserve special consideration in recidivism control? Perhaps very young offenders should be released as adults or incarcerated instead of killed, regardless of their likelihood of recidivism, simply out of compassion.

Even if likely recidivists deserve no special consideration, how high an example of conduct should the state set by the way it punishes offenders? If, for instance, the state is to represent the supreme value of human life, is it not hypocritical for the state to kill even serious wrongdoers? How far should human beings, whether in government or not, be trusted to decide who deserves to live and who to die, or to decide that some people deserve not only to be confined but to be confined under bare subsistence conditions? Is expedience a valid basis for deciding how to treat those who behave immorally? To what degree does one wrong justify another, or do ends justify means?

Even after all these issues have been decided, who deserves to be incapacitated as a probable recidivist? Does someone twice convicted of drunk driving deserve such treatment? Is it the amount of harm done by the offender or risked by the offender's acts to be determinative, and who draws the line? Whoever happens to sit in a legislature? Impartial "professionals" in each case? A jury of those who do not know the defendant? Jurors who know the offender? Victims? The possibilities are almost endless—both for who sets what standards for seriousness of offenses and how high the probability of recidivism should be to warrant incapacitation. The policy decision to control recidivism considers none of these moral issues.

Finally, although Americans especially regard certain sanctions as "cruel and unusual," it might be more humane to disable potential recidivists in such a way that they could return to the community physically incapable of carrying out their offenses. For instance, burglars could be crippled or branded to make them readily visible, armed robbers and pickpockets lose the use of their hands, counterfeiters and forgers blinded, and especially violent persons made quadruplegic. Of course, such an approach would probably cause the community more trouble and expense than it saved in recidivism. Imagine taking care of all those physically disabled persons! But once the principle is accepted that the physically able recidivist is intolerable and irredeemable, the relative humaneness of various sanctions can be reconsidered.

CONCLUSION

With recidivism, we have finally found a measure of criminality that can be controlled. And yet, employing this knowledge raises basic, especially troublesome moral issues. To be effective, the control of recidivism requires punishments so severe as to seem, to many, barbarous. Furthermore, if much recidivism is to be controlled, the task will be monumental unless we are prepare to adopt the expedient of continuously killing off large numbers of people.

In the last analysis, trying to control much recidivism would probably be self-defeating. Recall Chapters 4 through 7. Thus far,

U.S. criminal justice officials have only gradually escalated the level of punishment they inflict. The normal official U.S. response to mandatory life imprisonment would be to curtail severely the rate of arrest, prosecution, and conviction. If this obstacle to controlling recidivism were overcome, it would imply that the climate of U.S. society had changed radically, that it now tolerated violence and personal harm more than ever. Such a change in social climate would probably imply dramatic rises in crime rates, with more and more recidivism to be controlled, and with control lagging behind growth. In the long run, it appears unlikely that even recidivism greatly can be controlled without the major restructuring of U.S. society discussed in Chapters 4 through 7.

REFERENCES

American Friend's Service Committee. 1971. *Struggle for Justice.* New York: Hill and Wang.

Bailey, William C. 1966. "Correctional outcome: an evaluation of 100 reports." *Journal of Criminal Law, Criminology, and Police Science* 57 (June): 153–160.

Belkin, Jacob, Alfred Blumstein, and William Glass. 1973. "Recidivism as a feedback process: an analytical model and empirical validation." *Journal of Criminal Justice* 1 (March): 7–26.

Berntsen, K., and Karl O. Christiansen. 1965. "A resocialization experiment with short-term offenders." Vol. 1, pp. 35–54, in Karl O. Christiansen (ed.), *Scandinavian Studies in Criminology.* London: Tavistock.

British Home Office Statistical Research Unit. 1964. *The Sentence of the Court.* London: Her Majesty's Stationery Office.

California Bureau of Criminal Statistics. 1969. *Crime and Delinquency in California.* Sacramento, Calif.: Bureau of Criminal Statistics.

Empey, Lamar T., Maynard L. Erickson, and Max C. Scott. 1964. "The Provo experiment: evolution of a community." Pp. 29–38, in *Correction in the Community.* Sacramento: Calif.: State Board of Corrections.

Fairwether, Leslie. 1975. "The evolution of the prison." Pp. 13–40, in United Nations Social Defense Research Institute, *Prison Architecture.* London: Architectural Press.

Federal Bureau of Investigation. Annual. *Crime in the United States: Uniform Crime Reports.* Washington, D.C.: United States Government Printing Office.

Gottfredson, Don M. 1975. "Correctional decision-making." Pp. 82–91, in Don M. Gottfredson (ed.), *Decision-Making in the Criminal Justice System: Reviews and Essays*. Washington, D.C.: United States Government Printing Office.

Greenberg, David F. 1977. "The correctional effects of corrections: a survey of evaluations." Pp. 111–148, in David F. Greenberg (ed.), *Corrections and Punishment*. Beverly Hills, Calif.: Sage.

Grygier, Tadeusz. 1966. "The effect of social action: current prediction methods and two new models." *British Journal of Criminology* 6 (July): 269–293.

Havel, Joan. 1963. *Special Intensive Parole Unit, Phase IV: A High Base Expectancy Study*. Sacramento: California Department of Corrections.

———, and Elaine Sulka. 1962. *Special Intensive Parole Unit, Research Report No. 3*. Sacramento: California Department of Corrections.

Hood, Roger, and Richard Sparks. 1970. *Key Issues in Criminology*. New York: McGraw-Hill.

Indiana Penal Code. 1977. *Burns Indiana Statutes Annotated*. Title 35.

Lemert, Edwin M. 1972. *Human Deviance, Social Problems, and Social Control*. Englewood Cliffs, N.J.: Prentice-Hall (2nd ed.).

Lipton, Douglas, and Judith Wilks. 1975. *The effectiveness of correctional treatment: a survey of treatment evaluation studies*. New York: Praeger.

Mannheim, Herman, and Leslie T. Wilkins. 1955. *Prediction Methods in Relation to Borstal Training*. London: Her Majesty's Stationery Office.

Monahan, John. 1978. "Prediction research and the emergency commitment of dangerous mentally ill persons: a reconsideration." *American Journal of Psychiatry* 135 (February): 198–201.

Moseley, William H. 1977. "Parole: how it is working." *Journal of Criminal Justice* 5 (Fall): 185–203.

Neithercutt, M. G., William M. Moseley, and Ernst A. Wenk. 1975. *Uniform Parole Reports: A National Correctional Data System*. Davis, Calif.: National Council on Crime and Delinquency Research Center.

O'Leary, Vincent. 1972. "Issues and trends in parole administration in the United States." *American Criminal Law Review* 11 (Fall): 97–140.

Palmer, Ted. 1974. "The Youth Authority's Community Treatment Project." *Federal Probation* 38 (March): 3–14.

President's Commission on Law Enforcement and Administration of Justice. 1967. *Task Force Report: Corrections*. Washington, D.C.: United States Government Printing Office.

Rothman, David J. 1971. *The Discovery of the Asylum: Social Order and Disorder in the New Republic*. Boston: Little, Brown.

Schwitzgebel, Ralph K. 1972. "Limitation on the coercive treatment of offenders. " *Criminal Law Bulletin* 8 (May): 267–320.

Van Dine, Stephan, Simon Dinitz, and John P. Conrad. 1977. "The in-

capacitation of the dangerous offender: a statistical experiment." *Journal of Research in Crime and Delinquency* 14 (January): 22–34.
Von Hirsch, Andrew. 1976. *Doing Justice: The Choice of Punishments.* New York: Hill and Wang.
Waller, Irvin. 1974. "Conditional and unconditional discharge from prison." *Federal Probation* 38 (June): 9–14.
Wenk, Ernst A., and Robert L. Emrich. 1972. "Assaultive youth: an exploratory study of assaultive experience and assaultive potential of California Youth Authority wards." *Journal of Research in Crime and Delinquency* 9 (July): 171–196.
Wilkins, Leslie T. 1969. *Evaluation of Penal Measures.* New York: Random House.
———. 1974. "Current aspects of penology: directions for corrections." *Proceedings of the American Philosophical Society* 118 (June): 235–247.
———. 1975. "Putting treatment on trial." *Hastings Center Report* 5 (February): 35–48.
Wolfgang, Marvin E., Robert M. Figlio, and Thorsten Sellin. 1972. *Delinquency in a Birth Cohort.* Chicago: University of Chicago Press.

FOOD FOR THOUGHT

1. Should anything but reconviction be counted as recidivism? Why or why not?

2. What kinds of research studies on recidivism, if any, do you think would still be worth doing?

3. If all prison sentences were for life, who should pass sentence? Using which criteria?

5. Should capital or corporal punishment be used, and in which cases?

6. What kinds of help or treatment should persons be trained and employed to give offenders?

CHAPTER ELEVEN

Controlling Criminality Rates: A Review

AN EXERCISE IN FUTILITY

When you were a child, did you have a wind-up toy that walked or rolled along? Remember what happened when it ran into a wall? Sometimes it would bounce back and forth a few times and then stop against the wall. Other times, the walking toys especially would keep going but move nowhere. In many ways, these toys resemble the field of criminology. As described in Chapter 1, positivism has prevailed for the last century in Western criminology. Overwhelmingly, criminological research has focused on why some people are criminals or potential criminals, and tried rehabilitation of offenders or potential offenders. As we found in Chapters 8 to 10, this research has produced little useful information. Errors in all explanations and predictions of criminality remain sizable. The one exception is this: false positives can be minimal in predicting that property offenders with lengthy prior records beginning early in their youth will continue to commit crimes if left at liberty. The little that is known about what makes criminals different from the rest of us implies success in just one form of treatment or control of criminality: incapacitating likely recidivists permanently. All that we know about criminality is that persistent offenders (especially property offenders) are probably irredeemable. Their recidivism will probably stop some time, but not now and not because of any treatment we give them.

This is all we have known about criminality for over a century (Rothman, 1971; Duesterberg, 1979). It is all we are likely to know for the foreseeable future.

Those who persist in trying to explain criminality and find its cure are like the wind-up toy soldier who has hit the wall but keeps marching. They are going nowhere. If only they turned in a different direction, they might have a chance to progress. There are so many other directions to pursue that the criminologists who are up against the wall need not pursue any particular ideological line if they turn away from positivism; many choices will lie before them. But for now, much of criminological research is an exercise in futility.

WHO IS RESPONSIBLE FOR CRIME?

I have discussed problems of controlling criminality with many people. One response stands out: "You mean criminals should just be allowed to get away with everything!" Many of us naturally assume that those who have done wrong should be punished—held responsible for their acts. The only exception should be made for those who are incapable of exercising responsibility because of youth, insanity, mental retardation, and so on. Because we are morally committed to holding persons responsible for their actions and taking care of the irresponsible, we are led to identify criminals and treat them as different. We ourselves would be morally irresponsible if we failed to hold others accountable for their conduct.

Our ideas about responsibility are a little confused. If you tell someone, "You are responsible for your own life," you are in effect saying, "Don't expect me to get involved in your affairs." And yet, when we say that we hold criminals responsible for their acts, we imply that we will take over the management of their affairs. We say that we want people to behave responsibly, but in the realm of crime control, we assert that the only persons who qualify for our good treatment or help rather than for punishment are those who have acted irresponsibly. And when we punish to deter or treat to help, we try to teach persons to act responsibly by taking over the responsibility for their lives.

People are to be taught responsibility or held accountable by taking responsibility away from them, and may avoid punishment by showing that they have acted irresponsibly. How inconsistent this is.

Do you see a flaw in this logic? There *is* one. Our response to criminality shows that we accept wrongdoing only if the actors are irresponsible. If they are responsible for their actions, we expect them to behave properly. Thus, we are internally consistent if we take away responsibility from those who fail to exercise it properly. Also, if irresponsible people are held for treatment, we have taken nothing away from them but simply filled a void. Right? Wrong. If this were so, we would have no moral reason for punishing people for anything they did while they were already being punished or treated for criminality. If we have taken over responsibility for the criminal's affairs, then we must be held responsible and punished for what the criminal does during and after treatment.

Furthermore, the logic of the responsibility ethic implies that criminals are irredeemable. When do wrongdoers become worthy of managing their own affairs? When they prove themselves capable of doing so? If so, give wrongdoers a probationary period in which to attempt self-management; if they behave responsibly, they are redeemed. Right? Wrong. What does probation mean, if not that we are assuming ultimate responsibility for people in case they misbehave? Logically, if criminals are to be able to redeem themselves, official control of their behavior must end while they remain as yet unredeemed.

This is not to say that offenders under positivist crime control can never be accepted in the outside world. I myself have seen a few ex-convicts gain eminent middle-class respectability. However, these persons seem to have redeemed themselves by proving that their behavior was immune to crime control and by meeting middle-class standards of behavior of their own choice. The exceptional ex-offenders with this strength of will probably could have succeeded just as quickly without the "help" of the criminal justice system.

The contradiction of the positivist approach to crime control is this: If crime control teaches wrongdoers anything, it is how to get along without responsibility. If crime control is based on the moral imperative of holding persons responsible for their acts, then crime control is logically unattainable. That is, if someone breaks the law, that is in positivist terms a failure of crime control, not an opportunity for control. Again, we are up against the wall.

This does not rule out morally responsible crime control. If people hurt each other or get into disputes, responsibility can be presumed to be shared by those doing the harming, those harmed, and third-party mediators. As Parnell (1978), an anthropologist, has put it, this presumption implies a moral obligation to try to *settle* rather than to *process* disputes. He observed approaches to handling disputes in Oaxaca, Mexico. There, dispute processing was handled by the district courts; attempts at settlement by village elders. While dispute *processing* emphasized blaming someone for wrongdoing, dispute *settlement* stressed restoring harmony so that the disputants could live together peaceably.

The distinction is illustrated by an encounter I had with a former colleague. He strongly believed that teachers had a moral obligation to "maintain quality control" by giving low grades to many students. At the end of one term, he asked me how many C's I had given. I replied, "I taught the course so well that I didn't have to give any." Recall, from Chapter 1, the problem of naming any one thing as *the* cause of an event, as in deciding whether the sun or body chemistry is the cause of a sunburn. Is the teacher or the student responsible for a bad grade? If a student's performance is to be improved, it will require a behavior change in both the student and the teacher. From the mid 1960s to the mid 1970s, this premise guided formal education in the People's Republic of China (see Yee, 1973, for an account of this approach).

If crime control proceeded from the moral premise that everyone involved in a conflict was accountable, the issue of whom to hold responsible or to blame would no longer arise. Instead, the issue would be to determine the role of each party in resolving the conflict. For instance, a vandal might work to repair the damage to the property, while the property owner showed the vandal how to do the best job. As in traditional China, the matter might end with a ceremony of reconciliation (Van der Sprenkel, 1962).

And so, when asked whether criminals should be allowed to get away with wrongdoing, I reply: "No, they should be just as responsible for the harm they do as anyone else. However, that does not mean wasting effort by finding fault, laying blame, or punishing or treating them."

UNPREDICTABILITY AS A HUMAN VIRTUE

The inability of criminologists to explain, predict, or treat criminality is not all bad. Schumacher (1974) elevated the unpredictability of individual behavior to the level of moral principle:

a. Full predictability (in principle) exists only in the absence of human freedom, i.e. in "sub-human" nature. The limitations of predictability are purely limitations of knowledge and technique.
b. Relative predictability exists with regard to the behaviour pattern of very large numbers of people doing "normal" things (routine).
c. Relatively full predictability exists with regard to human actions controlled by a plan which eliminates freedom, e.g. railway timetable.
d. Individual decisions by individuals are in principle unpredictable. (pp. 192–193)

It is a truism that individuals should be able to deviate from what is expected of them. Most of us find the prospect of 1984 (Orwell, 1971, originally published in 1949) fearsome. This lack of freedom is exactly what is implied by predictability of behavior. If you know exactly how someone is going to behave in the future, how can that person be said to be free to choose how she or he behaves?

The technology for 1984 is already available to us; Schumacher's statement was intended to warn us not to use it. But the stalemate in criminological research indicates that 1984 is far away. Even though many criminologists have tried to predict and change individual behavior, even though advanced behavior control technology has been tried out in recent years (London, 1971) and computers have been fed piles of data from which to make lightning calculations, no way has been found to control human behavior except through continued personal interaction. Without intimacy, without sharing responsibility for social control throughout communities, it is impossible (so far) to change behavior permanently. With intimacy, everyone can be affected by everyone else; it becomes hard to distinguish the controller from the controlled. Criminological research has indicated that individual behavior is unpredictable and uncontrollable not only *in principle* but also *in fact*. If this can be considered a failure of human knowledge, it can also be seen as a triumph of human will.

THE FALLACY OF AFFIRMING THE CONSEQUENT

As mentioned in Chapter 1, it is fallacious to conclude that what has not yet been found cannot or will not be found. By the logic of science, the possibility cannot be ruled out that fairly accurate predictions and effective treatments of criminality will someday be discovered.

Let us imagine a science fiction scenario of an effective treatment of criminality. An offender's memory might be erased and reprogramed to provide the person with a completely new (and socially successful) personal history. The latest "entry" in the history would be undergoing surgery for a brain tumor, perhaps, just before moving to a new community. Although the new history might include the fact that the subject had no living family, official family records would have to be created and other persons in old places in the new history reprogramed to have memories of those ties, too. Perhaps these others could be offenders as well. Making the new histories remain credible might be complex, but it is conceivable that offenders could be rehabilitated in this manner.

However, given the long history of trying to explain, predict, and treat criminality, the chances of such a breakthrough seem remote. As we have seen, the problems are not merely those of needing more data and further research. Major conceptual barriers must be overcome. A new moral foundation for controlling criminality needs to be developed if the present "responsibility ethic" is to be transcended. As Wenk and Emrich (1972) have shown (see Chapter 10), minute details of personal life—each unrelated to (i.e., statistically independent of) the others—must be accurately measured before it becomes possible to predict or otherwise control rare events like future criminal acts with reasonable accuracy. Otherwise, the Draconian measures that would be needed to control widespread recidivism—the only currently known way to control criminality—would be worse than crime itself. As mentioned at the close of Chapter 10, more crime and recidivism would be created than controlled.

TURNING AWAY FROM THE WALL

In discussing the politics of crime control, I have noted that social change can probably not be forced. Therefore, we cannot expect that those criminologists whose work consists of trying to explain, predict, and treat criminality will just give up their efforts, no matter how futile the efforts are shown to be. If the control of criminality in the United States is ever to give way to the control of crime, it will probably involve the death of the positivist position. I maintain hope that the new generation of American criminologists will begin with the knowledge and confidence that new ideas for crime control are worth imagining and trying—even if many of them fail, too.

The problem of continued success in crime control is like that of sustaining a physical chain reaction. At first, nuclear physicists explained the relatively low level of energy emitted by radioactive materials (as in luminous clock numbers using radium) as follows: Atomic nuclei split when hit by particles called neutrons. In a radioactive material, the nuclei were composed of enough particles so that the split nuclei released more than one neutron. Whether any particular neutron encountered another nucleus, which was also moving around unpredictably, was mere chance. The space between nuclei was relatively large—like the distances between stars in the universe. Thus, even with a lot of neutrons flying about, the chance of splitting nuclei was small indeed.

On the other hand, when a nucleus did split, relative to the space occupied by one atom, the release of energy was enormous—like the energy that would be released in our solar system if the sun blew apart. If a way could be found to get a high percentage of nuclei to split simultaneously, the amount of energy released would be thousands of times greater than that of a conventional explosive like TNT. The problem nuclear physicists faced was how to create this simultaneous split even though they could not arrange for nuclei to be in the right place at the right time.

This is like the problem of sustaining successful crime control. Any crime control strategy that has not already failed may be used somewhere in the social system at the right time to prevent crime. However, it takes a practically simultaneous impact on many elements of the social system to have a significant impact on crime control. Even when potentially successful crime control strategies are implemented, the opportunities for failure are so great that success is a matter of mere chance.

To sustain a chain reaction, nuclear physicists arranged to have a large number of neutrons flying around at once. Thus, it did not matter which neutron encountered which nucleus; there would be enough simultaneous hits to release a greater multiple of neutrons. Eventually, so many chance hits would occur simultaneously that the enormous energy characteristic of an atomic bomb would be released.

Two factors could be manipulated simultaneously to raise the firing rate of neutrons to a "critical" level. Either the mass of the radioactive material or the density of the mass could be increased. Ideally, this would mean arranging any mass in a sphere so that the average distance between nuclei was minimized.

Similarly, the way to maximize the chances of successful crime control is (a) to maximize the number of strategies implemented at any one time (b) in such a way as to maximize the number of social elements that will be changed immediately. Thus, the best sustained success in crime control will come when we use many different simultaneous crime control strategies, each designed to have a broad impact on the society.

New ideas and experiments in the United States would be encouraged if the major funding source of crime control experiments —the Law Enforcement Assistance Administration (L.E.A.A.) of the Justice Department—changed its funding procedure. Whisenand (1977) gives a good overview of the kinds of crime control projects L.E.A.A. currently funds. Each project proposal is elaborately screened before funding decisions are made. The screening process is so costly that L.E.A.A. feels unjustified in giving small grants. Instead, a few projects are funded, each costing hundreds of thousands or even millions of dollars. Suppose, instead, that L.E.A.A. screened each proposal more superficially—simply to make sure of its sincerity—and gave out smaller funds for each project—say, no more than $50,000. Most experiments would fail, just as they do now. Thus, nothing much would be lost. But because so many more experiments would be funded, the possibility of some success could be substantially increased.

In sum, if Americans could get over their fear of failure in trying to control crime in any one new way, they would be more likely to succeed overall. And if fear and caution were reduced so that the experiments were modest, then failure would probably cause less harm, and less fear about crime control experiments would occur.

This book is written largely to encourage those beginning the study of crime to try to make the hope of successful crime control a reality. As a criminologist, your greatest weapon is your imagination. We need approaches to crime control that have not yet been tried and evaluated.

CONCLUSION

Chapters 8 to 10 have reviewed the Western tradition in criminology. In keeping with this tradition, findings on criminality are usually taught as though:

a. the findings were worth memorizing by every criminologist, and
b. research to explain, predict, or evaluate treatment of criminality was all that real criminologists ever did. Accordingly,
c. if you wanted to become a criminologist, this is the kind of work you, too, would have to do.

It is certainly worth knowing what criminologists have discovered about criminality and its treatment. One should understand the Western tradition of criminology well enough to know how it can or cannot help in crime control. However, in this book, I have a different goal. I hope to give new criminologists a sense of freedom and creativity, so that they can avoid marching to the wall like so many toy soldiers. I hope to give good reasons for criminologists to set out in new directions.

REFERENCES

Duesterberg, Thomas J. 1979. *The Social Origins of Criminology in Nineteenth-Century France.* Bloomington, Ind.: University of Indiana (dissertation).
London, Perry. 1971. *Behavior Control.* New York: Harper & Row.

Orwell, George. 1971. *1984*. New York: New American Library.

Parnell, Philip C. 1978. "Village or State? Competitive legal systems in a Mexican judicial district." Pp. 315–350, in Laura Nader and Harry F. Todd, Jr. (eds.), *The Disputing Process—Law in Ten Societies*. New York: Columbia University Press.

Rothman, David J. 1971. *The Discovery of the Asylum: Social Order and Disorder in the New Republic*. Boston: Little, Brown.

Schumacher, E. F. 1974. *Small Is Beautiful: A Study of Economics As If People Mattered*. London: Sphere Books.

Van der Sprenkel, Sybille. 1962. *Legal Institutions in Manchu China*. London: Athlone Press.

Wenk, Ernst A., and Robert L. Emrich. 1972. "Assaultive youth: an exploratory study of the assaultive experience and assaultive potential of California Youth Authority wards." *Journal of Research in Crime and Delinquency* 9 (July): 171–196.

Whisenand, Paul M. 1977. *Crime Prevention: A Practical Look at Deterrence of Crime*. Boston: Holbrook Press.

Yee, Albert H. 1973. "Schools and Progress in the People's Republic of China." *Educational Researcher* 2 (July): 5–15.

FOOD FOR THOUGHT

1. Think of the last few times you have had arguments, fights, or other conflicts with people. If you blamed other people or yourself for the trouble, how might you have responded instead? What difference would it have made had you done so? If you responded without blaming or finding fault what difference do you think these tactics made?

2. Suppose you knew a twenty-year-old man who had just been released from a one-year term in prison. This had followed his second burglary conviction as an adult (since turning eighteen). He had an extensive juvenile record, beginning with a charge of shoplifting when he was thirteen. He had had nine years of formal schooling, and had never worked at or been trained for a skilled job. What would he have to do, and how long would it take, for him to redeem himself in your eyes?

3. What points *in favor* of attempts to control criminality can you think of that have not been mentioned?

4. What other science fiction scenario for successful treatment of criminality can you imagine?

5. Do you think a career in criminology would be worthwhile? What would be your purpose in pursuing such a career?

6. Imagine yourself an aide to a U.S. legislator. What kinds of laws for treating criminality would you recommend?

PART FOUR

GENERAL PERSPECTIVES

CHAPTER TWELVE

A Note
on Cost-Benefit Analysis

Cost-benefit analysis is implicit in the question, "How much crime control activity is enough or too much?" For instance, we may decide that we have paid enough for police, courts, or prisons to balance the returns or benefits we receive. However, a formal cost-benefit analysis is rare. As mentioned in Chapter 2, this technique is in its infancy. Most of the work has been done by economists, and is quite tentative. Economic models have not really been applied to crime control planning. Instead, economists are beginning to develop models to suggest how cost-benefit analysis *might* be applied. The various models are similar to one another. To see what these models can and cannot do, we will examine a model that has been developed by Becker (1976).

On the other hand (see Chapter 2), some social scientists have applied cost-benefit analysis to evaluating particular programs for the treatment of criminality. One of these evaluations, of a pretrial diversion project in Washington, D.C., called Project Crossroads, is notable for its complexity and thoughtfulness (Holahan, 1971). The analysis attempts to show that the expense of the project was outweighed by its benefits to potential victims, to offenders, and to the criminal justice system. To explore the potential of cost-benefit evaluations of treatment programs, this study, too, will be examined.

As we shall see, cost-benefit analyses have heuristic value. They sensitize us to issues of crime control that we might otherwise overlook. At the same time, cost-analyses beg at least as many questions as they resolve. Thus, it would probably be a mistake (the fallacy of misplaced precision) to use such analysis to determine what should be tried or rejected in the realm of crime control.

COST-BENEFIT ANALYSIS IN PLANNING

Becker (1976) can be a little intimidating to the lay reader. He translates deterrence theory into mathematical equations and derives optimal crime control strategies by calculus. The use of mathematical language has its advantages. It enables more to be said in less space, and helps to ensure that the analysis is internally consistent. In this section, the formal language of the equations will be translated into more understandable language.

What basic requirements would be needed to decide how many offenses to punish? Becker attempts to answer this question. His model assumes that a criminal justice system punishes and thereby begins to deter the most serious offenses in a society *first*. Hence, as the criminal justice system expands to punish more offenses, the new offenses it handles will be less costly to society than the earlier ones.

In addition, Becker assumes that as the criminal justice system expands, new cases become more and more expensive. It is easiest to solve and punish the most serious offenses. With the later offenses, each case becomes more costly.

Because the offenses outside of a criminal justice system are less damaging to victims and more costly to pursue than those the system already attacks, the "marginal" or extra costs to society of leaving offenses alone decreases as one goes from the more serious to the less serious offenses.

On the other hand, Becker apparently assumes that the deterrent value of sanctions rises more and more as caseloads increase. That is, the "marginal revenue" of increasing caseloads rises as new cases are taken on.

These assumptions allow Becker to define the optimal caseload for a criminal justice system. The optimum is the point at which the marginal costs to society of leaving a kind of offense alone equal the marginal return from adding the offense to the criminal justice caseload. Beyond this point, offenses are not costly enough to justify official action. Thus, Becker treats a society that is controlling crime much as economists treat a firm making products for sale. In theory, the rational firm will produce just as much as it takes for the marginal cost of production to equal the marginal revenue for sales. Similarly, the rational society will go after just enough kinds of offenses for the marginal cost to equal the marginal return on expanding criminal justice caseloads.

Becker applies this argument to two issues: (a) How far should the criminal justice system go to increase the probability of punishment for offenses? (b) How much time, money, and effort should the criminal justice system devote to punishing more severely? Citing some evidence that (a) sureness brings more deterrence than severity, (b) Becker tentatively concludes that it is preferable to add cases rather than punishment to an expanding criminal justice system.

Becker's analysis is remarkably detailed and comprehensive, and should be read in its entirety. Here, let us consider what we gain and lose from his form of cost-benefit analysis.

Becker does not apply data to his model. He falls short of testing how well it could be used in practice to decide on an optimal level of criminal justice activity. Had he done so, he would have found the task almost impossible.

For one thing, we do not have adequate data for estimating the deterrent effects of increased criminal justice activity. Becker cites the work of economists Ehrlich (1967) and Smigel (1965) as attempts at such estimates, acknowledging that their data bases may be shaky. He is correct. Ratios of convictions to arrests or offenses known in various jurisdictions have been related to "offenses known" rates. If the conviction ratio for an offense is higher in one jurisdiction than another and the "offenses known" rate for the offense is lower, it has been assumed that this indicates the deterrent effect of conviction. The assumption is questionable. It is plausible to assume that jurisdictions with more offenses to handle have a harder time maintaining high conviction rates. As argued in Chapters 6 and 7, if these jurisdictions tried to convict more people, they could expect still higher "offenses known" rates and still lower conviction rates as criminal justice activity increases. The deterrence analyses probably reflect not deterrence but the fact that jurisdictions with less crime have an easier time responding to it.

To estimate the deterrent effects of increased convictions adequately, data would have to be gathered from each jurisdiction. The jurisdiction would have to experiment with obtaining more and fewer convictions from year to year, and obtain victimization data to see whether victimization rates increased or decreased as a consequence. And if the hypotheses of Chapters 6 and 7 were supported by such data, more convictions *per capita* in a jurisdiction would lead to higher, not lower, victimization rates. If data were gathered adequate to estimating deterrent effects of increased criminal justice activity for Becker's model, those data would probably not fit the assumptions of his model anyway.

In addition, definitions of costs and benefits are open to question. For instance, Becker assumes that it is a societal cost to hire more criminal justice personnel to expand criminal justice activity. In a society with an unemployment problem, might it not be considered a societal cost to *fail* to provide criminal justice jobs for citizens? We have repeatedly confronted this political issue in planning crime control strategies. In order to articulate his model, Becker has to gloss over the problem. And although Becker acknowledges that offenders may gain from crime, he glosses over this problem too, by treating the fruits of crime simply as damage in his model.

Becker's model reflects the problem of trying to optimize criminal control activity. For a logically tight model, rigid, limited, and limiting assumptions must be made as to what crime control data mean. If the model were applied, it would be the beginning, not the end, of arguments as to whether the indicated level of crime control activity were really optimal.

On the other hand, Becker's and other such optimization models do have heuristic value. They dramatize the possibility that even though a strategy may succeed, there may still come a point at which its marginal returns—in relation to the marginal costs of failing to employ it—fail to justify its use. Because these models make assumptions of crime control planning explicit, they draw our attention to assumptions that we might otherwise overlook, and give us a chance to consider them further. For these reasons, formal optimization models are useful—not to determine what we ought to do but to raise questions about what we are thinking of doing.

COST-BENEFIT ANALYSIS IN EVALUATION

Holahan's (1971) cost-benefit analysis of Project Crossroads, a pretrial diversion project, mentioned earlier, is praiseworthy. His study rises above the ritualism characteristic of much recent social science research. All too often, one researcher will use the same variables—collect the same kind of data—as others and analyze it in the same way. The only things that change are the time and place from which the data are drawn. (The relationships among the data change only a little.) By contrast, Holahan created an original research design. He had to; there were no other cost-benefit analyses of pretrial diversion projects to copy. While the study might not prove that the expense of Project Crossroads is socially justified, as Holahan suggests it does, it is still a delight to see an honest, imaginative attempt to address a difficult question.

Project Crossroads was one of the early pretrial diversion projects funded by the Manpower Administration of the U.S. Department of Labor. The idea was to find jobs for offenders with little or no prior record, prevent their being stigmatized as criminals, and thereby discourage recidivism. Project Crossroads began in September 1968. The cost-benefit evaluation covered the 460 participants in the program from its inception until April 1970. Participants were selected by interview from among adults charged with "lesser" property offenses (misdemeanors) who had no prior adult (eighteen years old or over) record of convictions. Those deemed eligible for the program were offered a chance to volunteer.

Participants agreed to plead guilty to the charges against them. Their cases were then adjourned for ninety days. During this time, they received intensive counseling, job placement, remedial education, and "other services." If, meanwhile, they got into trouble, they would be terminated from the program and sentenced by the court. If their counselors had doubts about how well they were doing at the end of the ninety days, their cases could be continued. But in most instances, at the end of ninety days, upon recommendation of their counselors, the trial judge dismissed the charges against them—leaving them with no record of having been convicted of a crime.

The September 1968–April 1970 budget for Project Cross-roads was $233,256, which Holahan implies was given to the project in one sum when the program began. Holahan's question was: Did the program yield more than $233,256 in social benefits during the period, discounted to September 1968, at interest rates of either 5, 10 or 15 percent? (That is, for example, a project benefit in September, 1969, then worth $105, would have been discounted at a 5 percent interest rate. Thus, it was worth $100 in September 1968, when the program received its funds.)

Holahan set out to determine three sets of figures, the September 1968 values of: (a) reduced judicial and corrections costs from diversion of cases out of the criminal justice system through the program, (b) savings in criminal justice system costs by the program's reduction of recidivism, and (c) contribution of the program to participants' earnings.

To estimate reduced costs by diversion, Holahan had to compare the experimental group to a "control" group—a group of defendants who had not participated in the program. The control group consisted of defendants whose cases had been heard in the Washington, D.C., courts during the six months prior to September 1968. Holahan's description of how the sample was chosen is a bit confusing. He says that selection was random, but also that defendants in this group were chosen for their similarity to program participants in age, lack of prior adult convictions, offense category, and eligibility for personal bond. Perhaps he is referring to a "stratified random sample," in which the selection is skewed to yield particular proportions of different categories of persons.

Then Holahan calculated the criminal justice savings of the diversion program. To begin with, he estimated what it would cost the taxpayers for a defendant to (a) be arraigned (i.e., have a hearing to enter a preliminary plea of guilty or not guilty), (b) have a bench (nonjury) trial, (c) have a jury trial, (d) be kept on probation, and (e) to be incarcerated. Holahan does not list these figures in his report, but from other figures he does provide, it appears that his estimates of costs of criminal justice activity per defendant range from about $35 per arraignment to about $2,000 per incarceration.

Holahan does not tell us how he arrived at these estimates. It was probably a complicated procedure, which first involved figuring out how much of the salaries and fees of various officials, and use of buildings and equipment, was allocable to each activity for the jurisdiction as a whole for a specific period, such as a fiscal year, and then dividing the total by the number of defendants who received that form of treatment in the jurisdiction during the period. It must have been either an accountant's dream or nightmare come true!

It has already been suggested that the money spent to pay officials might be considered a benefit rather than a cost to society. But let us assume that their pay is a societal cost. For the most part, criminal justice costs are fixed. It makes little difference, especially in a large city, to the expense of running an arraignment court whether a few defendants more or less are run through it. A few more defendants in a morning may make the proceedings a bit more rushed, but the judge or magistrate would probably do nothing extra for the taxpayers even with some additional leisure. In most cases, even the defense attorney is a public defender who would be paid just as much to appear for twenty defendants as for twenty-five. (Besides, if the usual pretrial diversion procedure was followed in Project Crossroads, participants went through arraignments in order to have their cases continued for ninety days.)

The situation with other criminal justice activities would be analogous. The problems are even worse in trying to measure the cost of probation and incarceration per person, for the conventional figures for caseloads or inmate populations on given days fail to reflect differences in lengths of sentences. In any case, a strong argument can be made that diverting as many defendants from the criminal justice system as Project Crossroads did saved Washington, D.C., taxpayers nothing.

Holahan nonetheless multiplied the difference between the percentage of program participants and control group defendants passing through each stage of the criminal justice system, by the number of program participants, by the cost per defendant of providing each procedure as estimated by Holahan. In other words: (percentage participants undergoing procedure—percentage control group undergoing procedure) $\times$ (460) $\times$ (cost of procedure/defendant). Adding the products for each criminal justice activity together, Holahan concluded that Project Crossroads had reduced judicial and corrections costs for defendants by a total of $115,494.25. This was worth $109,995 discounted at 5 percent interest, $104,995 at 10 percent interest, or $100,430 at 15 percent interest, in September 1968. Holahan concluded that diversion alone had paid back the taxpayers for almost half the cost of Project Crossroads.

About 70 percent of both the participants and the controls who were rearrested were charged with one of four offenses: robbery, burglary, larceny (theft), or auto theft. Holahan estimated what recidivism for each of these offenses cost the District of Columbia criminal justice system per defendant, and multiplied it by the product of the difference between the percentage of program participants and control group defendants being rearrested for the offense, times the number of program participants. In other words: (cost/defendant) $\times$ (percentage participant rearrested— percentage control group rearrested) $\times$ (460). The sum of the figures he obtained for each of the four offenses led Holahan to conclude that Project Crossroads had saved the taxpayers $216,963 discounted at 5 percent interest, $198,448 at 10 percent interest, or $182,634 at 15 percent interest, in the cost of handling recidivism.

Holahan's description of his estimation procedure indicates that he multiplied percentages of those arraigned, tried with and without juries, placed on probation, and incarcerated for each of the four offenses in the District of Columbia, by his earlier estimates of the average cost per defendant of each of these activities, in order to obtain the average criminal justice activity cost of rearresting a suspect. Apart from whether any particular recidivist should be reckoned as a societal cost in criminal justice activity, Holahan's estimates were apparently based on figures which included the cases of those rearrested who had lengthy prior records. Chances are that those rearrested in the program and control groups, who had only one prior conviction, at least at first rearrest, were not as severely treated as other defendants in the District of Columbia. Thus, in yet another way, Holahan exaggerated the amount saved by having less recidivism in the program group than in the control group.

Holahan is not explicit about his measure of recidivism. However, his summary suggests that he probably counted all those arrested for any of the four offenses as of the time—after April 1970 and before the 1971 publication of the study—that his data were collected. If this is so, then those in the control group had a longer period in which to be rearrested than those in the program. As Holahan acknowledges, the difference in recidivism rates he found between program participants and control defendants is not large: 26 percent for program participants and 36.4 percent for control defendants. If program participants had had as long to recidivate as control group defendants, the difference might have decreased substantially.

Holahan admits that despite his attempts to match program participants with controls, there might have been some unmeasured factors—inherent in the interviewing or in volunteering for the program—that made program participants different from controls regardless of what happened in the program. This possibility can probably be discounted. Given all the problems of predicting and influencing recidivism (see Chapter 10), there is little chance that program participants were any less predisposed to recidivate than controls.

It is possible that program counselors concealed or otherwise intervened to prevent the rearrest of program participants, especially during their ninety-day continuances. If so, the program might actually have affected recidivism. However, as argued in Chapter 10, this effect would probably disappear as the program became established and counselors settled into routines.

Holahan did not try to measure the cost of recidivism to victims. The loss to victims could be said to be offset by the gain to offenders, with the net social loss equaling zero. Since, as we have seen, one can argue that the gain realized by employees of the criminal justice system offsets the operating cost of the system, Holahan could have pursued his logic a step further and concluded that the net social cost of recidivism was zero. Hence, Project Crossroads could not have saved society *any* expense by preventing recidivism.

Holahan despaired of drawing a meaningful comparison between job progress among control group defendants and program participants. In any case, tracking down the employment records of control group members would have been too big a job. Accordingly, Holahan tried to gauge the increase in earnings that the program gave its participants in the year following their participation. He is not explicit about how he discriminated increased earnings due to program counseling and job placement from earnings the participants would have gotten without the program's help. Still, he concludes that earnings for the 460 participants were increased a total of $45,854 during their ninety-day counseling periods and $102,577 during the succeeding year.

Although the estimation procedure is again not described, Holahan also figured that 2.6 percent more of the program participants could be expected to hold jobs for five more years because of reduced recidivism among them. This added $77,438 to the social benefit attributed to Project Crossroads. Holahan's totals of earnings benefits of the program were $216,964 discounted at 5 percent, $198,448 at 10 percent, or $182,634 at 15 percent.

There is room for doubt as to how much the program actually contributed to the earnings of its participants. Also, unless new jobs were created by the program, it is possible that jobs filled by participants were taken away from others, who instead got worse jobs or no jobs at all. It could be argued that this cost should have been subtracted from Holahan's earnings benefit figures.

In all, Holahan calculated the benefits of Project Crossroads to have been $517,240 discounted at 5 percent (a benefit-cost ratio of 2.2), $474,172 at 10 percent (a benefit-cost ratio of 2.0), or $439,138 at 15 percent (a benefit-cost ratio of 1.8). Holahan's study was extremely intricate and imaginative. However, his conclusion—that Project Crossroads yielded substantial net benefits to society—is highly problematic. The study scarcely constitutes proof that Project Crossroads is, on balance, socially worthwhile.

Holahan's cost-benefit analysis nonetheless has heuristic value, too. For the study to be done in the program's name, its directors had to define their objectives and make themselves accountable for their work. This kind of accounting allows those who favor other objectives to discuss what is being done and what should be done in a program. This facilitates experimentation and change. The outstanding feature of cost-benefit analysis is that it discourages crime control personnel from resting on their laurels. Thus, it stimulates thoughtfulness and debate on how to treat crime or criminality. That in itself is a substantial contribution to criminology.

THE FALLACY OF MISPLACED PRECISION

Suppose you had a month's vacation and decided to use it to travel. What strategy would you adopt? Would you plan your trip carefully in advance, poring over guidebooks and figuring out how many days each stop would be worth? Or would your plans at best be tentative, so that your length of stay in each place could vary, depending on how interesting you found each stop? While planning is worthwhile, it would probably be a mistake to commit yourself in advance to a rigid timetable. Things would unfold as the costs and benefits of each stop became apparent. While structuring the trip in advance might facilitate your travel, you could not foresee exactly what you would experience as costs and benefits until you arrived.

The same principle applies to crime control planning and evaluation. It may facilitate your work to take stock of costs and benefits as you go, and to try to foresee (roughly) the relative gains and losses of proceeding in various directions at various speeds. However, you may be surprised about what you and others consider costs and benefits, and about how long you decide to maintain your crime control efforts in new places. It is fallacious to believe that we will be more successful if we commit ourselves to rely on advanced estimates of goals. It is a fallacy of misplaced precision if our planning prevents us from being flexible—from redefining costs and benefits as the results of our planning unfold.

Suppose you were trying to be as precise as possible in cutting and fitting pieces of a cabinet together. Measuring and cutting all the pieces at once would be an instance of misplaced precision. With a little error in your instruments or technique, one piece might turn out to be too small. Therefore, the preferable approach would be to cut the pieces a little bigger than you believe they should be, fit them, and then gradually plane, sand, or file them down as needed. The greatest precision in planning comes from allowing room for error, adjustment, and redefinition as you proceed. The fallacy of misplaced precision is that one gets closer to one's goal by defining all the parameters and fully predetermining one's course. If you get too committed to knowing exactly what you *will be* doing, you pass up chances to know what you *are* doing.

Although it entailed no cost-benefit analysis, the design of decision guidelines for the U.S. Parole Commission illustrates how one might try to plan for the future without precluding continual reassessment of one's progress. The designers of the guidelines found that parole decisions followed a pretty clear pattern: If one knew the length of an inmate's prior record, the offense behind the most recent conviction, and whether the inmate had a record of disciplinary infractions, one could predict with fair accuracy how many months the inmate would be incarcerated before being released on parole. The designers of the guidelines translated this pattern into a table which indicated to parole board members when inmates would normally be released. The Parole Commission agreed that parole would be granted as indicated in the table unless written reasons were given for departing from the guidelines in special cases.

There was a catch. The parole board members were told that they were *expected* to deviate from the guidelines and give written reasons for doing so in about 15 percent of the cases. Every six months, the board was to meet together to review these reasons and to consider revising the guidelines—to reconsider parole decision-making policy. Hence, room to rethink decision making was built into future plans. This procedure has yielded at least one major change in the guidelines since their inception (Gottfredson et al., 1978). Use of guidelines has since been extended to sentencing (Wilkins et al., 1978).

Similar mechanisms might well be built into optimization strategies of crime control. This could keep us from becoming complacent that we are doing the best we can because our models tell us to.

It is not even a good survival strategy to use cost-benefit analysis as a rigid guide to action, at least, not if Darwin (1968, originally published in 1859) is correct. He argued that different species had a better chance of surviving if they adapted to changes in the environment. According to this proposition, the more human beings behave in certain predetermined ways, the worse the chances for survival of the human species. The more open human beings are to change, the greater their life expectancy as a species. If, therefore, cost-benefit analyses are used by crime control planners to open the door to disagreement and to discovery of error, they may contribute to human survival. If, on the other hand, cost-benefit analyses are used to justify a set of rules, these rules—if effective—threaten human survival.

REFERENCES

Becker, Gary S. 1976. "Crime and punishment: an economic approach." Pp. 5–65, in Lee R. McPheters and William B. Stronge (eds.), *The Economics of Crime and Law Enforcement.* Springfield, Ill.: Charles C. Thomas.

Darwin, Charles. 1968. *Origin of Species.* New York: Penguin.

Ehrlich, Isaac. 1967. "The Supply of Illegitimate Activities." New York: Columbia University (unpublished manuscript).

Gottfredson, Don M., Leslie, T. Wilkins, and Peter B. Hoffman. 1978. *Guidelines for Parole and Sentencing.* Lexington, Mass.: Lexington Books.

Holahan, John F. 1971. "Cost-benefit analysis." In *Project Crossroads: A Final Report to the Manpower Administration of the U.S. Department of Labor.* Washington, D.C.: United States Government Printing Office.

Smigel, Arleen. 1965. *Crime and Punishment: An Economic Analysis.* New York: Columbia University (master's thesis).

Wilkins, Leslie T., Jack M. Kress, Don M. Gottfredson, Joseph C. Calpin, and Arthur M. Gelman. 1978. *Sentencing Guidelines: Structuring Judicial Discretion—Report on the Feasibility Study.* Washington, D.C.: United States Government Printing Office.

FOOD FOR THOUGHT

1. How would you decide how much of a crime control activity is enough? Try following Becker's lead: select an activity you would like to see implemented, list its costs and benefits, and try to figure out how you would measure them and weigh them against one another.

2. Suppose a criminal court trial judge were to ask for your guidance. The judge admits to you that he or she is uncertain about how to decide whether to imprison defendants or put them on probation. What kinds of preliminary decisions would you advise the judge to make about costs and benefits?

3. Who should have the authority to define costs and benefits for evaluating a crime control program like Project Crossroads?

4. After reading about the cost-benefit analysis of Project Crossroads, do you believe the program should be continued? What additional information would aid you in this evaluation?

5. What can and should be done to keep cost-benefit planning from inhibiting debate over which crime control experiments should be implemented?

6. What can and should be done to keep cost-benefit evaluations from rationalizing questionable programs?

CHAPTER THIRTEEN

The Potential
for Crime Control:
A Review

By now, it is time to take stock of what you have learned and thought about. Therefore, this chapter is a review. You have already read about crime control and its alternatives in various societies throughout the world. You have read about research findings and ideas from persons trained in anthropology, architecture, economics, engineering, genetics, history, law, medicine, philosophy, political science, psychiatry, psychology, social work, and sociology. You have considered analogies to criminology from biology and physics. You have read analyses based on the assumptions and concepts of statistical theory—in its pure form, a branch of mathematics. It is not hard to understand what these various disciplines have to offer criminology. And yet, it is a different matter to synthesize all this material into an integrated picture of issues of crime control.

While reading this book, you have probably come up with many new ideas. Thus, you may have synthesized this material differently from me. That would be admirable. There is no one appropriate way to interpret these data. Still, it may be helpful to review the material as I see it—not to dictate what it must mean but to show what it might mean.

THE SYSTEMS APPROACH

Toward the end of Chapter 1, I referred to systems theory, particularly Wilkins' deviance amplification model. I owe a great debt to Wilkins for giving me a perspective from which to think about crime control. I have learned a great deal not merely from his research findings and conclusions, but from trying to understand his approach to the study of crime control. He has pioneered the application of a systems approach to criminology—an approach I now use as well. The systems approach is basic to the organization of this book. Let us consider what a systems approach means.

Wilkins was involved in the early development of systems analysis in research by the British Royal Air Force on flight safety in World War II. Traditionally, when a plane had crashed, investigators had focused on what the pilot might have done wrong. The early systems analysts found this perspective a little limiting. Suppose the pilot had accidentally retracted the landing gear instead of feathering the props (turning the propeller blades so that they would not pull air over the wings)? More crashes might be prevented in the future if the instrument panel were redesigned. This would work better than disciplining the pilot. As Wilkins puts it, the big breakthrough came when investigators decided to ignore who or what caused the crash, and instead looked at the crash as an outcome of an interaction process between people and machinery. The key issue for systems analysis to resolve was: where, in the process leading to the crash, would intervention minimize the chance of future crashes?

It was possible that the chances of recurrence without intervention were small enough, compared to the cost and effectiveness of any intervention, that no change was warranted. This problem should be familiar by now: that of a tradeoff between false positives and false negatives—between type I and type II error. Which was the preferable risk: doing nothing (risking type II error) or doing more than was needed (risking type I error)? The systems analysts continually confronted this problem.

Wilkins shows the difference between traditionalists, who search for causes of events, and systems analysts thus: The traditionalist would look at footprints in the snow and ask who caused them; the systems analyst would look at the footprints without assuming that a person had caused them any more than the snow had done. In criminology, the traditionalist seeks to find out what causes crime; the systems analyst looks at how probabilities of crime, or response to crime, might be changed in a society by intervening at various points in the crime production process.

This is almost the same as the distinction drawn in this book between controlling criminality and controlling crime. But not quite. While it is true that those who attempt to explain, predict, and treat criminality are traditionalists rather than systems theorists, there are also traditionalists who reject this approach. These people simply assume that the cause of crime lies elsewhere than in the criminal, rather than rejecting the notion of causality itself. This leads to arguments over whether the *real* cause of crime lies in the criminal, in social conditions like poverty, or in other persons, like the ruling class. This produces a lot of scholarly debate, but few new ideas for controlling crime.

Some people refer to the traditional approach as the medical approach or model in criminology. That is a misnomer. Think of where we would be if medical researchers had not adopted a systems approach. Suppose those trying to prevent polio had treated a virus as the cause of the disease. It would have been a mind-boggling task to attempt to kill, isolate, or otherwise incapacitate all the polio viruses floating through the air. Instead, medical researchers focused on the interaction of virus and human organism. They determined that if the human organism were sufficiently exposed even to dead polio virus, the later interaction with a live virus would be effectively interrupted, and the chances of catching the disease would be virtually eliminated. If criminologists responded to crime as medical scientists commonly respond to disease, crime control would probably be much more successful.

I have defined crime as an outcome of an interaction process between criminal justice officials and other members of a society, in which one party is blamed and criminal justice officials take charge of that person's affairs. In this system, as we saw in Chapters 5 to 7, the more a society becomes kind to strangers and strange to kind, the higher crime and criminality rates per inhabitants will rise. Geographical, occupational, and familial mobility are integral elements in crime production. Some features of the crime production system are quite familiar to most of us: Situations are more likely to be defined as crimes among the poorer classes; among persons who are found guilty of first offenses early in life and more likely to be blamed for later crimes; and with property offenses, which are far more common than offenses against the person in large, complex societies like the United States. It does not help to call poverty, individual characteristics, or societal complexity causes of crime, but it does help to see that any strategy that hopes to work will probably have to change these elements of the society.

THE POTENTIAL FOR CRIME CONTROL

This book has emphasized the development and evaluation of ideas for crime control in the United States. This is not because U.S. crime control problems are unique. It is merely because I am more familiar with these problems and practices than those of other societies—which, in turn, makes it easier to give criticism and advice. I trust that much of the information about crime control in the United States is applicable to other societies. However, others must be the judge.

Chapter 7, the review of crime control strategies, is more optimistic than Chapter 11, the review of strategies for controlling criminality. And yet, the conclusions of the two chapters are closely interrelated. It is argued in Chapter 11 that crime control strategies based on giving special treatment to criminals or delinquents are bound to fail. Criminality cannot be contained in this manner. However, as argued in Chapter 7, if Americans became less mobile, became less tolerant of strangers and kinder to intimates, rates of crime per population would probably decrease, *and* rates of criminality would change accordingly. This contingency was discussed in Chapter 8. Incarceration rates per population might well be decreased if they were treated like conviction, arrest, and "offenses known" rates of crime. If fewer offenses are reported by police, and fewer arrests made and convictions obtained, fewer people will be sent to jail or prison. In Chapter 9, the cross-cultural self-reporting comparisons lent some support to the proposition that as victimization rates and other crime rates decline, self-reporting rates will follow suit. And although, as we saw in Chapter 10, there is no known way to change an offender's probability of recidivism, if fewer people are arrested and convicted in the United States, there will be fewer candidates for recidivism. If Americans can achieve sustained reductions in rates of crime per population, they are bound to achieve some control of criminality as well.

Control of crime implies control of criminality, but not the reverse. This problem was encountered in Chapter 10, when the conclusion was reached that too much incapacitation of recidivists would cause increases in crime rates and ultimately in the number of recidivists to control. A more punitive, more criminogenic social order is needed to support severer control of criminals. Further, trying to prevent crime by treating criminals is like trying to improve quality control in automobile production by building more repair shops for cars that break down. Remaking products probably will not improve the process that first created them.

It is not surprising that U.S. criminology is based on holding individuals responsible for crime, even given the problems with this approach, discussed in Chapter 11. Individualism is a hallmark of the American form of democracy. It is the basic tool Americans have used to try to overcome the injustice of aristocratic social orders, where unequal wealth and power are fixed at birth. The premise of the U.S. Declaration of Independence, "that all men are created equal," is taken to mean that one's social position should depend solely on individual effort. This premise is a two-edged sword. If those who do well do so on their own initiative, then those who do poorly have only themselves to blame. Hence, as a matter of principle in the American democratic ideology, criminals are presumed to have achieved their own degradation in a just society. If the society is in some respects unjust, if some persons become criminal because they were born disadvantaged, then these individuals must be helped to achieve a fair starting position from which to rise or fall on their own merits. Hence, if the individual criminals in American society do not deserve to be punished or degraded for their sins, then they deserve to be individually helped or treated for their problems.

Some Americans have realized that this premise is contradictory in two ways. First of all, if merit is to be earned by individual effort, those who get ahead by being helped or treated have only given further evidence that their social advancement is undeserved or unjust. In American ideology, it is no blessing to be called "disadvantaged"; this label confirms that the individual is socially unworthy and unproven. This is another way of saying, as was noted in Chapter 11, that by the terms of American criminal justice ideology, the criminal is irredeemable.

Second, as long as democracy is seen as giving worthy individuals an opportunity to rise in the social order, some individuals, *and their children*, must deserve being poorer and less powerful than others. That is, even if the social order is perfectly just, at any given time some people have more than others, and hence have advantages in getting even further ahead. The only escape from this contradiction is to move from the premise that all persons are created equal to the premise that all persons deserve equal opportunity to have their needs met—throughout their lives—which implies the central premise of the communist version of democracy: "From each according to his ability, to each according to his need."

It is the human fate to live with contradictions. It may well be utopian ("utopian" meaning that it applies to "no place") to presume that a social order can be made fair and just according to communist principles. But when individualism becomes a matter of principle, as it is in the United States, the implication is that the social order improves as individuals become kinder to strangers and stranger to their own kind. That is, the social order becomes more just the less individuals are rewarded based on the strength of their family, coworkers, and friends, and the more their progress is achieved independently of their social environment. In American terms, the less the progress of individuals depends on others and the more on what they do for themselves, the more just the social order. Individuals who show more compassion toward some than others, who help some more than others, contribute to discrimination and inequality and violate the principle that all persons are created equal.

Beginning in Chapter 5, we saw what may happen when persons become kind to strangers and strange to their intimates: crime stands to increase by virtually any measure. If the Japanese manage to control crime more effectively than Americans, it is in part because social power and social favors are a traditional Japanese birthright.

Criminologists are challenged to figure out how democracy and crime control might be made compatible. One conclusion seems safe: if crime control is to be achieved, it will require a fundamental reordering of U.S. society.

Fundamental change is sometimes confused with drastic change. They are not the same. Think of the alarm clock with the screw to reset its speed. If we turn the screw slightly, the clock will slow down only a little, perhaps a minute or two a day. This is not a drastic change but it is a fundamental one, for the speed of every piece in the mechanism has been changed. Similarly, a fundamental reordering of American society need not be drastic. Suppose the mobility of Americans were slowed just a bit, so that the annual divorce rate per married families, and rates of changes of job and residence, declined by several percentage points. If the rates were maintained at this lower level for a few years, rates of crime might start to decline a bit, too. On the average, Americans would have become a little kinder to their own kind and stranger to strangers, but this fundamental change in the social order would not be drastic.

In Chapter 7, it was mentioned that the only U.S. precedent for drastic changes in crime rate trends was set during two national calamities: the Great Depression and World War II. Doubts were expressed that Americans would wish at present to make fundamental social changes, whether or not the changes were drastic. This is in part because Americans are generally prosperous enough to afford crime as a basic cost of doing business the American way. It remains to be seen when or whether Americans will decide that crime, loneliness, social purposelessness of life, and the attendant anxiety and depression cost more than it is worth to give up prosperity and freedom to move around from person to person and place to place. However, if Americans did want to make fundamental changes in their social order, the changes could, in theory, be subtle and gradual instead of drastic and sudden. For instance, a gradual but fundamental change might occur in a middle-class suburban neighborhood if a set of cooperatives were formed: pooling labor and equipment for home improvement, maintenance and repairs; buying groceries; babysitting; house watching when homes were vacant; carpooling. Gradually, as relationships became firmer and more trustworthy, savings might be pooled to form a low-interest loan fund for the members, and the members might train one another in skills like family counseling (so as to help families through periods of strain without separation and divorce). Membership in such a neighborhood could become so precious that residents would pass up attractive job opportunities just to stay there.

Crime control need not be such an imposing task. It will probably not be accomplished by gimmicks like having people from different states come together for a month or so, to become sensitive to each other and to develop a sense of community, only to end the exercise and go their separate ways. On the other hand, each of us is able to become a sophisticated criminologist who weighs the pros and cons of various approaches to crime control and acts accordingly. How willing are you to stay with one family or job or neighborhood, despite the troubles or the notion that the grass is greener elsewhere? At the very least, you can affect what a group does to control crime by controlling the actions of one of its members: yourself. That is more control than none at all.

Another American cultural trait accompanies individualism: impatience. Anything worth accomplishing has to be accomplished RIGHT NOW. Unless you believe that anything worthwhile is achieved by the group, you have no reason to believe that the little you or anyone else does as an individual may eventually have social significance. The distinctiveness of American impatience was revealed in the recent war in Vietnam. It took Americans little more than a decade to conclude that the war could not be won. It took *one thousand* years of perseverance for the Vietnamese to fight their way to national independence. Unlike typical Americans, typical Vietnamese are not individuals alone; their identity resides largely in their ancestors and descendants as well. Vietnamese who die for a cause still live in their descendants, who can be expected to act as though of one life and one purpose. While the typical American can take comfort only from what "I have done," the typical Vietnamese considers what "we have done and will do."

This is like deciding: Which comes first, the chicken or the egg? The more Americans trust that others share their interests, the more U.S. criminologists will tend to act on their own principles without requiring immediate change. The more Americans become kinder to their own kind on their own initiative, the easier it will be for them to believe that others share their interests. How can one result be achieved unless the other has been achieved first? The only way to break the impasse is for each of us to risk relying on others in the hope that the favor will be returned. In the realm of crime control, there seems to be no escape from taking responsibility for one's own actions (as opposed to holding others responsible for doing what one wants). Time and again (as we saw especially in Chapters 8 through 11), attempts at crime control have failed when directed at "them" rather than "us." As individualists, most Americans are pessimistic about their capacity to help bring about social change. But if the chances of an individual's changing his or her own immediate social environment to achieve crime control are slim, the chances of controlling crime by going after other persons—criminals—seem even slimmer.

By helping themselves, criminologists can help persons in other communities, too. They can publish their evaluations of their own crime control experiments, in the hope of getting ideas and evaluations back from others in the bargain. The Law Enforcement Assistance Administration (L.E.A.A.), to its credit, has taken pains to gather and disseminate ideas, research findings, and evaluations of crime control throughout the United States. Some of these reports, like those of mediation services—e.g., the night prosecutor program in Columbus, Ohio, described in Chapter 5— can and do inspire innovative crime control experiments in other communities. It is too bad, however, that many of the evaluations are written to prove to L.E.A.A. that its funding works wonders. This encourages evaluators to conclude quickly that much crime has been prevented and that an experiment is a crime control messiah. This is sad, because we can learn a great deal from our failures as well as from our successes.

The point here is that crime control *is* possible even in the United States. As asserted in Chapter 11, all that is needed is enough people trying enough experiments in reorganizing their own communities. After reaching a critical mass of ideas and experiments, success can be built upon success.

In Chapter 3, it was considered problematic to find a strategy that would change every kind of crime rate as desired at once. Still, it is not so hard to *conceive* of how to achieve control by various measures of crime and criminality simultaneously. The trick is to make people kinder to their own kind and stranger to strangers.

But the problem of planning error remains. We may think we have found a way to make members of a community kinder to their own kind such as by setting up mediation services. No matter how careful our planning, though, we cannot preclude the possibility of failure. It is impossible to avoid error in changing all measures of crime and criminality at once. Perhaps the police will resent the mediation services, and will report increased offenses to show that they are failing. Perhaps a major employer will move out of the community, costing many residents their jobs, raising unemployment, and thereby predation, so that victimization rates increase. The number of large and small events that can confound the best laid plans is astronomical. The odds are excellent that there will be a major error in any honestly evaluated crime control experiment. This is what makes success in crime control depend so heavily on large numbers of ideas and experiments generated at the same time. Only then will the chances for success increase. Here, ultimately, is how American crime control will be achieved—if at all.

A CALL FOR CRIMINOLOGISTS

By now, you are already an expert criminologist. Others may have had some experience you have not. They may have designed questionnaires, or fed data and programs into computers, or analyzed data directly from computer printouts, or calculated statistics by hand, or been in police squad cars, courts, jails or prisons, or have talked to more officials or inmates than you have, or even been officials or inmates themselves. Experiences like these may be rewarding and help generate and shape crime control ideas. However, the ideas, predictions, and evaluations of experienced criminologists are no more likely to be right or worthwhile than your own. Your ideas and opinions about controlling crime deserve as much respect and attention as theirs. As you have seen, the more ideas and opinions you contribute to criminology, the greater the chances that effective, acceptable means to control crime will be found.

I hope you will continue doing criminology. As a career criminologist, I find the field to be more exciting and rewarding the longer I pursue it. It will be still more exciting and rewarding for me the more you add to it. That is my selfish reason for writing this book in hopes of stimulating your interest in the study of crime.

Consider the possibility of making a career of criminology yourself. Although I am less familiar with other countries, I do know that in the United States at this time, jobs for criminologists are plentiful. I have tried to convey my enthusiasm for my teaching and research career in this book. Unlike some fields, such as history and psychology, there are more than enough openings in colleges and universities for those entering the market with doctorates in criminology and criminal justice. There are also many jobs for those with master's degrees, especially if they have some practical experience in working with the criminal justice system. A number of private research firms hire criminologists to do evaluations and consultations for criminal justice agencies and programs. Experimental community crime control programs hire criminologists, too. At national, state, and local levels, there are jobs for criminal justice planners who help decide how federal crime control funds are to be disbursed, and who sometimes plan and carry out evaluations of experimental programs themselves. Law enforcement agencies, courts, and correctional agencies who have experimental projects or who want to implement them hire their own researchers and planners to coordinate these efforts. And the number of openings for criminal justice officials, such as police, probation and parole officers, and correctional workers and administrators, continues to expand.

It is common for those who do these jobs to gain formal training not only in criminology or criminal justice but in law, psychology, social work and sociology, too. To give you an idea of the diversity of backgrounds in criminology, the department in which I work includes persons trained in anthropology, Chinese language and literature, criminal justice, English literature, forensic science, history, law, police administration, political science, psychology, social work, and sociology. Architects, economists, geographers, and philosophers commonly work in the field as well.

There is a lot of work in criminology, and there are a lot of ways to prepare for it.

In criminology, you have a chance to be a pioneer in work of vital social importance. May you continue to be a criminologist!

FOOD FOR THOUGHT

1. What ideas for crime control would you like to develop further?

2. As a citizen, what crime control experiments might you help try to implement in your own community?

3. What kind of career as a criminologist might interest you?

4. Now that you have read this introduction to criminology, what else would you like to read about and explore in the field?

The U.S. Criminal Justice Process

The following chart was designed in 1967 by the President's Commission on Law Enforcement and Administration of Justice to depict the flow of cases through the U.S. criminal justice process. Many of the terms used in the chart are defined in footnotes; most are not. To supplement the chart, definitions of the terms wholly or partially undefined in the chart follow the chart in alphabetical order. In each of the definitions, terms defined elsewhere in the list are printed in CAPITAL LETTERS, while terms defined in footnotes in the chart are referred to by note number.

There is an error in the chart, indicating that information and arraignment in misdemeanor cases follow a preliminary hearing. Preliminary hearings are given only to some defendants charged with felonies. Information and arraignment on a misdemeanor can follow a preliminary hearing only if the prosecutor has reduced charges.

To understand the criminal justice process, try following the chart step by step, referring to definitions of terms as you proceed.

Acquitted. As a matter of constitutionally guaranteed due process (Fifth and Fourteenth Amendments) in the United States, criminal defendants are presumed innocent until proven guilty beyond a reasonable doubt. Thus, in cases in which defendants fail to plead guilty and the PROSECUTION fails to establish guilt beyond a reasonable doubt at TRIAL, defendants are not "found innocent" but are "acquitted" or "found not guilty."

A GENERAL VIEW OF THE CRIMINAL JUSTICE SYSTEM

This chart seeks to present a simple yet comprehensive view of the movement of cases through the criminal justice system. Procedures in individual jurisdictions may vary from the pattern shown here. The differing weights of line indicate the relative volumes of cases disposed of at various points in the system, but this is only suggestive since no nationwide data of this sort exists.

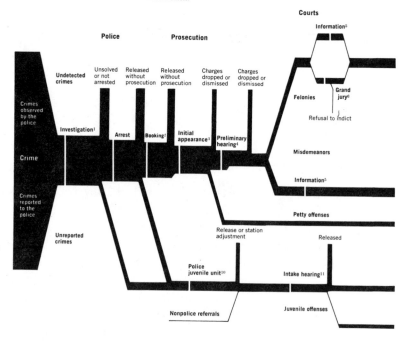

1 May continue until trial.
2 Administrative record of arrest. First step at which temporary release on bail may be available.
3 Before magistrate, commissioner, or justice of peace. Formal notice of charge, advice of rights. Bail set. Summary trials for petty offenses usually conducted here without further processing.
4 Preliminary testing of evidence against defendant. Charge may be reduced. No separate preliminary hearings for misdemeanors in some systems.
5 Charge filed by prosecutor on basis of information submitted by police or citizens. Alternative to grand jury indictment; often used in felonies, almost always in misdemeanors.
6 Reviews whether Government evidence sufficient to justify trial.

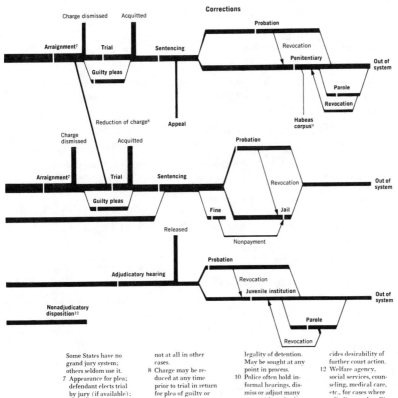

Corrections

Charge dismissed   Acquitted

Probation

Arraignment[7]   Trial   Sentencing

Revocation

Penitentiary

Out of system

Guilty pleas

Parole

Revocation

Reduction of charge[8]   Appeal

Habeas corpus[9]

Charge dismissed   Acquitted   Probation

Arraignment[7]   Trial   Sentencing

Revocation

Out of system

Guilty pleas   Fine   Jail

Released

Nonpayment

Probation

Adjudicatory hearing

Revocation

Juvenile institution

Out of system

Nonadjudicatory disposition[12]

Parole

Revocation

Some States have no grand jury system; others seldom use it.

7 Appearance for plea; defendant elects trial by jury (if available); counsel for indigent usually appointed here in felonies, often

not at all in other cases.

8 Charge may be reduced at any time prior to trial in return for plea of guilty or for other reasons.

9 Challenge on constitutional grounds to

legality of detention. May be sought at any point in process.

10 Police often hold informal hearings, dismiss or adjust many cases without further processing.

11 Probation officer de-

cides desirability of further court action.

12 Welfare agency, social services, counseling, medical care, etc., for cases where adjudicatory handling not needed.

Adjudicatory hearing. For juveniles (see JUVENILE OFFENSES), the equivalent of a criminal TRIAL for adults. Under the U.S. Constitution as currently interpreted by the Supreme Court, juveniles in adjudicatory hearings are entitled to all major due process rights given adults in TRIALS except the right to have a case heard by a jury. While TRIALS are generally open to public view, adjudicatory hearings are generally closed to the public.

While adults found guilty at TRIAL are said to have been "convicted," juveniles found guilty of delinquent acts are said to have been "adjudicated delinquent" and those found guilty of status offenses said to have been "adjudicated children (CHINS) or persons in need of supervision (PINS)."

Juveniles adjudicated delinquent, CHINS, or PINS are then subject to a dispositional hearing in which a PROBATION officer presents a report of a "presentence investigation" and the defendant (or defendant's counsel) has a chance to be heard. Following this, SENTENCING occurs.

Juveniles not proven guilty beyond a reasonable doubt in adjudicatory hearings are found "not guilty" (or ACQUITTED) and released from juvenile court custody.

Appeal. Removal of a case to a higher court for review and possible reversal of a possible error or injustice committed by a lower court. Although in rare instances an appeal may be had before SENTENCING of a defendant or in some jurisdictions a prosecutor may appeal for a higher sentence of a convicted defendant, criminal appeals are generally taken by defendants following conviction and SENTENCING.

The U.S. Supreme Court has interpreted the due process clauses of the Fifth and Fourteenth Amendments to the Constitution to give every convicted and sentenced defendant one appeal as a matter of right, including provision of legal counsel and payment of expenses of getting the trial record together for defendants too poor to pay these expenses for themselves.

Lawyers distinguish issues of fact—those of what the defendant has or has not done—from issues of law—those of what the law defines as CRIME and of what procedure is to be followed in prosecuting and trying defendants. Although jurisdictions occasionally give defendants the right to have completely new trials following conviction and SENTENCING for minor offenses, U.S. courts of appeal usually consider only whether errors of law have been made and, except in outrageous cases, refrain from considering issues of fact about a defendant's guilt or sentence. If an appellate court finds that a defendant has been harmed by an error of law, it "reverses" the conviction or sentence and "remands" the case for another prosecution at the prosecutor's discretion.

A few states have only a single appellate (supreme) court, but most states and the federal system have two levels of appellate courts. In most cases, the higher level appellate courts have discretion as to whether to hear appeals from the lower level.

In addition to these "direct" appeals, every U.S. jurisdiction gives defendants whose time for direct appeal has passed and who are serving sentences a limited "collateral" appeal, which most commonly consists of a petition for a writ of *habeas corpus* (to release the petitioner from custody; see chart n. 9).

State defendants who allege violation of federal constitutional rights have some access to federal appellate courts, such as from the highest court of the state to the U.S. Supreme Court on direct appeal or to the lowest-level federal courts (U.S. Districts Courts) on collateral appeal.

Charges dropped or dismissed. A charge is *dropped* by a prosecutor who decides not to pursue a PROSECUTION some time after formal charging but before permission of a judge not to pursue the case is required. At some point, from the filing of a formal charge until arraignment (n. 7), depending on the law of the jurisdiction, charges can be withdrawn only by a judge's granting a motion to *dismiss* the charges. If a judge dismisses charges *without prejudice*, the prosecutor may subsequently reinitiate prosecution on the same charges. Charges that are dismissed *with prejudice* cannot be reprosecuted.

Corrections. Corrections denotes the systems and personnel to whose custody sentenced defendants are remanded. It encompasses a wide range of punishment and treatment alternatives, including JAILS, PENITENTIARIES, PROBATION, PAROLE, and a variety of community treatment programs.

Corrections is distinguished from "detention," in holding in JAIL of defendants who cannot obtain or afford bail pending TRIAL.

Courts. TRIAL and appellate courts are charged with administration of the criminal law. They are run by elected or appointed judges, and have clerks and other administrative staff. PROBATION officers are members of the staff of trial courts.

Although prosecutors have considerable discretion as to whether and how to prosecute cases, every stage of a PROSECUTION, from the filing of formal charges (n. 5) and an initial appearance (n. 3) through SENTENCING, operates—in theory, at least—at the direction of TRIAL judges or magistrates. During this time, the defendant has a federal constitutional right (under the Sixth and Fourteenth Amendments) to assistance of counsel, provided free of charge to those deemed unable to afford lawyers' fees.

Crime. A crime is a wrongful act (*actus reus*) that with few exceptions must have been committed by someone consciously (with a guilty mind, or *mens rea*), which is made punishable by law as an offense against the public interest.

Crimes observed by the police. The POLICE may find evidence of a CRIME without having had a complaint of the CRIME from a private citizen. If they so choose, the POLICE may then investigate the possible CRIME or make an ARREST "proactively" or on their own initiative (see, by contrast, CRIMES REPORTED TO THE POLICE).

This proactive (as opposed to "reactive") law enforcement is most common with public order offenses like disturbing the peace, in traffic enforcement, and to a lesser extent, in enforcing the law against so-called "crimes without victims" (see UNDETECTED CRIMES).

Crimes reported to the police. The larger (and throughout the last century, increasing) proportion of "offenses known" to the POLICE (see Chapters 3 and 5) and of ARRESTS stem from information provided to the POLICE by citizen complainants. Other than public order offenses, traffic offenses, and "CRIMES without victims" (see CRIMES OBSERVED BY THE POLICE and UNDETECTED CRIMES), U.S. police today seldom discover evidence of CRIMES on their own initiative. Instead, they wait to be radio-dispatched to interview citizens who have called for POLICE assistance. In other words, most law enforcement is "reactive" rather than "proactive."

Felonies. Originally, at English common law, felonies were the CRIMES punishable by death.

Today in the United States, felonies are those offenses punishable (or punished in Minnesota; see MISDEMEANORS and Chapters 4 and 8) by more than a year of incarceration in a PENITENTIARY.

Fine. State and federal statutes provide that a monetary penalty of no more than a specified amount may be imposed either in lieu of or in addition to another sentence, such as incarceration.

The U.S. Supreme Court has held it unconstitutional to incarcerate those who cannot afford to pay to work off the fines.

Grand Jury. Although "blue ribbon" panels of politically notable citizens occasionally may be drawn to aid prosecutorial investigations (see PROSECUTION) by making special reports, grand juries in the criminal justice system are generally selected randomly from voter rolls, as are petit juries that decide issues of fact in TRIALS. (As a matter of fact, in many communities, these juries are made up of repeaters from selected segments of the community, such as state workers in a state's capital city.)

While trial or petit juries are composed of six or twelve members (plus alternates) for a single case, grand juries may be composed of twenty-three jurors who hear a number of cases at a session, with some lesser figures constituting a quorum and approximately three-fourths of the full body being required to vote in favor of an indictment to return a "true bill."

In FELONY cases, the prosecutor usually has the option of preceding the arraignment (see chart, n. 7) with an information (see chart, n. 5) or a grand jury indictment (see n. 6 and REFUSAL TO INDICT). When prosecutors choose to give the responsibility for a FELONY PROSECUTION to someone else, cases will usually be referred to the grand jury rather than filing an information as a matter of policy.

In a grand jury hearing of a case, the prosecutor presents evidence unopposed by any representative of the defendant. A defendant, without legal representation in the grand jury room, may be heard as a volunteer only at the discretion of the prosecutor. In order that an indictment be returned (a "true bill" instead of "no bill"), a prosecutor is supposed to persuade the requisite number of grand jurors that uncontradicted evidence establishes "reasonable" or "probable cause" to believe the defendant guilty of the CRIME charged by the prosecutor.

Grand juries usually hear each case and reach decisions within a few minutes, returning true bills in more than nine of ten cases. This has led to the charge that grand juries are merely prosecutorial rubber stamps.

Guilty pleas. At any time between arraignment (see chart, no. 7) and conviction, an acknowledgment of guilt by a defendant, which, if deemed informed and voluntary, implies that the defendant can be regarded by the state as guilty of the admitted CRIME for purposes of SENTENCING.

Juvenile offenses. Juvenile offenses fall under two headings: delinquent acts (acts that would be CRIMES if committed by adults) and status offenses (like truancy or running away from home, made sanctionable only for juveniles). In the United States, the law varies from state to state as to the age at which a person becomes an adult rather than a juvenile for criminal justice processing purposes (somewhere between ages fifteen and eighteen). In some states, defendants of juvenile age charged with serious delinquent acts may be bound over by a juvenile judge for prosecution as adults (e.g., at age fourteen where the criminal law age of adulthood is normally seventeen). There are no juvenile offenses in U.S. federal law.

Misdemeanors. Originally, at English common law, misdemeanors included all CRIMES not punishable by death (see FELONIES).

Today in the United States, misdemeanors are generally those offenses that can be punished by a term of incarceration no longer than one year in JAIL. *Gross* misdemeanors may include offenses punishable by more than ninety days but no more than one year in JAIL. In the State of Minnesota, whether a CRIME is a misdemeanor or a FELONY is determined by the length of the actual sentence (see SENTENCING) imposed rather than by the length of sentence the law allows for the offense (see Chapters 4 and 8).

In some jurisdictions (including Minnesota), a CRIME punishable or punished by no more than fifteen days in JAIL is said to be a "violation" rather than a misdemeanor.

Nonpayment. Since the chart was drawn up (in 1967), the U.S. Supreme Court has held it unconstitutional to incarcerate defendants who cannot afford to pay fines for nonpayment. However, those deemed capable of paying fines may generally serve time in JAIL or in a PENITENTIARY in lieu of paying a fine.

Jail. Jails are usually operated by county sheriffs or by city POLICE in the United States, although in Connecticut and Rhode Island, jails are operated by the state governments (see Chapter 8). Jails are used to detain defendants who cannot obtain or afford bail pending TRIAL, and to house sentenced defendants. Usually, if a sentence of incarceration is longer than a year, the defendant is committed to a PENITENTIARY rather than to a jail.

It has often been recommended that detainees (defendants held pending TRIAL) be housed separately from jail inmates who are serving sentences. This recommendation has not been implemented in many jails.

Juvenile institution. A number of jurisdictions maintain separate facilities for keeping children who cannot make bail in custody pending their juvenile court hearings. These institutions are known as juvenile detention centers. In addition, separate facilities are maintained by the states for juveniles adjudicated delinquent or PINS (see JUVENILE OFFENSES) whom the judge commits to state institutions. These facilities are generally called "schools" (e.g., training schools, industrial schools, schools for boys, schools for girls) or sometimes "camps" (e.g., forestry camps).

In many jurisdictions, defendants old enough to have been tried as adults but under the age of twenty-one who are sentenced to incarceration (see Chapter 8) are sent to juvenile institutions as "youthful offenders."

Nonpolice referrals.   Referrals to JUVENILE UNIT officers or juvenile PROBATION officers by sources other than POLICE officers, including private citizens, schools, and social welfare agency personnel (n. 12).

Police juvenile unit.   Larger police departments are likely to have specialized units of nonuniformed officers known variously as juvenile officers, juvenile aid officers, or youth aid officers. Once possible juvenile offenders are identified, usually by patrol officers, school personnel, social welfare workers, or family members, cases may initially be referred to the juvenile unit officers. In some cases, juvenile unit officers are assigned to work in specific public schools.

Parole.   Parole is a supervised, conditional release of a prison inmate into the community before the expiration of his or her term.

Parole and parole REVOCATION are granted at the discretion of representatives of an appointed body known as a parole board or commission.

Each parolee is assigned to the caseload of a parole officer, who monitors whether the parolee is meeting the conditions of parole. Besides avoiding further trouble with the police or prosecutors, common conditions of parole include such demands as regular visits to the parole officer, not leaving the jurisdiction or getting married without the parole officer's permission, not "consorting with known felons" (see FELONIES), and not using drugs or alcohol.

Penitentiary.   Penitentiaries are also known as prisons or, more recently, as "correctional facilities" or "institutions." In the United States, penitentiary systems are run by the governments of states and of the United States, in contrast to JAILS, which are usually run by county or municipal governments. Penitentiaries are used to house only sentenced felons (see SENTENCING and FELONIES).

Petty offenses.   Also known as violations, petty offenses are those in some jurisdictions carrying lesser penalties (generally no more than fifteen days in JAIL) than MISDEMEANORS. In cases in which only a FINE is to be imposed upon conviction, some jurisdictions provide for summary hearings in front of magistrates or judges without necessarily providing defendants with assistance of legal counsel. The summary procedure (n. 3) is most commonly used to hear cases of alleged traffic violations.

Police.   The police are employed to enforce the law by investigating possible violations of the law and making arrests. Accordingly, the police are generally given a more extended right of arrest and authorized to use greater force to enforce the law than are private citizens.

U.S. police are employed by municipalities, and by the states. Counties employ sheriffs and sheriffs' deputies, who have full POLICE powers and, in addition, usually run county JAILS.

It is sometimes claimed that the United States has no federal police force, because federal law enforcement agents, like agents of the Federal Bureau of Investigation and the Drug Enforcement Agency, supposedly investigate only CRIMES that have already occurred instead of mobilizing themselves to detect CRIMES before or during their commission. This distinction is tenuous at best. Law enforcement officers are given special powers to enforce only the laws of the state or federal system in which they are employed.

Probation. Probation is a SENTENCING option available to an adult or juvenile judge, in which a convicted defendant is RELEASED into the community upon conditions the judge specifies, to be monitored by the probation staff of the judge's court as an alternative to incarceration (see Chapter 8). Arrest on a new charge is a violation of the conditions of probation. Conditions of probation may also include regular visits to a probation officer, participation in a community treatment program, and prohibition from associating with other offenders, among others. A probation officer who believes a probationer has violated a condition of probation may arrest the defendant and initiate REVOCATION proceedings.

Prosecution. The process of disposing of a case in the COURTS, from the filing of a formal charge by an appointed or elected official, known variously as a prosecutor, district attorney, United States Attorney or attorney general, or a member of that person's staff, preparatory to an initial appearance (n. 3), and thence to SENTENCING or APPEAL. The U.S. prosecutor has absolute discretion as to whether to initiate formal court proceedings on behalf of the state.

Reduction of charge. A prosecutor may either drop certain charges against a defendant or prosecute for a less serious offense than that originally charged. It is common practice for U.S. prosecutors to reduce charges in exchange for defendants' agreement to plead guilty to the lesser charges (see the discussion of plea bargaining in Chapter 4).

Refusal to indict. To obtain an arraignment in a FELONY case (see chart, no. 7), a state prosecutor has the option of proceeding by information (see chart, n. 5) or indictment. By the terms of the U.S. Constitution's Fifth Amendment, federal prosecutors are limited to proceeding by indictment.

An indictment is issued by requisite vote of a GRAND JURY agreeing that there is "probable" or "reasonable cause" to believe that the accused is guilt of a CRIME or CRIMES charged.

If less than the requisite number of grand jurors vote to indict, the result is said to be a "no bill" or "refusal to indict."

A "refusal to indict" leaves it open to the prosecutor to refile charges to reinitiate charges.

Released. A person who is set free from custody, supervision, or a court's jurisdiction is said to have been released.

Revocation. PROBATION or PAROLE may be revoked for failure of a probationer or parolee to meet the conditions of remaining at liberty. The PROBATION or PAROLE officer who has probable cause to believe that a condition has been violated may arrest the probationer or parolee and initiate revocation proceedings. The authority who granted PROBATION (the sentencing judge) or PAROLE (the PAROLE board) then holds a revocation hearing. If the hearing authority concludes that a condition has been violated, the authority may revoke PROBATION or PAROLE and commit the violator to incarceration.

The maximum term of incarceration for a violator whose PAROLE has been revoked is the amount of time that had remained of the violator's maximum sentence (see SENTENCING) when PAROLE was originally granted.

In the case of PROBATION, if the SENTENCING judge had imposed a suspended sentence (see SENTENCING) when originally granting PROBATION, the violator is committed for that period of time (subject to PAROLE). If no suspended sentence was imposed at the time of the original grant of PROBATION, the hearing officer (judge) has the power to impose any sentence of incarceration within statutory limits for the offense of which the probationer was originally convicted. The most common basis for revocation is arrest for a new offense.

Sentencing. Criminal defendants who are found guilty at TRIAL or who enter GUILTY PLEAS are subject to a decision of the TRIAL judge (or in some jurisdictions, especially in capital cases by petit juries, see GRAND JURY) as to what penalty, up to the maximum prescribed for the offense(s) convicted, to sentence the defendant.

Before sentence is passed, the defendant is entitled to be heard through counsel. Especially in FELONY cases, a PROBATION officer reports the results of a presentence investigation.

In many of the criminal PROSECUTIONS resulting in GUILTY PLEAS, the prosecutor recommends a bargained-for sentence to the sentencing judge or jury.

Trial.   The counterpart of an ADJUDICATORY HEARING for a person who is a juvenile at criminal law, at which the guilt of an adult (according to criminal law) must be established beyond a reasonable doubt in the United States to the satisfaction of a judge, or if the defendant so elects, to a petit jury (see GRAND JURY).

In a trial, after a jury is selected if the defendant elects to have one, (1) the prosecutor makes an opening statement of what the state intends to prove, (2) counsel for the defense makes an opening statement of what reasonable doubts of guilt the defendant will try to establish, (3) the prosecution presents its witnesses and leaves them to be cross-examined by defense counsel (or the defendant, in the absence of constitutionally protected right of assistance of counsel). Then the prosecution presents a closing argument in favor of conviction, followed by a closing argument on behalf of the defendant. If a petit jury is hearing the case, the trial judge then instructs the jury in the legal criteria upon which the jury is to reach a verdict of guilty or not guilty. The judge or jury, whichever is the trier of fact, decides whether the guilt of the defendant has been established beyond a reasonable doubt (resulting in conviction) or not (resulting in acquittal). Odds heavily favor conviction in any U.S. trial.

Undetected crimes.   As opposed to UNREPORTED CRIMES, undetected CRIMES are those like drug offenses, with willing "victims" (known as victimless CRIMES), in which no one involved complains to criminal justice officials.

Unreported crimes.   As opposed to UNDETECTED CRIMES, those CRIMES that neither the victim nor anyone on behalf of a victim reports to criminal justice officials.

Definitions of Crimes

Almost all crimes in the United States are defined by statute. Every state has a section of its statutes known as a "penal code" or "criminal code" or "penal law" which contains most of the definitions of crimes for the jurisdiction, and sets the legal limits on punishments that can be imposed on convicted defendants. Scattered among other statutes, such as those on health and safety, may be some other definitions of crimes as well. The U.S. federal government has many of its definitions of crime compiled in Title 18 of the United States Code, but as yet has no comprehensive criminal code.

Definitions of crimes and penalties vary widely from one jurisdiction to another. Within each jurisdiction, hundreds of offenses are defined. Following the basic definitions of crimes, there may be other sections of a code that further define elements of the crimes. This appendix is not intended to be a comprehensive list of definitions of crimes. Listed below are the basic definitions of a few of the more serious or common offenses, together with the penalties provided in the California Penal Code. This list will give you an idea of how crimes are defined by law.

First, to illustrate the range of offenses covered by the California Penal Code, here is its Table of Contents of definitions of crimes and punishments:

CALIFORNIA PENAL CODE
PART 1   OF CRIMES AND PUNISHMENTS

Here, then, are some of the provisions of the California Penal Code:

Aggravated Assault. This common term does not appear in the California Penal Code and has no fixed legal meaning. It refers to something more heinous than simple assault, and thus is covered by *Assault With a Deadly Weapon* and *Mayhem*, below.

Assault. Section 240. Assault defined

Assault defined. An assault is an unlawful attempt, coupled with a present ability, to commit a violent injury on the person of another.

Section 241. Assault; punishment

An assault is punishable by fine not exceeding five hundred dollars ($500), or by imprisonment in the county jail not exceeding six months, or by both. When it is committed against the person of a peace officer or fireman, and the person committing the offense knows or reasonably should know that such victim is a peace officer or fireman engaged in the performance of his duties, and such peace officer or fireman is engaged in the performance of his duties, the offense shall be punished by imprisonment in the county jail not exceeding one year or by imprisonment in the state prison not exceeding two years.

As used in this section, "peace officer" refers to any person designated as a peace officer by Section 830.1, Section 830.2, or by subdivision

(a) of Section 830.6, as well as any policeman of the San Francisco Port Authority and each deputized law enforcement member of the Wildlife Protection Branch of the Department of Fish and Game.

Assault and Battery. Instead of having the crimes of assault and battery separately defined in their statutes, as in the California Penal Code, many jurisdictions define "assault and battery" as a single offense. See *Assault* and *Battery*.

Assault With a Deadly Weapon. Section 245. Assault with deadly weapon or force likely to produce great bodily injury; punishment

(a)   Every person who commits an assault upon the person of another with a deadly weapon or instrument or by any means of force likely to produce great bodily injury is punishable by imprisonment in the state prison not exceeding 10 years, or in county jail not exceeding one year, or by fine not exceeding five thousand dollars ($5,000), or by both such fine and imprisonment. When a person is convicted of a violation of this section, in a case involving use of a deadly weapon or instrument, and such weapon or instrument is owned by such person, the court may, in its discretion, order that the weapon or instrument be deemed a nuisance and shall be confiscated and destroyed in the manner provided by Section 12028.

(b)   Every person who commits an assault with a deadly weapon or instrument or by any means likely to produce great bodily injury upon the person of a peace officer or fireman, and who knows or reasonably should know that such victim is a peace officer or fireman engaged in the performance of his duties, when such peace officer or fireman is engaged in the performance of his duties shall be punished by imprisonment in the state prison not exceeding 15 years; provided, that if such person has previously been convicted of an offense under the laws of any other state or of the United States which, if committed in this state, would have been punishable as a felony, he shall be punished by imprisonment in the state prison for five years to life.

As used in this section, "peace officer" refers to any person designated as a peace officer by Section 830.1, Section 830.2, or by subdivision (a) of Section 830.6, as well as any policeman of the San Francisco Port Authority and each deputized law enforcement member of the Wildlife Protection Branch of the Department of Fish and Game.

Battery.   Section 242.   Battery defined

Battery defined.   A battery is any willful and unlawful use of force or violence upon the person of another.

Section 243.   Battery; punishment

A battery is punishable by fine of not exceeding one thousand dollars ($1,000), or by imprisonment in the county jail not exceeding six months, or by both. When it is committed against the person of a peace officer or fireman, and the person committing the offense knows or reasonably should know that such victim is a peace officer or fireman engaged in the performance of his duties, and such peace officer or fireman is engaged in the performance of his duties, the offense shall be punished by imprisonment in the county jail not exceeding one year or by imprisonment in the state prison for not less than one nor more than 10 years.

As used in this section, "peace officer" refers to any person designated as a peace officer by Section 830.1, Section 830.2, or by subdivision (a) of Section 830.6, as well as any policeman of the San Francisco Port Authority and each deputized law enforcement member of the Wildlife Protection Branch of the Department of Fish and Game.

Burglary.   Section 459.   Definition

Every person who enters any house, room, apartment, tenement, shop, warehouse, store, mill, barn, stable, outhouse or other building, tent, vessel, railroad car, trailer coach, as defined in Section 635 of the Vehicle Code, any house car, as defined in Section 362 of the Vehicle Code, inhabited camper, as defined in Section 243 of the Vehicle Code, vehicle as defined by the Vehicle Code when the doors of such vehicle are locked, aircraft as defined by the Harbors and Navigation Code, mine or any underground portion thereof, with intent to commit grand or petit larceny or any felony is guilty of burglary. As used in this section, "inhabited" means currently being used in dwelling purposes, whether occupied or not.

Section 460.   Degrees; construction of section

1.   Every burglary of an inhabited dwelling house, trailer coach as defined by the Vehicle Code, or building committed in the nighttime, is burglary of the first degree.

2.   All other kinds of burglary are of the second degree.

3.   This section shall not be construed to supersede or affect Section 464 of the Penal Code.

Section 461.   Punishment

Burglary is punishable as follows:

1.   Burglary in the first degree: by imprisonment in the state prison for two, three, or four years.

2.   Burglary in the second degree: by imprisonment in the county jail not exceeding one year or in the state prison.

Excusable Homicide (see also *Justifiable Homicide, Manslaughter, Murder*).   Section 195.   Excusable homicide.

EXCUSABLE HOMICIDE.   Homicide is excusable in the following cases:

1.   When committed by accident and misfortune, in lawfully correcting a child or servant, or in doing any other lawful act by lawful means, with usual and ordinary caution, and without any unlawful intent.

2.   When committed by accident and misfortune, in the heat of passion, upon any sudden and sufficient provocation, or upon a sudden combat, when no undue advantage is taken, nor any dangerous weapon used, and when the killing is not done in a cruel or unusual manner.

Grand Theft.   See *Theft.*

Homicide.   Homicide literally means the killing of one person by another. When homicide is excusable (see *Excusable Homicide*) or justifiable (see *Justifiable Homicide*), it is not a crime. Criminal homicide includes *Manslaughter* and *Murder*.

Justifiable Homicide (see also *Excusable Homicide*). Section 196.   Justifiable homicide; public officers

JUSTIFIABLE HOMICIDE BY PUBLIC OFFICERS.   Homicide is justifiable when committed by public officers and those acting by their command in their aid and assistance, either—

1.   In obedience to any judgement of a competent Court; or,

2.   When necessarily committed in overcoming actual resistance to the execution of some legal process, or in the discharge of any other legal duty; or,

3.   When necessarily committed in retaking felons who have been rescued or have escaped, or when necessarily committed in arresting persons charged with felony, and who are fleeing from justice or resisting such arrest.

Section 197.   Justifiable homicide; any person

Homicide is also justifiable when committed by any person in any of the following cases:

1.   When resisting any attempt to murder any person, or to commit a felony, or to do some great bodily injury upon any person; or

2.   When committed in defense of habitation, property, or person, against one who manifestly intends or endeavors, by violence or surprise, to commit a felony, riotous or tumultuous manner, to enter the habitation of another for the purpose of offering violence to any person therein, or,

3.   When committed in the lawful defense of such person, or of a wife or husband, parent, child, master, mistress, or servant of such a person, when there is reasonable ground to apprehend a design to commit a felony or to do some great bodily injury, and imminent danger of such design being accomplished; but such person, or the person in whose behalf the defense was made, if he was the assailant or engaged in mutual combat, must really and in good faith have endeavored to decline any further struggle before the homicide was committed; or,

4.   When necessarily committed in attempting, by lawful ways and means, to apprehend any person for any felony committed, or in lawfully suppressing any riot, or in lawfully keeping and preserving the peace.

Larceny.   Larceny is the same as *Theft.*

Manslaughter (see also *Excusable Homicide, Justifiable Homicide,* and *Murder.*) Section 192.   Manslaughter, voluntary, involuntary, and in driving a vehicle defined; construction of section

Manslaughter is the unlawful killing of a human being, without malice. It is of three kinds:

1.   Voluntary—upon a sudden quarrel or heat of passion.

2.   Involuntary—in the commission of an unlawful act, not amounting to felony, or in the commission of a lawful act which might produce death, in an unlawful manner, or without due caution and circumspection, provided that this subdivision shall not apply to acts committed in the driving of a vehicle.

3.   In the driving of a vehicle—

    a   In the commission of an unlawful act, not amounting to felony, with gross negligence; or in the commission of a lawful act which might produce death, in an unlawful manner, and with gross negligence.

b   This section should not be construed as making any homicide in the driving of an automobile punishable which is not a proximate result of the commission of an unlawful act, not amounting to a felony, or of the commission of a lawful act which might produce death, in an unlawful manner.

Section 193.   Manslaughter; punishment

Manslaughter is punishable by imprisonment in the state prison for two, three or four years, except that a violation of subsection 3 of Section 192 of this code is punishable as follows: In the case of a violation of subdivision (a) of said subsection 3 the punishment shall be either by imprisonment in the county jail for not more than one year or in the state prison, and in such case the jury may recommend by their verdict that the punishment shall be by imprisonment in the county jail; in the case of a violation of subdivision (b) of said subsection 3, the punishment shall be by imprisonment in the county jail for not more than one year.

   In cases where, as authorized in this section, the jury recommends by their verdict that the punishment shall be by imprisonment in the county jail, the court shall not have authority to sentence the defendant to imprisonment in the state prison, but may nevertheless place the defendant on probation as provided in this code.

Mayhem.   Section 203.   Definition

   Every person who unlawfully and maliciously deprives a human being of a member of his body, or disables, disfigures, or renders it useless, or cuts or disables the tongue, or puts out an eye, or slits the nose, ear, or lip, is guilty of mayhem.

Section 204.   Punishment

MAYHEM, HOW PUNISHABLE.   Mayhem is punishable by imprisonment in the State Prison not exceeding fourteen years.

Murder (see also *Excusable Homicide, Justifiable Homicide,* and *Manslaughter*). Section 187.   Murder defined; death of fetus

a   Murder is the unlawful killing of a human being, or a fetus, with malice aforethought.
b   This section shall not apply to any person who commits an act which results in the death of a fetus if any of the following apply:
   1   The act complied with the Therapeutic Abortion Act, Chapter 11 (commencing with Section 25950) of Division 20 of the Health and Safety Code.

2 The act was committed by a holder of a physician's and surgeon's certificate, as defined in the Business and Professions Code, in a case where, to a medical certainty, the result of childbirth would be death of the mother of the fetus or where her death from childbirth, although not medically certain, would be substantially certain or more likely than not.

3 The act was solicited, aided, abetted, or consented to by the mother of the fetus.

c Subdivision (b) shall not be construed to prohibit the prosecution of any person under any other provision of law.

Section 189.   Murder; degrees

All murder which is perpetrated by means of a destructive device or explosive, poison, lying in wait, torture, or by any other kind of willful, deliberate, and premeditated killing, or which is committed in the perpetration of, or attempt to perpetrate, arson, rape, robbery, burglary, mayhem, or any act punishable under Section 288, is murder of the first degree; and all other kinds of murders are of the second degree.

As used in this section, "destructive device" shall mean any destructive as defined in Section 12301, and "explosive" shall mean any explosive as defined in Section 12000 of the Health and Safety Code.

Section 190.   Murder; degrees; punishment

Every person guilty of murder in the first degree shall suffer death, confinement in state prison for life without possibility of parole, or confinement in state prison for life. The penalty to be applied shall be determined as provided in Sections 190.1, 190.2, 190.3, 190.4, and 190.5. Every person guilty of murder in the second degree is punishable by imprisonment in the state prison for five, six, or seven years.

Petty (or *Petit*) *Theft.*   See *Theft.*

Rape.   Section 261.   Rape defined

Rape is an act of sexual intercourse, accomplished with a female not the wife of the perpetrator, under either of the following circumstances:

1.   Where the female is under the age of eighteen years;

2.   Where she is incapable, through lunacy or other unsoundness of mind, whether temporary or permanent, of giving legal consent;

3.   Where she resists, but her resistance is overcome by force or violence;

4.   Where she is prevented from resisting by threats of great and

immediate bodily harm, accompanied by apparent power of execution or by any intoxicating narcotic, or anaesthetic substance, administered by or with the privity of the accused;

5. Where she is at the time unconscious of the nature of the act, and this is known to the accused;

6. Where she submits under the belief that the person committing the act is her husband, and this belief is induced by any artifice, pretense, or concealment practiced by the accused, with intent to induce such belief.

Section 264. Rape; punishment; recommendation of jury; discretion of court

Rape is punishable by imprisonment in the state prison not less than three years, except where the offense is under subdivision 1 of Section 261 of the Penal Code, in which case the punishment shall be either by imprisonment in the county jail for not more than one year or in the state prison for not more than 50 years, and in such case the jury shall recommend by their verdict whether the punishment shall be by imprisonment in the county jail or in the state prison; provided that when the defendant pleads guilty of an offense under subdivision 1 of Section 261 of the Penal Code the punishment shall be in the discretion of the trial court, either by imprisonment in the county jail for not more than one year or in the state prison for not more than 50 years.

The preceding provisions of this section notwithstanding, in any case in which defendant committed rape and, in the course of commission of a rape other than as defined in subdivision 1 of Section 261, with the intent to inflict such injury, inflicted great bodily injury on the victim of the rape, such fact shall be charged in the indictment or information and if found to be true by the jury, upon a jury trial, or if found to be true by the court, upon a court trial, or if admitted by the defendant, defendant shall suffer confinement in the state prison from 15 years to life.

Robbery. Section 211. Definition

ROBBERY DEFINED. Robbery is the felonious taking of personal property in the possession of another, from his person or immediate presence, and against his will, accomplished by means of force or fear.

Section 211a. Degrees

All robbery which is perpetrated by torture or by a person being armed with a dangerous or deadly weapon, and the robbery of any person who is performing his duties as operator of any motor vehicle, streetcar, or trackless trolley used for the transportation of persons for hire, is robbery in the first degree. All other kinds of robbery are of the second degree.

Section 213.   Punishment

Robbery is punishable by imprisonment in the state prison, as follows:

1.   Robbery in the first degree for not less than five years.
2.   Robbery in the second degree, for not less than one year.

The preceding provisions of this section notwithstanding, in any case in which defendant committed robbery, and in the course of commission of the robbery, with the intent to inflict such injury, inflicted great bodily injury on the victim of the robbery, such fact shall be charged in the indictment or information and if found to be true by the jury, upon a jury trial, or if found to be true by the court, upon a court trial or if admitted by the defendant, defendant shall suffer confinement in the state prison from 15 years to life.

Theft.   Section 484.   Theft defined

a   Every person who shall feloniously steal, take, carry, lead, or drive away the personal property of another, or who shall fraudulently appropriate property which has been entrusted to him, or who shall knowingly and designedly, by any false or fraudulent representation or pretense, defraud any other person of money, labor or real or personal property, or who causes or procures others to report falsely of his wealth or mercantile character and by thus imposing upon any other person, obtains credit and thereby fraudulently gets or obtains possession of money, or property or obtains the labor or service of another, is guilty of theft. In determining the value of the property obtained, for the purposes of this section, the reasonable and fair market value shall be the test, and in determining the value of services received the contract price shall be the test. If there be no contract price, the reasonable and going wage for the service rendered shall govern. For the purposes of this section, any false or fraudulent representation or pretense made shall be treated as continuing, so as to cover any money, property or service received as a result thereof, and the complaint, information or indictment may charge that the crime was committed on any date during the particular period in question. The hiring of any additional employee or employees without advising each of them of every labor claim due and unpaid and every judgment that the employer has been unable to meet shall be prima facie evidence of intent to defraud.

b   Except as provided in Section 10855 of the Vehicle Code, intent to commit theft by fraud is presumed if one who has leased or rented the personal property of another pursuant to a written contract fails to return the personal property to its owner within 20 days after the owner has made written demand by certified or registered mail following the expiration of the lease or rental agreement for return of the property so leased or rented, or if one presents to the owner identification which bears a false or fictitious name or address for the purpose of obtaining the lease or rental agreement.

c   The presumptions created by subdivision (b) are presumptions affecting the burden of producing evidence.

d   Within 30 days after the lease or rental agreeement has expired, the owner shall make written demand for return of the property so leased or rented. Notice addressed and mailed to the lessee or renter at the address given at the time of the making of the lease or rental agreement and to any other known address shall constitute proper demand. Where the owner fails to make such written demand the presumption created by subdivision (b) shall not apply.

Section 487.   Grand theft defined

Grand theft is theft committed in any of the following cases:

1.   When the money, labor or real or personal property taken is of a value exceeding two hundred dollars ($200); provided, that when domestic fowls, avocados, olives, citrus or deciduous fruits, nuts and artichokes are taken of a value exceeding fifty dollars ($50); provided, further, that where the money, labor, real or personal property is taken by a servant, agent or employee from his principal or employer and aggregates two hundred dollars ($200) or more in any 12 consecutive month period, then the same shall constitute grand theft.

2.   When the property is taken from the person of another.

3.   When the property taken is an automobile, firearm, horse, mare, gelding, any bovine animal, any caprine animal, mule, jack, jenny, sheep, lamb, hog, sow, boar, gilt, barrow or pig.

Sometimes peculiar anomalies appear in the law. For instance, the California Penal Code has a series of sections defining theft of other objects as grand theft, too. Here is an example:

Section 487g.   Grand theft; stealing dog for purposes of sale, medical research, or other commercial uses

Every person who feloniously steals, takes, or carries away a dog of another for purposes of sale, medical research, or other commercial uses, is guilty of grand theft.

Section 488.   Petty theft defined

Theft in other cases is petty theft.

Section 489.   Grand theft; punishment

Grand theft is punishable by imprisonment in the county jail for not more than one year or in the state prison for not more than 10 years.

Section 490.   Petty theft; punishment

Petty theft is punishable by fine not exceeding five hundred dollars, or by imprisonment in the county jail not exceeding six months, or both.

Author Index

Reference page numbers are in italic type. References to works by more than one author include the first author's name in parentheses.

Administrative Office of the Courts, 177, *193*
Aichhorn, A., 17, *25*
Akers, R. L., 202, *241*
Alabama Supreme Court, 10, *25*
American Bar Association, 84, *90*, 97, *115*
American Friends Service Committee, 183, *193*, 245, 256, 264, 266, *268*
Andenaes, J. (Christie), 209–10, 237, *241*
Aronowitz, S., 159, *165*

Bailey, W. C., 256–57, *268*
Baum, B. (Galliher), 82, *90*
Bayley, D. H., 99, 103, 114, *115*, 133, *139*
Beattie, R. H., 58–59, *68*
Beccaria, C., 4–5, 9, 11, 19, *25*, 129, *140*, 148, *165*
Becker, G. S., 47, *49*, 285, 286–89, *297*
Belkin, J., 246–47, *268*
Bentham, J., 5, *25*

Berger, A. S., 211, *241*
Berk, R. E. (Rossi), 74, *91*
Berkman, A., 4, 8, *25*, 29, 45, *49*
Berman, H. J., 8, *25*
Berntsen, K., 257, *268*
Biderman, A. D., 37, *49*, 120, *140*
Black, D. J., 36, *49*, 94, *115*
Blackmore, J., 232, *241*
Blumstein, A., 131, 132, *140*, 174, 177, *193*; (Belkin), 246–47, *268*
Bodde, D., 6, *25*
Bodine, G. E. (Hardt), 216, *242*
Boland, B., 132, *140*
Bonger, W., 22, *25*, 183–84, *193*
Bose, C. E. (Rossi), 74, *91*
Bottomley, A. K., 80, 81, *90*
Brantingham, Patricia L., 109, *115*
Brantingham, Paul J. (Brantingham), 109, *115*; (Faust), 18, *26*
Briar, S. (Piliavin), 22, *26*
British Home Office Statistical Research Unit, 247, 254–56, *268*

Subject Index